A YEAR
OF
BEER

A YEAR
OF
BEER

260
SEASONAL
HOMEBREW
RECIPES

Compiled by Amahl Turczyn

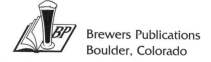

Brewers Publications
Boulder, Colorado

Brewers Publications, Division of the Association of Brewers
PO Box 1679, Boulder, CO 80306-1679
(303) 447-0816; Fax (303) 447-2825

Printed in the United States of America
10 9 8 7 6 5 4 3 2 1

ISBN 0-937381-53-5

Library of Congress Cataloging-in-Publication Data
A year of beer: 260 seasonal homebrew recipes / compiled by Amahl Turczyn.
    p. cm.
  Includes index.
  ISBN 0-937381-53-5 (alk. paper)
  1. Brewing—Amateurs' manuals.   I. Turczyn, Amahl.
TP570.Y43 1997
641.8'73—dc21   97-13169
                                                                      CIP

Technical Editor: Phil Fleming
Book Project Editor: Theresa Duggan
Copy Editor: Kim Adams
Cover and Interior Designer: Vicki Hopewell
Cover Photo by Michael Lichter, Michael Lichter Photography

Please direct all inquiries or orders to the above address.

CONTENTS

INTRODUCTION

The Background of Seasonal Brewing

Generally speaking, you can brew any style of beer at any time of the year if you have the proper equipment and the desire to do so. But there are two good reasons to craft particular styles of beer during certain times of the year: (1) tradition and (2) a practical consideration of your locale's temperature.

Many countries and regions have long brewing histories and ancient traditions of drinking distinct styles of beer during specific months or seasons. For example, bock and its many variations are seasonal beers. Plain bock is typically consumed from September to early November, at which time the slightly drier Oktoberfest style makes its annual debut. For the Christmas season the spicy clovey weizenbock is enjoyed. May also has its own bock beer, maibock. Maibock is lighter colored and often hoppier than the traditional bock but it still possesses the clean malty strength of the original. Many of these brewing seasons also incorporate religious holidays. In Bavaria, Pauline monks have brewed doppelbock, an extra-strong version of bock, for centuries to provide nourishment during their fasting at Lent. Today, the now secularized Paulaner brewery makes its own version of this style named *Salvator* (savior) and commemorates the tradition by tapping the first barrel of the season three or four weeks before Easter.

Other countries have similar versions of bock, too. Northern France has a rich malty bière de garde called bière de Mars to enjoy in May. In Italy, Moretti brews its own delicious doppio malto version of dopplebock, for the frigid Mediterranean winter. The Dutch brew bock for late September to early October, much like the German tradition, and several old-world brewing nations like Switzerland and Norway reserve their own particularly strong version of bock for the Christmas season.

One can enjoy these styles at other times of the year—I myself can easily put down a good Oktoberfest any day. But for those brewers wishing to adhere to the practices of our brewing ancestors, who perfected so many delicious styles of ale and lager, it's valuable to know that a light hoppy kölsch or a Berliner weisse is not the appropriate tipple when it's snowing outside, or a Russian imperial stout the thing after a game of tennis in the heat of August.

By now, you can probably begin to guess some of the criteria for when it is appropriate to drink a particular style of beer. Lighter, more thirst-quenching beers are best for warm weather and summer. Heartier darker brews with a higher alcohol content make better winter warmers. It's no mistake that primarily warm-climate countries like Africa, China, Japan, and Australia have adopted lighter lagers as their preferred beers. Even the United States and Canada, though by no means warm countries, have adopted light lagers as their standard beers, because beer was neither seen as a sustaining drink nor á safe septic drink in times of widespread disease, like dopplebock was to the Pauline monks and to the Cistercian monks in eleventh- and twelfth-century Belgium.

As homebrewers, we want to brew as many different styles from the world of beer as we can, and hopefully, enjoy them at the proper time of year. However, many of us aren't equipped to brew good beer in warm climates. Lagers prove especially difficult in the summer, as that particular yeast requires lower temperatures for clean fermentation. This has been a problem for centuries and is the cause for many traditional guidelines, which suggest when to brew what.

One might go as far as to say that lager yeast developed as a result of the practice of storing beer at low temperatures for long periods of time—not the other way around. Bavarian brewers stored their beer in the spring in Alpine caves, otherwise it spoiled in the summer heat. These cold-resistant strains of lager yeast survived the storage period and continued to work throughout the process. The yeast's less conspicuous flavor produced beer with a cleaner maltier flavor. As a result, higher-temperature, top-fermenting yeasts fell out, went dormant, and were eventually squeezed out of the process. We now call this process lagering, from the German word *lagerung* (storage).

Likewise, warm-fermenting ale yeasts also developed from region-specific brewing methods. British brewers originally thought the thick foam that rose to the surface of fermenting beer was detrimental to its quality, so they skimmed it off and threw it away. Eventually, some brewer discovered transferring this foam to the next batch produced a cleaner faster fermentation, because skimming encourages the selection of flocculant yeast strains over bottom-fermenting types. Thus, the more heat-tolerant ale yeasts became commonly used.

So how can these two subcategories of yeast help you brew good beer year-round without breaking tradition? Simple. Brew lagers in the winter, when your ale yeasts won't be able to take the cold, and brew ales in the spring and fall, when heat-tolerant strains work best. Summer brewing can be risky, depending on your location and equipment, but there are many styles of beer that can withstand a little warmth in your brewery.

HOW TO USE THIS CALENDAR

Each line on the calendar represents a reasonable period of time to brew each beer style—from the time you brew it to the time you can enjoy it. These total times include conditioning, regardless of whether you use bottles or kegs to age your beer.

This calendar blends traditional brewing times with practical suggestions for a consistent annual brewing schedule. You can brew some styles almost any time of year, like pale ale, while you can brew others, like Oktoberfest, to enjoy at a certain time of year. You can indulge in some ales, like mild, within the same month they are made, assuming a healthy pitching rate, proper fermentation temperature, and adequate wort aeration. But other styles, like mead and imperial stout, need a year of conditioning at traditional gravity, or, like lambic, aged well beyond a year's time. Use this chart as a guideline—it isn't set in stone. Lengthen or shorten times depending on your own brewery's conditions, equipment, and the original gravity of your beer.

What to Brew and When to Brew It

What to Brew	Winter Dec.	Jan.	Feb.
Altbier	🍺		
Barley Wine	🍺		🍾
Belgian Strong Ale/Trappist Ale	•————————🍺		
Belgian White			
Bière de Garde/Saison			🍾
Bitter			
Bock		🍾	
Brown Ale, United States	🍺		
Brown Ale, United Kingdom			
California Common			
Doppelbock	•————————————🍺		
Dortmunder	🍺		
Dunkelweizen			
Extra Special Bitter	🍺		
Eisbock	•————————————🍺		
Festbier			
Fruit Beer			
Imperial Stout	🍺	🍾	
India Pale Ale			
Kölsch			
Lambic	•————————————🍺		
Lager, United States			
Maibock			🍾
Märzen/Oktoberfest			🍾
Mead	🍺🍾————————————		
Mild Ale			
Munich Helles/Dunkles		🍾————————	
Old Ale			
Pale Ale			
Pilsener			🍾
Porter			🍾——🍺
Red Ale			🍾——🍺
Scotch Ale	🍺		
Scottish Ale			
Schwarzbier	🍾————————🍺		
Smoked Beer			
Spiced Ale	🍺		
Stout, Dry		🍾————————🍺	
Stout, Specialty			
Weisse, Berliner			
Weizen			
Weizenbock	🍺		

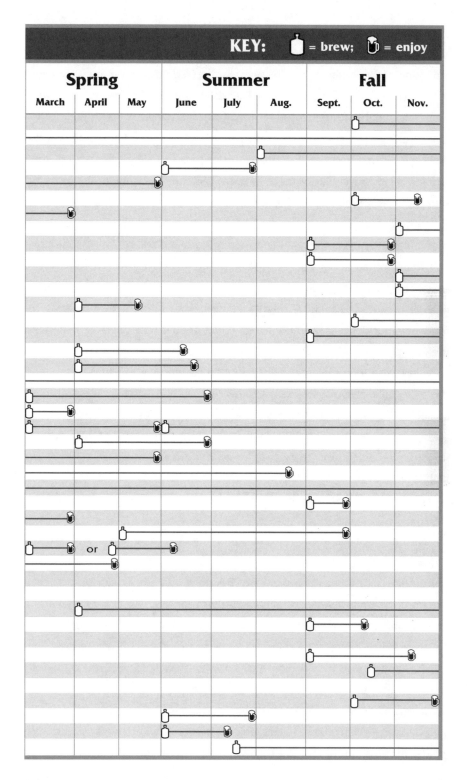

WARM-WEATHER BREWING

Please note this information assumes you have a reasonable room temperature in your brewing space. The beers suggested for summer brewing have yeasts with a higher heat tolerance, and any phenolic or estery off-flavors you get at higher fermentation temperatures are consistent with their flavor profiles. If your house gets beyond 72 °F (22 °C), try to find some way to keep your fermenters cool or abstain from brewing altogether until it gets cooler. Also, do not attempt to brew a Märzen/Oktoberfest at the traditional suggested time and expect to lager it all summer if you don't have the refrigeration space. This particular style, like the French bière de Mars, was meant to be kept very cold for a long time and will probably spoil during four months of ambient summer temperatures. An acceptable temperature range for many yeasts is 72 °F (22 °C), but remember your fermentation also produces heat. At high kraeusen, your fermenter's temperature may rise four degrees, and the esters you'll get are only tolerable in certain Belgian specialty ales and perhaps weizenbock.

You also increase chances of infection by brewing in warm weather—be especially conscious of sanitation. Brew smaller batches (for example, reduce 10-gallon batches to 5) and keg condition with forced carbonation, rather than bottle condition, to decrease the risk of something funky getting in your beer and to minimize your losses if it does.

ENJOYING WORLD BEER STYLES
Winter

December—Dozens of countries celebrate the Christmas season with strong drink, and the brewing nations are no exception. Try a true Trappist ale from one of the six monastic breweries of Belgium or a strong seasonal spiced ale from the United States. In Britain, barley wine is an excellent and warming sipping beer as is an imperial stout. In Germany, weizenbock is the first in a long line of bock beers. Sample a seasonal bock from Norway or Switzerland. This is also the time to sample a few bottles of mead. Sweet and still are the choices of style for this time of year to celebrate solstice, Kwaanza, Christmas, or any other winter holidays.

January—Many beer lovers enjoy stronger darker beers during the colder months. Strong porters are favorites in Slavic countries, and eisbocks are popular in Germany. Belgians consume the rich intensely malty Scotch ales in January, and the British have a variety of winter warmers to help fight the cold. In the United States, many breweries produce a strong version of spiced ale for the season.

February—February includes Valentine's Day, for which fruity Belgian lambics are appropriate. Meads and braggots, thought to have aphrodisiac qualities as well as a warming alcohol content, are also suitable drinks. Also, the Mardi Gras season is a time for much revelry in Germany, and in many other countries. Enjoy a good bock or several strong Belgian ales.

Spring

March—A big month to consume and produce beer is March. Märzen and bière de Mars are traditionally produced, not consumed, in March. In many countries, tradition dictates that March is the last month of the brewing season, so production is in full swing to put away reserves for the summer and following season. It is also the Lent season, and in Germany, this has always been associated with doppelbock. As March marks the end of the coldest weather, it is also a good month to indulge in a strong version of bock beer, eisbock. On the last Saturday of this month, the Eisbock Festival in Kulmbach, Germany, taps the year's new batch of this style. In Ireland, Irish red ale and dry stouts or porters are drunk in celebration of Saint Patrick's Day.

April—Standard bocks are in season during April as the weather begins to change. Helles and dunkel bocks replace dopplebock as the preferred beer in Germany. For a lighter brew, try a soft hoppy kölsch from Cologne or a Belgian golden ale. Likewise, a British pale ale may lighten spirits dampened by wet weather.

May—Maibock is the obvious choice for this month, and the Germans switch bocks once again. Festivals involving beer abound worldwide. Cinco de Mayo, in Mexico, is rejoiced with the crisp malty Mexican version of the Vienna-style lager. Celebrate the delicate flowery Saaz hop with Czech Pilseners that were brewed in February when the year's new hop harvest arrived. In Scotland, the oldest brewery of that nation, Traquair House, has its own beer festival—reason enough to open a few bottles of hearty Scotch ale.

Summer

June—When summer finally hits, it's good to have a tart, thirst-quenching fruit beer, perhaps made with wheat, in the tradition of a Belgian-style lambic. As fruit beer gains popularity in the United States, several interpretations of this style are widely available. In northern Germany, Berliner weisse is the favorite summer drink, laced with fruit syrups to cut some of the lactic tartness of this refreshing style. Bavaria has its own renown specialty in the wheat beer category: hefeweizen. Have some of your own hefeweizen on tap for the warmer months. Its higher fermentation temperatures make it easy to brew in summer—bottle conditioning ensures a longer shelf life, even at summer temperatures—and it's one of the few beer styles that you can quaff for breakfast without raising eyebrows among fellow beer aficionados. With the coming of the summer solstice, many may want to raise a glass of chilled sparkling mead.

July—American ales and lagers are appropriate for the heat of July and August. Served very cold, they are refreshing and light-bodied enough to beat the warmest Independence Day weather. France's Bastille Day makes a perfect opportunity to sample a saison or a bière de garde. India pale ale is another hot-weather beer, held over from the winter months. It may be a stronger beer than you're used to this time of year, but the liberal use of hops makes it dry and satisfying. Witbier, or Belgian-style white, has a cloudy sediment with voluminous carbonation and a hint of tartness. Not unlike German wheat beer, it gains its spicy character from the addition of coriander and/or orange peel more than from the phenolic character of its yeast.

August—High cereal adjunct ales and lagers are popular choices this month for their light body and flavor—variations on the light lager are ideal choices. For a change, try a Caribbean-, Mediterranean-, Asian-, or South Pacific–style lager—the differences from our own versions are often subtle but are worth seeking out.

Fall

September—As things finally begin to cool down a bit, brewers begin to plan their recipes for the coming season. Amber ales or California common lagers in the United States and bitters in the United Kingdom are appropriate beers in strength and color for the advent of fall. The German equivalent, altbier, is also a fine medium-strength brew. Oktoberfest is traditionally celebrated at the end of September, so no one will say anything if you decide to tap that keg of Märzen a tad early. Several beer festivals also occur in northern Belgium this month, so a Flemish-style specialty ale is not out of order.

October—Perhaps the biggest month in the beer calendar, October marks the beginning of the new brewing season. Copious amounts of Oktoberfest are consumed worldwide, but darker lagers like schwarzbier are also appropriate as the days shorten. Apart from the world-renown German festival, the Great American Beer Festival® happens at the beginning of this month in Denver, Colorado. British ESBs are an excellent choice for British ale lovers, as are English mild and Scottish ales.

November—Colder weather prompts many to turn to stronger winter-style beers. In England, old ales are popular this month. Likewise, brown ale and sweeter stouts are good drinks to enjoy in a warm pub. Americans share their own versions of brown and stout, generally a bit stronger, with family and friends at Thanksgiving. In Germany, one might be tempted to sample a rauchbier or smoked lager, originally from the town of Bamberg. It is certainly rich and flavorful enough to go with any hearty winter fare.

NOTE ON THE RECIPES

The recipes included in *A Year of Beer* are largely from the American Homebrewers Association National Homebrew Competitions (NHC). These recipes are designated by NHC, and the place, category, year, and brewer's name are given. Most of the recipes are 1994, 1995, and 1996 competition entries; however, older winners are occasionally included because they were such good recipes. For more information about the NHC call (303) 447-0816. About a quarter of the recipes come from various club-only competitions, Boston Beer Company's World Homebrew Contest, *Zymurgy*® magazine, and individual brewers. Charlie Papazian also developed four new recipes for *A Year of Beer*.

Since every brewer uses different equipment and materials, there are often slight deviations in efficiency from brew house to brew house. It is wise to read every recipe thoroughly. The given amounts are not absolute. For example, you can adjust a specified amount of grain to obtain a better yield.

Two things are helpful to remember if you choose to do so: (1) preserve the character of a recipe by increasing or decreasing only the amount of base malt (usually pale); and (2) remember if you make a drastic change in malt, adjust your bitterness. For those brewers who want to double or triple a recipe's yield, remember you cannot always double the number of hops—get out the calculator and do some math to achieve the same bitterness. To help track your modifications, there is a beer log located in appendix A.

Note on Judges' Comments

These judges are each designated as recognized, certified, national, or master. During the competitions, they do not have access to the beer or mead recipes nor do they see fellow judges' comments. Therefore, please take into consideration that discrepancies sometimes arise in their analyses. It's all part of the judging process. Also, the term "okay" is frequently used in these analyses. Okay denotes that the characteristic being discussed is allowable within the style's parameter.

Reap the benefits from *A Year of Beer* and brew a superior batch of homebrew. Whether you are just embarking on this hobby or are a seasoned veteran, this is the perfect opportunity to gather new recipes and ideas from award-winning brewers. Good luck with your brewing endeavors!

WINTER

MEAD

Mead is made from the fermentation of honey and water with a wine, sherry, lager, ale, or mead yeast. Other traditional ingredients include fruit, herbs, and spices. The final gravity determines whether mead is dry, medium, sweet, or very sweet. Further subcategories, based on additional ingredients, include melomel (any fruit), cyser (apples), pyment (grapes), braggot (less than 50 percent malt fermentables), metheglin (any herbs or spices), and hippocras (spices and grapes). Meads are sparkling or still.

While beer always undergoes a long boil (with the possible exception of Berliner weisse), mead traditionally does not. Many meadmakers still follow this practice to preserve the delicate aromas and flavors of raw honey. Note, however, that this greatly increases the risk of infection. Some brewers choose to heat the mixture of honey and water to 160–175 °F (71–79 °C) to kill any harmful bacteria. Fresh raw honey has such a high concentration of sugars that it is usually sterile, but once diluted, it's a viable medium for a host of wild yeasts and bacteria.

Making mead is more similar to winemaking than brewing. It is a simpler process, but proper aging is essential—at least one year from bottling time. If storage takes place above cellar temperatures (55 °F [13 °C]), mead may ferment more in the bottle, causing slight carbonation. For sparkling meads, this is desirable, but for still versions, it may not be appropriate. Like winemakers, choose to use sulfites or pasteurization to stabilize your mead.

Urban Garden Metheglin

Gold Medal, NHC, Herb and Spice Mead, 1996
Mike Rivard, Chicago, Illinois

Ingredients for 2 Gallons

- 5 pounds clover honey
- 1 bunch lemon thyme
- 1 3-inch cinnamon stick
- 8 whole allspice
- 6 whole peppercorns
- Lalvin wine yeast No. EC-1118
- 2 teaspoons yeast nutrient

Original gravity:	1.120
Final gravity:	1.030
Boiling time:	—
Primary fermentation:	30 days at 65 °F (18 °C) in glass
Secondary fermentation:	5 months at 65 °F (18 °C) in glass
Age when judged:	5 months

Brewer's Specifics

Boil spices in 1 1/4 gallons of water and then steep for 60 minutes. Strain spices out and add honey to water.

Judges' Comments

"This metheglin is pleasantly balanced and lacks 'off' characteristics. Finishes pleasantly and carries with a nice blend of honey and pepper. Spices just at the flavor threshold—there, but not obnoxious."

"It is tough to sort out the individual components, but this mead does deliver a fine package. I would love this mead with a nice chicken or fish meal. Damn fine."

"All flavor comes through. Cinnamon, allspice, and peppercorn come in with a taste of honey. Good alcohol flavor. None of the ingredients are too overpowering."

"Good clean mead and very drinkable. No overpowering character. Honey comes through."

Hypocrite's Hippocras

Gold Medal, NHC, Still Mead, 1994
Kevin Stiles, Orefield, Pennsylvania

Ingredients for 1 Gallon
- 2 pounds clover honey
- 2 teaspoons malic acid
- 1 teaspoon cinnamon
- 1 teaspoon ginger
- 1 teaspoon orange peel
- 1 clove
- 18 fluid ounces Alexander's Gamay Beaujolais wine concentrate
- 2 Campden tablets
- Red Star Prise de Mousse yeast

Original gravity:	1.095
Final gravity:	1.000
Boiling time:	—
Primary fermentation:	13 days at 72 °F (22 °C) in glass
Secondary fermentation:	5 1/2 months at 72–53 °F (22–12 °C) in glass
Age when judged:	4 1/2 months

Judges' Comments
"Very astringent. Grape is there. Nice warming in aftertaste. Reasonable balance. This is a fascinating beverage! So many things going on. Tannins/astringency too much, but time will help. I don't think clove adds here."

"Honey is subtle but there. Cinnamon, clove, and alcohol combine to tickle the palate like pepper. Grapes give a pleasing tannic finish and add that wonderful color. Sweetness, acidity, and body are just right to accentuate the spices. Experiment with a different honey to further increase the aroma and deepen the flavor. I'm raving over this one! Congrats!"

"Big alcohol up front. Warming. Nice grape that gets overwhelmed by cinnamon first, then the rest of the spices. Nice medium dryness that carries in the warm lingering alcoholic finish. Nice job! I like the complexity and the honey-grape combination. I never really found the ginger or clove. You may increase them slightly next time."

After Dinner Dessert

Gold Medal, NHC, Fruit and Vegetable Mead, 1996
Michael Coen, Kenosha, Wisconsin

Ingredients for 5 Gallons
12	pounds generic clover/wildflower honey
6	pounds red raspberries
4	pounds orange blossom honey
3 1/2	pounds blueberries
4	teaspoons acid blend
4	teaspoons yeast nutrient
1 1/2	teaspoons Irish moss
	Wyeast No. 3184 sweet mead yeast

Original gravity:	1.100
Final gravity:	1.024
Boiling time:	—
Primary fermentation:	2 weeks at 66 °F (19 °C) in glass
Secondary fermentation:	5 1/2 weeks at 66 °F (19 °C) in glass
Tertiary fermentation:	5 weeks at 66 °F (19 °C) in glass
Age when judged:	13 months

Brewer's Specifics
Boil honey and Irish moss with 5 gallons of water for 20 minutes. Add fruit, yeast nutrient, and acid blend. Stabilize temperature at 160 °F (71 °C) for 15 minutes. Cool with wort chiller, pitch yeast starter, and aerate.

Judges' Comments
"Very good. Really like the berry flavor. Good job. This is sweet but could use more honey tones."

"Sweet. Fruity. Smooth finish. Good balance. Clean."

Mighty Fine Wine

Gold Medal, NHC, Traditional Mead and Braggot, 1996
Scott Mills, Loveland, Colorado

Ingredients for 5 Gallons
15 pounds wildflower honey
 1 tablespoon crushed coriander
 1 tablespoon dried orange peel
    Wyeast No. 3184 sweet mead yeast

Original gravity:	1.110
Final gravity:	—
Boiling time:	—
Primary fermentation:	60 days at 65 °F (18 °C) in glass
Secondary fermentation:	210 days at 65 °F (18 °C) in glass
Age when judged:	3 months

Judges' Comments
"Honey comes through very nicely."

"I would like a touch more alcohol to balance the sweetness, but very nice."

"Clean excellent honey presence and delicate smooth sweetness."

"Excellent mead. Wonderful balance. Good honey presence. Nice pH level."

Untitled

Gold Medal, NHC, Traditional Mead and Braggot, 1995
Paddy Giffen, Rohnert Park, California

Ingredients for 3 Gallons
12 1/2	pounds citrus honey
2	ounces The Beverage People™ mead yeast nutrient
	Prise de Mousse yeast

Original gravity:	1.121
Final gravity:	1.028
Boiling time:	—
Primary fermentation:	6 weeks at 68 °F (20 °C) in glass
Secondary fermentation:	4 months at 68 °F (20 °C) in glass
Age when judged:	3 months

Judges' Comments
"Good honey balance, but alcohol is a little prickly and hot. Very nice body. This is a nice sweet still mead."

"Very good balance. Orange comes through nicely. Very good!"

"Sweet, full, honey flavor. Good balance with alcohol flavor and warmth. Excellent mead."

Anointing Oil

Gold Medal, NHC, Still Mead, 1994
Byron Burch, Santa Rosa, California

Ingredients for 11 Gallons
36	pounds Meadmaker's Magic™ Canadian clover honey
10 1/2	ounces freshly squeezed lime juice
5	ounces tartaric acid
4	ounces The Beverage People™ yeast nutrient for meads
1	ounce The Beverage People pectic enzyme
1	tablespoon Irish moss
5	milliliters lime oil
20	grams The Beverage People Prise de Mousse wine yeast
10	gallons water

Original gravity:	1.108
Final gravity:	—
Boiling time:	5 minutes
Primary fermentation:	2 weeks at 75 °F (24 °C) in glass
Secondary fermentation:	2 weeks at 75 °F (24 °C) in glass
Age when judged:	4 months

Judges' Comments
"Nice honey flavor. Lime is present but more would be better. Very slight spritz. Good acidity to balance sweetness. More lime and this could score higher. A very good, clean, well-made mead. I personally believe this would be a better sparkling product."

"Slight carbonation gives a very nice mouthfeel. Lime comes through to balance the sweetness. Great job. Subtle lime. More bottle age will improve this tremendously. Excellent job. Terrific balance. A little more lime might make its presence better felt, but a terrific job nonetheless. Perhaps 5% more lime."

"Light lime nose. Honey, lime, acid balance is fine. Clean and to the point."

"Wonderful balance of honey and citrus fruit. The acidity is very nicely counterpointed. Excellent overall impression. Except for a little unexpected carbonation, this was great. I'd actually carbonate a little more on purpose."

Strawberry Kiss

First Place, Club-Only Competition, Sweet Mead, 1996
Hal Buttermore, Ann Arbor, Michigan

Ingredients for 5 Gallons

12 1/2   pounds wildflower/clover honey
9 1/2   pounds fresh strawberries
          Yeast Lab® sweet mead yeast

Original gravity:	—
Final gravity:	—
Boiling time:	—
Primary fermentation:	2 weeks at 65 °F (18 °C) in glass
Secondary fermentation:	2 years at 65 °F (18 °C) in glass
Age when judged:	—

It's My First Mead

Gold Medal, NHC, Still Mead, 1994
Andrew La Morte and Susanne Price, Littleton, Colorado

Ingredients for 10 Gallons

35	pounds clover honey
4 1/2	teaspoons yeast nutrient
2 1/2	teaspoons acid blend
2	teaspoons Irish moss
	Lalvin EC-1118 yeast

Original gravity:	1.140
Final gravity:	1.068
Boiling time:	—
Primary fermentation:	6 weeks at 68 °F (20 °C) in glass
Secondary fermentation:	9 months at 65 °F (18 °C) in glass
Age when judged:	6 months

Brewer's Specifics

Heat honey and water to 170 °F (77 °C) for 30 minutes. Oxygenate with pure oxygen for 15 minutes.

Judges' Comments

"Pleasant, vinous, and sweet. No major angularities or detractors. Might need a bit of acid in finish, but that's subjective. Very nice dessert mead. May lack a bit of complexity but really clean and drinkable. Good job."

"Light body. Very sweet all the way around. Clean flavor. Not as complex as I would like. Nothing to cry about though. Nice flavor. Easy to drink. No major flaws in taste."

"Veruyu" Mead

Silver Medal, NHC, Sparkling Traditional Mead, 1996
Byron Burch, Santa Rosa, California

Ingredients for 5 Gallons
21	pounds Meadmaker's Magic™ Canadian clover honey
4	tablespoons tartaric acid
1/4	teaspoon Irish moss
2	ounces The Beverage People™ yeast nutrient for meads
20	grams dry Prise de Mousse wine yeast

Original gravity:	1.136
Final gravity:	—
Boiling time:	5 minutes
Primary fermentation:	1 week at 75 °F (24 °C) in glass
Secondary fermentation:	2 weeks at 75 °F (24 °C) in glass
Age when judged:	4 months

Judges' Comments
"Great expression of honey. Clover predominates. Nice alcohol level."

"Great color [and] carbonation. Great. Slight layering."

"Great honey flavor. Wonderful sweetness. Could use more acid to help balance finish."

"Excellent mead. Nothing overpowers. Very well balanced."

SCHWARZBIER

Literally, schwarzbier is "black beer," as the style is called in other parts of the world. Bottom-fermented schwarzbier has a full body with a flavor like bitter chocolate from the roasted malts. It is opaque black with a moderate gravity of 1.042–1.056 (11–14 °Plato), yielding 4–5.5 percent alcohol by volume. The style generally has low to moderate bitterness and no hop flavor or aroma. Some malt sweetness is evident though heavily masked by roasted flavors. Fruitiness, esters, and diacetyl are inappropriate. This is a great beer to enjoy during cold weather.

Black Mariah

Gold Medal, NHC, Bavarian Dark, 1995
Paul Sullivan, Brooklyn, New York
(All-Grain)

Ingredients for 11 Gallons
- 15 pounds two-row Briess malt
- 2 pounds Ireks Munich malt
- 1 pound chocolate malt
- 1 pound Munton and Fison crystal malt
- 1/2 pound black patent malt
- 2 ounces Hallertau hops, 4.5% alpha acid
- 1 ounce Hallertau hops, 4.5% alpha acid
- 1 ounce Hallertau hops, 4.5% alpha acid
- yeast from Zip City Brewing Company
- 3/4 cup corn sugar (to prime)

Original gravity:	1.052
Final gravity:	1.010
Boiling time:	90 minutes
Primary fermentation:	3 weeks at 48 °F (9 °C) in glass
Secondary fermentation:	3 weeks at 40 °F (4 °C) in glass
Age when judged:	3 months

Brewer's Specifics
Mash grains at 152 °F (67 °C) for 90 minutes.

Judges' Comments
"Roasty malt. Sweetness a little high for style. Low bitterness from roast malt. Very drinkable. Smooth schwarzbier."

"Dry finish. Sharp roastiness present without excess. Lingering mellow bitterness. Across-the-board balanced. Malt firmness complements bitter chocolate flavors."

"I like the bitter chocolate. Nice rich maltiness without being too aggressive. Noble-spicy hops in background. Some dark-malt acidity in finish."

Beaver Creek™ Double Raven Lager

Gold Medal, NHC, German Dark Lager, 1996
Tom Bergman and Chas Peterson, Jefferson, Maryland
(All-Grain)

Ingredients for 6 1/2 Gallons
6	pounds Munich malt
5 1/2	pounds Klages malt
1	pound biscuit malt
1	pound crystal malt
1/2	pound CaraPils malt
1/2	pound aromatic malt
1/2	pound chocolate malt
1/2	pound CaraMunich malt
1/4	pound Belgian Special "B" malt
1	ounce Northern Brewer hop pellets, 8.9% alpha acid (60 minutes)
3/4	ounce Hallertau hops, 2.6% alpha acid (20 minutes)
1/2	ounce Mittelfruh hop pellets, 2.6% alpha acid (5 minutes)
	Wyeast No. 2206 Bavarian lager yeast
3/4	cup corn sugar (to prime)

Original gravity:	1.068
Final gravity:	1.022
Boiling time:	120 minutes
Primary fermentation:	12 days at 44 °F (7 °C) in glass
Secondary fermentation:	24 days at 44 °F (7 °C) in glass
Age when judged:	5 1/2 months

Brewer's Specifics
For the double decoction mash, the main mash temperature rests are at 122 °F (50 °C) for 30 minutes, 160 °F (71 °C) for 30 minutes, and 170 °F (77 °C) for 30 minutes.

Judges' Comments
"Medium malt sweetness. Low bitterness. Good beer. Could use a bit more roast malt and a bit more hop bitterness."

"Nice malty-roasted malt flavor. Could use a bit more hop bitterness. A very nice beer."

"Malt flavor is there. Hop bitterness is somewhat lacking. Needs more 'noble-type' hops maybe. Very good effort."

Black Heart

Bronze Medal, NHC, Schwarzbier, 1995
Delano and Katy DuGarm, Arlington, Virginia
(All-Grain)

Ingredients for 5 Gallons
- 9 pounds DeWolf-Cosyns Pilsener malt
- 1 pound aromatic malt
- 1 pound Munich malt
- 1/2 pound DeWolf-Cosyns chocolate malt
- 1/3 pound CaraPils malt
- 1/4 pound DeWolf-Cosyns roasted barley
- 1/4 pound black patent malt
- 1/4 pound CaraVienne malt
- 1 ounce Perle hops, 7.5% alpha acid (60 minutes)
- 1 ounce Crystal hops, 4.2% alpha acid (10 minutes)
- 1 ounce Crystal hops, 4.2% alpha acid
- Wyeast No. 2007 Pilsen lager yeast

Original gravity:	1.060
Final gravity:	1.025
Boiling time:	—
Primary fermentation:	7 days at 48 °F (9° C) in glass
Secondary fermentation:	7 days at 48 °F (9° C) in glass
Tertiary fermentation:	35 days at 32 °F (0° C) in glass
Age when judged:	4 months

Brewer's Specifics
Mash grains at 154 °F (68 °C) for 60 minutes.

Judges' Comments
"Black roast malt aroma. Almost a smoky quality to it. No substantial hop aroma. Full maltiness. Very rich. Black malt acidity in aftertaste. Very chewy, perhaps a bit too chewy. Hop character is okay."

"Well rounded. Creamy. Slightly sweet with balancing toastiness. Sharp without being harsh. Could be too sweet."

Untitled

Silver Medal, NHC, Bavarian Dark, 1994
Thomas Altenbach, Tracy, California
(All-Grain)

Ingredients for 10 Gallons

10	pounds pale malt
4	pounds light Munich malt
2	pounds toasted malt
2	pounds chocolate malt
1	pound flaked barley
1	pound dextrin malt
1	pound dark crystal malt
1/4	pound brown malt
3	ounces roasted malt
3	ounces black malt
1	ounce Perle hops, 9.1% alpha acid (60 minutes)
1/2	ounce Perle hops, 9.1% alpha acid (30 minutes)
1 1/2	ounces Mt. Hood hops, 6.3% alpha acid (10 minutes)
3	ounces Hallertau hops, 5.2% alpha acid (finish)
1	ounce Mt. Hood hops, 6.3% alpha acid (finish)
	Wyeast No. 2308 Munich lager yeast
1 1/2	cup corn sugar (to prime)

Original gravity:	1.056
Final gravity:	1.016
Boiling time:	120 minutes
Primary fermentation:	10 days at 50 °F (10 °C) in glass
Secondary fermentation:	19 days at 40 °F (4 °C) in glass
Age when judged:	7 months

Brewer's Specifics

Mash grains at 155 °F (68 °C) for 90 minutes.

Judges' Comments

"Roasted malt character. Some roasted malt bitterness. Medium sweetness high for style but balanced by roasted malts. An excellent beer."

"Clean tasting. Roasted malts and plenty of hops come through. A lingering smokiness in the finish. Good beer. Hop it less, and it will fit the style nicely."

"Too sweet for style. Nice balance otherwise. Roasty malt evident. Too sweet and perhaps a little big for style but excellent beer."

Big Black's Revenge

NHC, Schwarzbier, 1996
Tony Steenkolk, Boise, Idaho
(Extract/Grain)

Ingredients for 7 1/2 Gallons
       6   pounds amber extract malt
       5   pounds dark extract malt
       2   pounds 80 °L crystal malt
       1   pound chocolate malt
       1   pound black patent malt
  3 1/4   ounces Hallertau hop pellets, 3.5% alpha acid (60 minutes)
  1 1/4   ounces Hallertau hop pellets, 3.9% alpha acid (30 minutes)
  1 1/4   ounces Tettnang hop pellets, 3.4% alpha acid (15 minutes)
           Wyeast No. 2206 Bavarian lager yeast
           force-carbonate in keg

Original gravity:	1.063
Final gravity:	1.025
Boiling time:	60 minutes
Primary fermentation:	2 weeks at 55 °F (13 °C) in glass
Secondary fermentation:	4 weeks at 45 °F (7 °C) in stainless steel
Age when judged:	3 months

Brewer's Specifics
Steep grains at 170 °F (77 °C) for 30 minutes.

BOCK

Dunkel (dark) and *helles* (light) commonly designate traditional bock. Both subtypes are very clean and malty. The malt dominates both bouquet and flavor, though the dunkels have more caramel tones. Bock is always made with lager yeast strains, fermented cold, and lagered for at least two months. Hop profile is minimal, and bitterness is very restrained. "Noble-type" hops serve only to balance some of the malt sweetness (20–30 IBU). Roasted malt flavors are inappropriate for this style, so use dark caramel malt to give color (20–30 SRM for dunkel, 4–6 SRM for helles). Alcohol is fairly high—original gravity for both styles is 1.064–1.072 (16–18 °Plato), leaving an alcohol content between 6 and 7.5 percent by volume.

Thanksgiving Bock

Winner, Club-Only Competition, Traditional Bock, 1996
Bruce Stott, Rockville, Connecticut
(All-Grain)

Ingredients for 5 Gallons
5 1/2	pounds Durst Munich malt
4 1/2	pounds Briess pale malt
1	pound toasted Munich malt
1	pound wheat malt
1/2	pound 90 °L crystal malt
1/2	pound 40 °L crystal malt
4/5	ounce Northern Brewer hop pellets, 8.9% alpha acid (60 minutes)
1	ounce Liberty hop pellets, 3.9% alpha acid (30 minutes)
	Wyeast No. 2206 Bavarian lager yeast
3/4	cup corn sugar (to prime)

Original gravity:	1.066
Final gravity:	1.021
Boiling time:	75 minutes
Primary fermentation:	3 weeks at 45–50 °F (7–10 °C) in glass
Secondary fermentation:	2 weeks at 45–50 °F (7–10 °C) in glass
Age when judged:	5 months

Brewer's Specifics
Single decoction mash rests are at 122 °F (50 °C) for 30 minutes, 142 °F (61 °C) for 15 minutes, and 157 °F (69 °C) for 20 minutes.

Judges' Comments
"Very effervescent. Excellent mouthfeel. Excellent brew."

"Full body. Great flavor. Excellent beer."

Bock

Winner, World Homebrew Contest, Bock, 1996
Meleq Kacani, Westlake Village, California
(All-Grain)

Ingredients for 5 Gallons
8 1/2 pounds Durst Munich malt
   1 pound Durst Pilsener malt
   1 pound Gambrinus honey malt
 1/2 pound Durst 50 °L caramel malt
 1/2 pound Durst 90 °L caramel malt
   4 ounces chocolate malt
   2 ounces black malt
   1 ounce Spalt hops (60 minutes)
   1 ounce Hallertau hops (60 minutes)
 1/4 ounce Hallertau hops (10 minutes)
   1 teaspoon chalk added to mash
     Wyeast No. 2206 Bavarian lager yeast

Original gravity:	1.066
Final gravity:	1.024
Boiling time:	—
Primary fermentation:	10 days at 50 °F (10 °C)
Secondary fermentation:	—
Age when judged:	2 months

Brewer's Specifics
Employ a two decoction mash. Mash-in at 100 °F (38 °C). Decoction rest is at 158 °F (70 °C) for 10 minutes. Boil for 15 minutes. Main mash rests are at 127 °F (53 °C) for 20 minutes, 154 °F (68 °C) for 30 minutes, and 170 °F (77 °C) for 10 minutes.

How I Survived Lent

NHC, Traditional Bock, 1996
Paul Lachmanek, Sierra Vista, Arizona
(Extract/Grain)

Ingredients for 5 Gallons
6 3/5   pounds Yellow Dog malt extract
3 1/3   pounds Home Brewery hopped dark malt
1   pound Alexander's amber malt
1/2   pound dark crystal malt
1/2   pound chocolate malt
1/2   pound Victory malt
1   ounce Saaz hop pellets, 5.3% alpha acid (60 minutes)
1   ounce Kent Goldings hop pellets, 5.5% alpha acid (60 minutes)
3/4   ounce Hallertau hop pellets, 4.1% alpha acid (60 minutes)
     Wyeast No. 2124 Bohemian lager yeast
3/4   cup dextrose (to prime)

Original gravity:	1.070
Final gravity:	1.018
Boiling time:	60 minutes
Primary fermentation:	11 days at 65 °F (18 °C) in plastic
Secondary fermentation:	—
Age when judged:	4 1/2 months

Brewer's Specifics
Steep grains at 155 °F (68 °C) for 20 minutes. Boil for 60 minutes.

Floyd's Bock

NHC, Doppelbock, 1996
Floyd Atherton Jr., Independence, Kansas
(Extract/Grain)

Ingredients for 5 Gallons

- 6   pounds amber dry malt extract
- 3   pounds dark dry malt extract
- 1/2 pound chocolate malt
- 3   ounces Tettnang hop pellets, 3.7% alpha acid (60 minutes)
- 1   ounce Hallertau hop pellets, 3.7% alpha acid (15 minutes)
-    Wyeast No. 2206 Bavarian lager yeast

Original gravity:	1.074
Final gravity:	1.022
Boiling time:	60 minutes
Primary fermentation:	14 days at 45 °F (7 °C) in plastic
Secondary fermentation:	3 days at 45 °F (7 °C) in glass
Age when judged:	2 months

Brewer's Specifics

Steep grains at 155 °F (68 °C) for 20 minutes. Boil for 60 minutes.

Carnival Bock

Bock, 1997
Charlie Papazian, Boulder, Colorado
(All-Grain)

Ingredients for 5 Gallons

5	pounds two-row pale malt
4	pounds Munich malt
2	pounds wheat malt
1/2	pound Victory (or Belgian aromatic) malt
1/2	pound chocolate malt
1/2	pound Belgian CaraMunich malt
5	HBU German Northern Brewer hops (75 minutes)
2 1/2	HBU German Hersbrucker-Mittelfruh hop pellets (20 minutes)
1	HBU Czech Saaz hop pellets (10 minutes)
1	ounce American Tettnang hops (1–3 minutes)
1/4	teaspoon Irish moss
	Wyeast No. 2206 Bavarian lager yeast
3/4	cup corn sugar (to prime)

Original gravity:	1.063
Final gravity:	1.018
Boiling time:	75 minutes
Primary fermentation:	2 days in glass
Secondary fermentation:	2 weeks at 50 °F (10 °C)
Tertiary fermentation:	2–4 weeks at 40 °F (4.4 °C)

Brewer's Specifics

Employ a step infusion mash to mash the grains. Add 13 quarts (12 liters) of 143 °F (62 °C) water to the crushed grain, stir, stabilize, and hold the temperature at 133 °F (56 °C) for 30 minutes. Add 6 quarts (6 liters) of boiling water. Add heat to raise temperature to 152 °F (66.7 °C). Hold for about 60 minutes.

After conversion, raise temperature to 167 °F (75 °C), lauter, and sparge with 4 gallons (15.1 liters) of 170 °F (77 °C) water. Collect about 7 gallons (26.5 liters) of runoff, add bittering hops, and bring to a full and vigorous boil.

The total boil time will be 75 minutes. When 20 minutes remain, add first flavor hops. When 10 minutes remain, add second flavor hops and Irish moss. After a total wort boil of about 75 minutes (or when wort has been reduced to about 5.5 gallons [21 liters]), turn off the heat, add aroma hops, and let steep 1–3 minutes. Then separate or strain out and sparge hops. Chill the wort to 60 °F (15.6 °C) and direct into a sanitized fermenter (if you use a carboy, you will need a 6.5-gallon [64.6-liter] carboy for primary fermentation). Aerate the cooled wort well. Add active yeast and ferment for 2 days in the primary. Then, transfer into a secondary fermenter, chill to 50 °F (10 °C), and allow to continue fermenting for 2 weeks or until fermentation is complete. Then drop temperature to 40 °F (4.4 °C) and lager for an additional 2–4 weeks.

When secondary aging is complete, prime with sugar and either bottle or keg. Let condition at temperatures above 60 °F (15.5 °C) until it is clear and carbonated.

Flavor Comments

The original gravity does not qualify this as a traditional German-style bock beer, but we're not going to Germany to drink it. You'll enjoy it in your own home and perhaps, as the name implies, celebrating Carnival or Mardi Gras. If you don't celebrate this event, then I'm sure you'll invent something to celebrate with this highly drinkable, smooth, malty bock. With a little less alcohol than German bock beers, this beer's malt and European hop characteristics are highlighted. And, the cold lagering adds a velvety smoothness absent of esters and harsh notes.

Boudoir Bock II

Reprinted from 1996 Special Issue of *Zymurgy*
Mick and Vi Walker, Fargo, North Dakota
(All-Grain)

Ingredients for 10 Gallons

24 1/2	pounds Belgian Munich malt
3 1/2	pounds two-row Pilsener malt
1	pound CaraVienne malt
1	pound CaraMunich malt
1/4	pound chocolate malt
25	IBU Hallertau hops (bitter)
1/2	ounce Hallertau hops (flavor)
	Wyeast No. 2308 Munich lager yeast
	force-carbonate in keg

Original gravity:	1.080
Final gravity:	1.026
Boiling time:	90 minutes
Primary fermentation:	3 weeks at 50 °F (10 °C) in glass
Secondary fermentation:	2 weeks at 45 °F (7 °C) in glass
Tertiary fermentation:	6 weeks at 38 °F (3 °C) in keg

Brewer's Specifics

Use a triple decoction mash. The main mash rest temperatures are at 100, 122, 149, and 167 °F (38, 50, 65, and 75 °C). The mash cooker rest temperatures are at 122, 149, and 160 °F (50, 65, and 71 °C).

Bock

Second Place, Club-Only Competition, Traditional Bock, 1996
Robert Dawson, New Carrollton, Maryland
(All-Grain)

Ingredients for 6 Gallons

8	pounds DeWolf-Cosyns Pilsener malt
8	pounds DeWolf-Cosyns Munich malt
1/2	pound DeWolf-Cosyns wheat malt
1/2	pound 10 °L caramel malt
9/10	ounce Perle hop flowers, 7.3% alpha acid (60 minutes)
3/5	ounce Perle hop flowers, 7% alpha acid (60 minutes)
3/4	ounce Ultra hop flowers, 3.3% alpha acid (30 minutes)
1/2	ounce Ultra hop flowers, 3.3% alpha acid (finish)
	Dominion lager yeast slurry
	force-carbonate

Original gravity:	1.070
Final gravity:	1.020
Boiling time:	60 minutes
Primary fermentation:	3 weeks at 46 °F (8 °C) in glass
Secondary fermentation:	2 weeks at 45 °F (7 °C) in glass
Tertiary fermentation:	2 months at 32 °F (0 °C) in stainless steel keg
Age when judged:	—

Brewer's Specifics

Employ a double decoction mash. Total mash time is 230 minutes.

August's Bock

NHC, Traditional Bock, 1996
Mike Bardallis, Allen Park, Michigan
(All-Grain)

Ingredients for 5 Gallons

9	pounds Briess two-row pale malt
3 1/2	pounds Briess Munich 20 °L crystal malt
1/4	pound Briess caramel malt
1/4	pound chocolate malt
7	HBU Northern Brewer hops, 8.2% alpha acid (60 minutes)
1/2	ounce Tettnang hops, 3.3% alpha acid (10 minutes)
	Wyeast No. 2308 Munich lager yeast
	force-carbonate

Original gravity:	1.069
Final gravity:	1.019
Boiling time:	90 minutes
Primary fermentation:	10 days at 48–50 °F (9–10 °C) in glass
Secondary fermentation:	60 days at 50–30 °F (10–4 °C) in stainless steel
Age when judged:	2 months

IMPERIAL STOUT

This very complex beer is rich with roasted malt flavors, fruity esters from the relatively warm fermentation, and alcohol. The color of imperial stout ranges from deep copper to opaque black. Full body is appropriate with a rich dominating maltiness. Bitterness is medium to high (50–80 IBU). Alcohol is usually very high, 7–9 percent by volume. Low levels of diacetyl are acceptable.

Rapid Run Stout

Silver Medal, NHC, Imperial Stout, 1995
James Gebhardt, Fargo, North Dakota
(Extract/Grain)

Ingredients for 5 Gallons

10 3/4	pounds six-row malt
6	pounds Briess dark malt extract syrup
1 1/4	pounds 80 °L crystal malt
1/2	pound chocolate malt
1/2	pound black patent malt
1/2	pound special roasted malt
1/4	pound black barley malt
1/4	pound wheat malt
1/4	pound CaraPils malt
2	ounces Bullion hops, 10.1% alpha acid (60 minutes)
2 1/2	ounces Cluster hops, 7% alpha acid (30 minutes)
3	ounces Mt. Hood hops, 2.3% alpha acid (2 minutes)
1/2	ounce Cascade hops, 5% alpha acid (2 minutes)
	Wyeast No. 1084 Irish ale yeast
3/4	cup dextrose (to prime)

Original gravity:	1.105
Final gravity:	1.030
Boiling time:	60 minutes
Primary fermentation:	30 days at 60 °F (16 °C) in glass
Secondary fermentation:	—
Age when judged:	5 months

Brewer's Specifics

Mash grains at 150 °F (66 °C) for 90 minutes.

Judges' Comments

"Alcohol evident (very!). Bitter but not any hop flavor. Very slight malt sweetness. Roast malt. Needs more late addition of hops for hop aroma and flavor. Bitterness is okay or perhaps a little high."

"Sweet with some licorice. Alcohol evident. Maltiness and bitterness very much there. A big beer with lots of malt and hops. Balance leans a bit toward the hops' side."

Rose's Russian Imperial Stout with Mayo

First Place, Club-Only Competition, Imperial Stout, 1995
Dick Van Dyke, Park Forest, Illinois
(Extract/Grain)

Ingredients for 5 Gallons

6 2/3	pounds Northwestern dark malt extract
5	pounds six-row malt
2	pounds 90 °L crystal malt
1	pound black patent malt
1	pound chocolate malt
1	pound Munich malt
1/4	pound wheat malt
5 1/2	ounces Eroica hops, 10.6% alpha acid (60 minutes)
1	ounce Chinook hops, 11.3% alpha acid (60 minutes)
1	ounce Kent Goldings hops, 4.7% alpha acid (45 minutes)
1	ounce Cascade hops, 4.9% alpha acid (45 minutes)
1	ounce Fuggles hops, 4.5% alpha acid (45 minutes)
1	ounce Chinook hops, 10.8% alpha acid (45 minutes)
1	ounce Kent Goldings hops, 4.7% alpha acid (30 minutes)
3/4	ounce Cascade hops, 4.9% alpha acid (30 minutes)
1	ounce Kent Goldings hops, 4.7% alpha acid (10 minutes)
1	ounce Fuggles hops, 3.4% alpha acid (10 minutes)
1	cup molasses
1	inch licorice stick
2	packages Red Star champagne yeast
2/3	cup corn sugar (to prime)

Original gravity:	1.107
Final gravity:	1.047
Boiling time:	60 minutes
Primary fermentation:	3 days at 65 °F (18 °C) in plastic
Secondary fermentation:	6 days at 63 °F (17 °C) in glass
Tertiary fermentation:	28 days at 63 °F (17 °C) in glass
Age when judged:	6 months

Brewer's Specifics
Mash all grains at 130 °F (54 °C) for 30 minutes. Raise temperature to 150 °F (66 °C) for 60 minutes and then 156 °F (69 °C) for 30 minutes.

Judges' Comments
"Molasses, licorice, roasted malt. Very nice beer. Well-made imperial stout."

Imperial Curmudgeon

Reprinted from 1991 Special Issue of *Zymurgy*
Dave Hammaker, Roaring Spring, Pennsylvania
(Extract/Grain)

Ingredients for 5 Gallons

6	pounds William's English dark malt extract
6	pounds William's Australian dark malt extract
2 1/4	pounds American rice extract
1 7/8	pounds crystal malt
1 2/3	pounds American dark malt extract
11	ounces black patent malt
9	ounces chocolate malt
6	ounces roasted barley
1	ounce Green Bullet hops, 10% alpha acid (45 minutes)
1	ounce Northern Brewer hops, 8.1% alpha acid (45 minutes)
1	ounce Pride of Ringwood hops, 8.9% alpha acid (45 minutes)
1	ounce Chinook hops, 11.9% alpha acid (45 minutes)
1	ounce Mt. Hood hops, 7.8% alpha acid (15 minutes)
1	ounce Cascade hops, 5% alpha acid (15 minutes)
3/4	ounce Mt. Hood hops, 7.8% alpha acid (steep)
3/4	ounce Cascade hops, 5% alpha acid (steep)
1/2	ounce East Kent Goldings hops, 5.9% alpha acid (steep)
2	teaspoons gypsum
	K-1 dry wine yeast
1/2	cup sugar (to prime)

Original gravity:	1.120
Final gravity:	1.050
Boiling time:	45 minutes
Primary fermentation:	2 weeks
Secondary fermentation:	2 months
Age when judged:	15 months

Judges' Comments

"Very rich aroma. Very full-flavored. This beer is very strong! Marked down only for its excessive strength. A barley wine?"

"Nice malty nose. Alcoholic. A wonderful beer. A lot of everything here, but it is well balanced."

Thameside Thumper

Bronze Medal, NHC, Imperial Stout, 1996
Ross Hastings, Edmonton, Alberta, Canada
(All-Grain)

Ingredients for 3 1/4 Gallons

10	pounds two-row pale malt
1 1/2	pounds roasted barley
1	pound unmalted barley
12	ounces 75 °L crystal malt
4	ounces CaraMunich malt
3	ounces chocolate malt
0.84	ounce Nugget hops, 11.8% alpha acid (60 minutes)
2 1/3	ounces Goldings hops, 5% alpha acid (20 minutes)
3/4	ounce Goldings hops, 5% alpha acid (dry)
	Wyeast No. 1028 London ale yeast

Original gravity:	1.088
Final gravity:	1.032
Boiling time:	80 minutes
Primary fermentation:	8 days at 67 °F (19 °C) in glass
Secondary fermentation:	25 days at 60 °F (16 °C) in glass
Age when judged:	1 month

Rasputin Imperial Russian Stout

Reprinted from 1996 Special Issue of *Zymurgy*
Peter Sidari, West Pittston, Pennsylvania
(Extract/Grain)

Ingredients for 6 1/2 Gallons

6 2/3 pounds Northwestern pale malt extract
6 2/3 pounds Northwestern amber malt extract
1   pound black patent malt
3/4 pound roasted barley
3/4 pound chocolate malt
2   ounces Galena bittering hops (24 HBU)
1   ounce Fuggles bittering hops (4.5 HBU)
1   ounce Cascade hops (finish)
1   ounce Hallertau hops (finish)
2   packages Edme ale yeast

Original gravity:	1.075
Final gravity:	1.018
Boiling time:	60 minutes
Primary fermentation:	2 weeks at 65 °F (18 °C)
Secondary fermentation:	6 weeks at 60 °F (16 °C)
Tertiary fermentation:	—

Brewer's Specifics

Add crushed grains to 2 gallons of water at 150 °F (66 °C) and hold for 45 minutes. Remove grains and bring to a boil. Add the extract and bittering hops. Boil for 60 minutes. Add finishing hops and boil for 15 more minutes. At same time, hydrate yeast with 1 cup of warm water at 100 °F (138 °C). Remove wort from heat, strain into 3 gallons of cold water and rinse hops with 170 °F (77 °C) water. Use enough water to bring total volume to 6 1/2 gallons.

Untitled

Finalist, NHC, Stout, 1996
Rich Bialkowski, Littleton, Colorado
(Extract/Grain)

Ingredients for 5 Gallons

6	pounds Northwestern dark malt extract syrup
3	pounds Munton and Fison extra dark dry malt extract
2 1/5	pounds Morgan's Master Blend Caramalt syrup
1	pound British 50 °L crystal malt
1/2	pound British chocolate malt
1/2	pound dextrin malt
1/2	pound German Munich malt
1/4	pound British roasted barley malt
0.15	pound Belgian black patent malt
3	ounces Bullton hop pellets, 8.5% alpha acid (60 minutes)
1	ounce Fuggles hops, 4.6% alpha acid (3 minutes)
6	teaspoons gypsum
	Wyeast No. 1084 Irish ale yeast
3/4	cup corn sugar (to prime)

Original gravity:	1.094
Final gravity:	1.027
Boiling time:	60 minutes
Primary fermentation:	7 days at 72 °F (22 °C) in glass
Secondary fermentation:	21 days at 72 °F (22 °C) in glass
Age when judged:	3 months

Brewer's Specifics

Mash grains at 156 °F (69 °C) for 35 minutes. Sparge, add extracts, and boil for 60 minutes.

Black Forest
Imperial Oatmeal Stout

Finalist, NHC, Specialty Beer, 1996
Dennis Garrett, Grand Forks, North Dakota
(Extract/Grain)

Ingredients for 5 Gallons

3 1/3	pounds John Bull amber malt extract
3 1/3	pounds John Bull dark malt extract
3	pounds pale barley malt
2	pounds flaked barley
1 1/2	pounds flaked oats
1	pound malted wheat
1	pound roasted barley
10	ounces light molasses added to boil
2 1/2	ounces Northern Brewer hop pellets, 8.1% alpha acid (60 minutes)
1	ounce Kent Goldings hop pellets, 5% alpha acid (15 minutes)
1/2	ounce Northern Brewer hop flowers, 7.7% alpha acid (15 minutes)
2	ounces Hallertau hop pellets, 3.2% alpha acid (5 minutes)
2	ounces white oak chips added to secondary (2 weeks)
1	stick brewer's licorice added to boil
	Brewer's Choice No. 1084 Irish ale yeast
1 1/4	cup light dry malt extract (to prime)

Original gravity:	1.082
Final gravity:	1.027
Boiling time:	60 minutes
Primary fermentation:	2 weeks at 70 °F (21 °C) in glass
Secondary fermentation:	—
Age when judged:	3 weeks

Brewer's Specifics

Mash grains at 136 °F (58 °C) for 90 minutes. Add 1 1/2 gallons of boiling water and hold at 156 °F (69 °C) for another 90 minutes. Sparge with 5 gallons of 170 °F (77 °C) water.

MUNICH HELLES/DUNKELS

This lager style is fuller in body than most classic European lagers and is a celebration beer in many parts of Bavaria. Heavier than its northern cousins, like Dortmunder, its accents are on malt rather than hops. It is pale to golden in color with medium body and malt sweetness. Low bitterness is acceptable for this style as is "noble-type" flavor and hop aroma. Fruity or estery character and diacetyl are inappropriate.

Lakewood Dunkel

Silver Medal, NHC, Munich Dunkel, 1996
Keith Weerts, Windsor, California
(Extract/Grain)

Ingredients for 5 3/5 Gallons

6	pounds Klages malt
3 1/2	pounds Munich malt
1/2	pound CaraPils malt
1/2	pound 80 °L crystal malt
1/2	pound Belgian CaraVienne malt
1/2	pound DME light malt extract
10	grams Hallertau hops, 4.6% alpha acid (60 minutes)
10	grams Northern Brewer pellets, 7.5% alpha acid (60 minutes)
15	grams Hallertau hops, 4.6% alpha acid (30 minutes)
10	grams Northern Brewer hop pellets, 7.5% alpha acid (5 minutes)
10	grams Hallertau hops, 4.6% alpha acid (5 minutes)
	Wyeast No. 2124 Bohemian lager yeast

Original gravity:	1.052
Final gravity:	1.015
Boiling time:	90 minutes
Primary fermentation:	10 days at 48 °F (9 °C) in glass
Secondary fermentation:	17 days at 32 °F (0 °C) in glass
Age when judged:	3 months

Brewer's Specifics

Mash grains at 154 °F (68 °C) for 90 minutes.

Central European Pils

Gold Medal, World Homebrew Competition,
Munich Helles, 1997
Rhett Rebold, Burke, Virginia
(All-Grain)

Ingredients for 12 Gallons

11	pounds German Pilsener malt
8	pounds Belgian Pilsener malt
1 1/2	pounds German Vienna malt
1 1/2	pounds CaraPils malt
3	ounces Saaz hops, 4.2% alpha acid (50 minutes)
1 2/3	ounces Saaz hops, 4.2% alpha acid (25 minutes)
4 1/2	ounces Saaz hops, 4.2% alpha acid (5 minutes)
	Wyeast No. 2124 Bohemian lager yeast
	force-carbonate in keg

Original gravity:	1.048
Final gravity:	1.013
Boiling time:	120 minutes
Primary fermentation:	18 days at 54 °F (12 °C) in glass
Secondary fermentation:	30 days at 38 °F (3 °C) in glass
Age when judged:	10 months

Brewer's Specifics

Mash grains at 152 °F (67 °C) for 180 minutes.

Judges' Comments

"Wonderful malt flavor. Nice hops. Clean finish. Great beer—most balanced I've had all day. Truly Munich."

"Great balance. Very good beer. Great balance on the side of bitterness toward a Dortmund export, but okay for style."

Untitled

**Finalist, World Homebrew Competition,
Munich Helles, 1997
Tom Sallese, Baltimore, Maryland
(Extract/Grain)**

Ingredients for 5 Gallons

- 4 pounds Alexander's pale malt extract
- 2 pounds American two-row pale malt
- 1 pound Vienna malt
- 1 pound dextrin malt
- 1/4 pound 40 °L crystal malt
- 1 ounce Perle pellets, 6.2% alpha acid (60 minutes)
- 1/2 ounce German Hallertau pellets, 4.7% alpha acid (5 minutes)
- Wyeast No. 2206 Bavarian lager yeast
- 3/4 cup corn sugar (to prime)

Original gravity:	1.055
Final gravity:	1.017
Boiling time:	60 minutes
Primary fermentation:	7 days at 55 °F (13 °C) in glass
Secondary fermentation:	7 days at 55 °F (13 °C) in glass
Tertiary fermentation:	14 days at 37 °F (3 °C) in glass

Brewer's Specifics

Mash grains at 152 °F (67 °C) for 60 minutes in 1 1/2 gallons of water.
Sparge with 2 gallons of water.

Bacher Brew #35

Silver Medal, NHC, Münchner-Style Helles, 1996
Don Bacher, Woodstock, Ontario, Canada
(All-Grain)

Ingredients for 10 Gallons

- 15.9 pounds Canadian two-row malt
- 0.66 pound Durst wheat malt
- 1.05 ounces Cluster pellets, 7.3% alpha acid (60 minutes)
- 0.18 ounce Saaz pellets, 2.0% alpha acid (25 minutes)
- 0.53 ounce Cascade pellets, 5.5% alpha acid (15 minutes)
- 1.06 ounces Cascade pellets, 5.5% alpha acid (3 minutes)
- 2.00 teaspoons gypsum
  distilled water
  Yeast Lab® L31 Pilsener yeast

Original gravity:	1.050
Final gravity:	1.016
Boiling time:	90 minutes
Primary fermentation:	12 days at 46 °F (8 °C) in glass
Secondary fermentation:	30 days at 46 °F (8 °C) in glass
Age when judged:	5 months

Brewer's Specifics

Mash grains at 126 °F (52 °C) for 30 minutes, 135 °F (57 °C) for 15 minutes, 150 °F (66 °C) for 15 minutes, 155 °F (70 °C) for 45 minutes, and 171 °F (77 °C) for 15 minutes. Sparge at 168 °F (76 °C).

Backyard Brown

Gold Medal, NHC, Munich Dunkel, 1994
John Rittenhouse, Folsom, California
(Extract/Grain)

Ingredients for 5 Gallons
- 10 pounds light malt extract
- 1 pound Munich malt
- 1 pound pale malt
- 1/2 pound 120 °L crystal malt
- 1/4 pound chocolate malt
- 2 ounces Hallertau hops, 3.7% alpha acid (60 minutes)
- 1 ounce Hallertau hops, 4.6% alpha acid (10 minutes)
- 1 ounce Hallertau hops, 4.6% alpha acid (finish)
- 1 teaspoon Irish moss (15 minutes)
- Wyeast No. 2206 Bavarian lager yeast
- 3/4 cup corn sugar (to prime)

Original gravity:	1.080
Final gravity:	1.040
Boiling time:	60 minutes
Primary fermentation:	2 weeks at 65 °F (18 °C) in glass
Secondary fermentation:	2 weeks at 40 °F (4 °C) in glass
Age when judged:	4 months

Brewer's Specifics
Mash grains at 155 °F (68 °C) for 60 minutes.

Judges' Comments
"Beautiful, malty, chocolate palate. Clean. Hop bitterness appropriate. A wonderful beer! I'll take a case."

"Good, malty, chocolate flavors. Back off on the flavor hops. I like this. Would be even better without the hop flavor and aroma."

"Big, roasty, caramel, malt character. Balance seems fine. Sweetness lingers. Excellent beer but lacks the big aroma that should go with it."

Drunkel

Gold Medal, NHC, Munich Dunkel, 1993
Jay Hersh, Medord, Massachusetts
(All-Grain)

Ingredients for 3 Gallons

2	pounds Ireks two-row Pilsener malt
1 1/2	pounds Ireks Munich malt
3/4	pound Ireks Vienna malt
1/2	pound aromatic malt
1/4	pound CaraPils malt
1/8	pound chocolate malt
1/2	ounce Tettnang hops (90 minutes)
1/2	ounce Styrian Goldings hops (5 minutes)
	Wyeast No. 2206 Bavarian yeast
	force-carbonate in keg

Original gravity:	1.046
Final gravity:	1.015
Boiling time:	90 minutes
Primary fermentation:	4 weeks at 48 °F (9 °C) in glass
Secondary fermentation:	12 weeks at 32 °F (0 °C) in stainless steel
Age when judged:	2 months

Brewer's Specifics

Mash grains at 130 °F (54 °C) for 30 minutes. Raise temperature to 152 °F (67 °C).

Judges' Comments

"Good job. Good malt character but could use some more. A little heavy on the roasted malt. Slightly bitter. Drying finish detracts. Clean."

"Sweet malt balanced with hops. Quite a bit of hops in finish. Slightly astringent. Very well-made beer."

"Nutty toasty flavor of malt blends very well with hops. Might be just a tad bitter. But very nice."

"Initial semisweet chocolate flavor dries out because of strong hop character. Needs a little more of the complex maltiness found in some beers of this style."

Brett's Dunkel

Finalist, NHC, Munich Dunkel, 1996
Joe Newcomer, Las Cruces, New Mexico
(All-Grain)

Ingredients for 6 Gallons

5	pounds Klages two-row malt
5	pounds Munich malt
1	pound 80 °L crystal malt
1	pound 40 °L crystal malt
1/2	pound Durst toasted malt
1/4	pound chocolate malt
1 1/2	ounces Hallertau Hersbrucker hop plugs, 4.5% alpha acid (60 minutes)
1/2	ounce Hallertau Hersbrucker hop plugs, 4.5% alpha acid (10 minutes)
10	grams chalk
	Wyeast No. 2124 Bohemian lager yeast
	force-carbonate in keg

Original gravity:	1.054
Final gravity:	1.016
Boiling time:	90 minutes
Primary fermentation:	14 days at 46 °F (8 °C) in stainless steel keg
Secondary fermentation:	21 days at 38 °F (3 °C) in glass
Tertiary fermentation:	6 weeks at 34 °F (1 °C) in stainless steel keg
Age when judged:	3 months

Brewer's Specifics

Mash grains at 155 °F (66 °C) for 30 minutes.

BARLEY WINE

This unusually strong ale requires extraordinary amounts of time to ferment and age, so plan ahead. The style yields 6–12 percent by volume alcohol content and is warming. The color of a barley wine ranges from copper to medium brown. Malty sweetness is appropriate with estery characters often pronounced. Bitterness varies from moderate to very high, though it is a good idea to have at least enough so that malt sweetness isn't cloying (40–75 IBU). Hop aroma and flavor vary from low to high, though malt usually replaces hop aroma when the beer has properly aged. High final gravities ensure a medium to full body. Low to medium diacetyl is okay.

Barley Wine #4

Gold Medal, NHC, Barley Wine, 1995
Gordon Olson, Los Alamos, New Mexico
(Extract/Grain)

Ingredients for 5 Gallons
- 12 pounds Briess two-row malt
- 4 pounds Alexander's pale malt extract syrup
- 1 pound toasted Briess malt
- 1 pound Ireks 20 °L light crystal malt
- 1 pound malted wheat
- 10 ounces CaraMunich 70 °L malt
- 8 ounces American six-row crystal malt
- 1 ounce chocolate malt
- 1 ounce Galena hop pellets, 13.8% alpha acid (90 minutes)
- 1 ounce Chinook hop pellets, 11.5% alpha acid (90 minutes)
- 1 ounce Nugget hop pellets, 12.8% alpha acid (90 minutes)
- 1 ounce Northern Brewer hop pellets, 7.5% alpha acid (60 minutes)
- 1 ounce Mt. Hood hop pellets, 3.9% alpha acid (15 minutes)
- 1 ounce Saaz hop pellets, 5.4% alpha acid (finish)
- 1 ounce Saaz hop pellets, 5.4% alpha acid (dry, 1 week)
- 1 teaspoon Polyclar® (15 minutes)
- 1/2 teaspoon Irish moss rehydrated (20 minutes)
-   CL-170 Classic British ale yeast
- 1/2 cup dextrose (to prime)

Original gravity:	1.097
Final gravity:	1.037
Boiling time:	90 minutes
Primary fermentation:	2 weeks at 65 °F (18 °C) in glass
Secondary fermentation:	2 weeks at 65 °F (18 °C) in glass
Age when judged:	6 months

Brewer's Specifics
Mash grains at 130 °F (54 °C) for 20 minutes. Add 1 gallon boiling water to raise temperature to 150 °F (66 °C). Hold between 152 and 156 °F (67 and 69 °C) for 90 minutes and then raise to 165 °F (74 °C) for 10 minutes. Collect 6 gallons wort and add extract. Boil 90 minutes, cool, aerate, and pitch a pint yeast starter.

Judges' Comments
"Sweet, malty, creamy taste. Not much bitterness comes through. Warming alcohol taste. On the malty sweet side of the scale but very drinkable."

Big Oak Barley Wine

Gold Medal, NHC, Barley Wine, 1996
Mike Harper, Oakdale, California
(Extract/Grain)

Ingredients for 5 Gallons

12	pounds Alexander's light malt extract
8	pounds Klages two-row malt
1	pound 20 °L caramel malt
1 1/10	ounces East Kent Goldings hops, 5.1% alpha acid (60 minutes)
9/10	ounce Northern Brewer hops, 8.2% alpha acid (60 minutes)
7/10	ounce Chinook hops, 12.5% alpha acid (60 minutes)
7/10	ounce Chinook hops, 12.5% alpha acid (30 minutes)
7/10	ounce Northern Brewer hops, 8.2% alpha acid (30 minutes)
7/10	ounce East Kent Goldings hops, 5.1% alpha acid (30 minutes)
7/10	ounce Willamette hops, 5.4% alpha acid (15 minutes)
2	ounces Cascade hops, 5.7% alpha acid (dry, 8 weeks)
	Wyeast No. 1056 American ale yeast
	force-carbonate in keg

Original gravity:	1.095
Final gravity:	1.024
Boiling time:	60 minutes
Primary fermentation:	7 days at 60–65 °F (16–18 °C) in glass
Secondary fermentation:	8 weeks at 60–64 °F (16–18 °C) in glass
Age when judged:	4 months

Brewer's Specifics

Mash grains at 158 °F (70 °C) for 60 minutes.

Black Acre Barley Wine

Silver Medal, NHC, Barley Wine, 1995
Kevin McCarty, Sicklerville, New Jersey
(Extract/Grain)

Ingredients for 6 Gallons

12	pounds pale malt extract
5	pounds two-row pale malt
1	pound CaraPils malt
1	pound Munich malt
1	pound Vienna malt
2	ounces chocolate malt
1 1/2	ounces black patent malt
1 1/2	ounces light dry malt extract
3	ounces Chinook hops, 10.1% alpha acid (70 minutes)
1	ounce Centennial hops, 9.9% alpha acid (70 minutes)
1	ounce Tettnang hops, 4.4% alpha acid (70 minutes)
1 1/2	ounces Kent Goldings hops, 5% alpha acid (20 minutes)
1/2	ounce Kent Goldings hops, 5% alpha acid (5 minutes)
	Wyeast No. 1728 Scottish ale yeast

Original gravity:	—
Final gravity:	—
Boiling time:	70 minutes
Primary fermentation:	3 days at 71 °F (22 °C) in glass
Secondary fermentation:	18 days at 71 °F (22 °C) in glass
Age when judged:	5 months

Brewer's Specifics

Mash grains at 153 °F (67 °C) for 90 minutes.

Judges' Comments

"Nice mohagany color. Clear. And a head that is small but lingers."

"Burnt flavor with some caramel. Some fruity flavors. Flavor should be malty sweet. Not much hops—needs more bittering [hops]."

"I like the beer but would reduce use of dark grain a bit and perhaps reduce alcohol a bit."

Chinook Barley Wine

Silver Medal, NHC, Barley Wine, 1996
Steve Valley, Shelton, Washington
(All-Grain)

Ingredients for 11 1/4 Gallons
34 3/4	pounds Great Western two-row malt
2	pounds Munton and Fison 50 °L crystal malt
5 1/2	ounces Northern Brewer pellet hops, 6.9% alpha acid (45 minutes)
10	ounces Cascade hops, 5.7% alpha acid (10 minutes)
2	ounces Northern Brewer pellet hops, 6.9% alpha acid (10 minutes)
5	ounces Cascade hops, 5.7% alpha acid (2 minutes)
2	ounces Cascade hops, 5.7% alpha acid (dry)
300	milligrams per liter sulfate
130	milligrams per liter gypsum adjusted to calcium
	Wyeast No. 1056 American ale yeast

Original gravity:	1.094
Final gravity:	1.030
Boiling time:	90 minutes
Primary fermentation:	12 days at 68–70 °F (20–21 °C) in stainless steel keg
Secondary fermentation:	10 days at 68–70 °F (20–21 °C) in stainless steel keg
Age when judged:	8 months

Brewer's Specifics
Mash grains at 148 °F (64 °C) for 75 minutes.

Barley Winer

Bronze Medal, NHC, Barley Wine, 1996
David Pappas and Gary Michel, Ocoee, Florida
(All-Grain)

Ingredients for 3 Gallons
9 9/10 pounds Northwestern Gold malt
   1 pound crystal malt
   1 pound pale malt
   5 ounces Chinook pellet hops, 12% alpha acid (60 minutes)
   1 ounce Cascade pellet hops, 5.1% alpha acid (30 minutes)
   1 ounce Cascade pellet hops, 5.1% alpha acid (5 minutes)
     Wyeast No. 1056 American ale yeast

Original gravity:	1.112
Final gravity:	1.050
Boiling time:	60 minutes
Primary fermentation:	2 weeks at 68 °F (20 °C) in glass
Secondary fermentation:	3 weeks at 65 °F (18 °C) in glass
Age when judged:	3 months

Brewer's Specifics
Mash grains at 155 °F (68 °C) for 60 minutes.

Spring Heaven

Silver Medal, NHC, Barley Wine, 1994
David West and Bill Pankratz, Milford, Michigan
(All-Grain)

Ingredients for 10 Gallons

30	pounds Munton and Fison pale malt
5	pounds Munich malt
3 1/2	pounds Munton and Fison crystal malt
2 1/2	pounds CaraPils malt
3	ounces Chinook hops, 11.3% alpha acid (60 minutes)
1	ounce Cascade hops, 5.9% alpha acid (60 minutes)
2	ounces Cascade hops, 5.9% alpha acid (20 minutes)
3	ounces Cascade hops, 5.9% alpha acid (finish)
4	ounces Cascade hops, 5.9% alpha acid (dry)
	Wyeast No. 1338 European ale yeast
	force-carbonate in keg

Original gravity:	1.090
Final gravity:	1.020
Boiling time:	60 minutes
Primary fermentation:	3 weeks at 68 °F (20 °C) in glass
Secondary fermentation:	2 months at 38 °F (3 °C) in stainless steel
Age when judged:	18 months

Brewer's Specifics

Mash grains at 150–155 °F (66–68 °C) for 90 minutes.

Judges' Comments

"Flavor hops seem a bit too intense. Cut back on ending hops some or just age this another couple of months. Cascade hops aplenty. Could cut back some to allow more malt to come through."

"A hint of licorice in the finish. Hop bitterness, flavor, and malty sweetness all nicely balanced."

Romulin Ale

Gold Medal, NHC, Barley Wine, 1993
Ray Call, Stockton, California
(All-Grain)

Ingredients for 6 Gallons
- 35 pounds pale malt
- 1 pound wheat malt
- 1/2 pound British caramel malt
- 1/2 pound toasted malt
- 1 1/2 ounces Chinook hops, 8.3% alpha acid (90 minutes)
- 1 1/2 ounces Centennial hops, 7.1% alpha acid (90 minutes)
- 1 1/2 ounces Kent Goldings hops (30 minutes)
- 2 ounces Kent Goldings hops (5 minutes)
- 2 ounces Kent Goldings hops (dry)
- Wyeast No. 1056 American ale yeast
- carbonate by kraeusening

Original gravity:	1.106
Final gravity:	—
Boiling time:	90 minutes
Primary fermentation:	9 days at 70 °F (21 °C) in glass
Secondary fermentation:	12 days at 70 °F (21 °C) in glass
Age when judged:	19 months

Brewer's Specifics
Mash grains at 158 °F (70 °C) for 75 minutes.

Judges' Comments
"Aroma is big, malty, fruity, alcohol, some hops, touch diacetyl. Wonderful. Hop bitterness expressed in middle is the only oddity. I wouldn't change a thing."

"Good malt and hop balance. Well aged and conditioned. Good head."

"Very clean malt. Some bitterness in finish. Alcohol shows. Good balance. Lacks true estery complexity. A little candylike. Very nice effort."

"Rich, malty, hoppy flavor. Somewhat astringent but will mellow with age."

"Overcarbonated. A very good well-aged barley wine. Prime with less or else not at all with long storage time."

BIÈRE DE GARDE/SAISON

Traditionally brewed toward the end of the brewing season and consumed in early summer, saison has an original gravity of 1.055–1.060 (13.75–15 °Plato) (according to a 1907 treatise on the style), but higher gravities are sometimes produced. It is a top-fermenting beer with medium body and a dry hoppy finish. A small proportion of wheat, raw oats, or rice is often added to the barley grist to add to mouthfeel and head retention. Sometimes spices like coriander are also added at the finish. Fermentation is fast and relatively warm with highly distinctive multistrain yeasts. Many brewers have success reculturing these yeasts from the 750-milliliter bottles of available brands. Authentic yeasts are essential in making a true example of the style. A saison is typically dry-hopped, always bottle-conditioned, and always highly carbonated, adding to the dry finish. It is very pale to orange gold in color.

Considered a provision beer and produced in generally the same region, though on the other side of the French-Belgian border, bière de garde may be thought of as the French counterpart to Belgian saison. Bière de garde is often stronger and maltier than saison, and uses either ale or lager yeasts for fermentation and is brewed to an original gravity of 1060–1076 (15–19 °Plato). Its color ranges from gold to reddish brown, and this style isn't as highly hopped as the saison style. Bitterness and aroma are fairly restrained.

Both styles deserve bottling in heavy 750-milliliter bottles with champagne corks to be opened on special occasions.

Saison Deneve

Belgian French Ale/Saison, 1997
Amahl Turczyn, Boulder, Colorado
(All-Grain)

Ingredients for 10 Gallons

- 8 pounds Hugh Baird pale malt
- 5 pounds Belgian Pilsener malt
- 3 pounds German Vienna malt
- 1 pound Belgian 20 °L crystal malt
- 3 ounces Kent Goldings hops, 5% alpha acid (75 minutes)
- 2 ounces Tettnang hops, 4.4% alpha acid (5 minutes)
- 2 pounds wildflower honey (3 minutes)
- Saison Dupont yeast, cultured from the bottle,
    or Wyeast No. 1214 Belgian Abbey ale yeast
- 3/4 cup corn sugar (to prime)

Original gravity:	1.063
Final gravity:	1.010
Boiling time:	75 minutes
Primary fermentation:	1 week at 72 °F (22 °C) in glass
Secondary fermentation:	2 weeks at 68 °F (20 °C) in glass
Tertiary fermentation:	—

Brewer's Specifics

Mash grains at 150 °F (66 °C) for 60 minutes. Bottle condition and age at least 2 months before enjoying.

Note: Saison yeasts recultured from the bottle, such as Saison DuPont, tend to attenuate very slowly after the first week of fermentation. Be sure to give your saison plenty of time in secondary—at least 2 weeks. You should also use heavy-gauge bottles, as the beer will continue to dry out and produce extra carbonation up to 2 months after bottling.—Ed.

Saison Falcon

First Place, Club-Only Competition, Saison, 1996
Tom Wolf, Valencia, California
(All-Grain)

Ingredients for 5 Gallons

12	pounds Belgian Pilsener malt
1	pound candi sugar
0.06	pound Belgian Special "B" malt
4/5	ounce Styrian Goldings hop pellets, 3.7% alpha acid (90 minutes)
1/6	ounce Hersbrucker hop pellets, 2.3% alpha acid (60 minutes)
1/6	ounce Mittelfruh hop pellets, 3.6% alpha acid (60 minutes)
1/6	ounce Saaz hop pellets, 2.6% alpha acid (60 minutes)
1/3	ounce Hersbrucker hop pellets, 2.3% alpha acid (finish)
1/3	ounce Mittelfruh hop pellets, 3.6% alpha acid (finish)
1/3	ounce Saaz hop pellets, 2.6% alpha acid (finish)
3/5	ounce coriander
4	gallons purified water
3	gallons boiled tap water
1	teaspoon gypsum
	Wyeast No. 1388 Belgian Strong Ale yeast
	force-carbonate in keg

Original gravity:	1.077
Final gravity:	1.015
Boiling time:	90 minutes
Primary fermentation:	7 days at 70 °F (21 °C) in glass
Secondary fermentation:	23 days at 70 °F (21 °C) in glass
Age when judged:	6 months

Brewer's Specifics
Employ an infusion mash at 150 °F (66 °C) for 90 minutes.

Judges' Comments
"Very nice beer. Very light on spice. Add more spice. This beer needs a higher starting gravity."

"Clear as a bell. Excellent head retention."

Troubled Waters Lager

NHC, Bière de Garde, 1996
Dennis Waltman, Atlanta, Georgia
(Extract/Grain)

Ingredients for 5 Gallons

5	pounds pale light malt extract
2	pounds dark malt extract
1 1/2	pounds Munich malt
1/10	pound black patent malt
1 1/2	ounces Saaz hop plugs, 3.3% alpha acid (60 minutes)
1	ounce Saaz hop plugs, 3.3% alpha acid (15 minutes)
1/2	ounce Saaz hop plugs, 3.3% alpha acid (4 minutes)
	Wyeast No. 2042 Danish lager yeast
3/4	cup corn sugar (to prime)

Original gravity:	1.060
Final gravity:	1.016
Boiling time:	60 minutes
Primary fermentation:	9 days at 50 °F (10 °C) in glass
Secondary fermentation:	21 days at 45 °F (7 °C) in glass
Tertiary fermentation:	21 days at 40 °F (4 °C) in glass
Age when judged:	4 months

Brewer's Specifics

Boil for 60 minutes. Steep grains at 170 °F (77 °C) for 30 minutes.

Untitled

Finalist, NHC, French Ale, 1996
Kenneth Butler, Kansas City, Kansas
(Extract/Grain)

Ingredients for 10 Gallons

6	pounds Spray Lite dry malt extract
5 2/5	pounds Alexander's wheat malt extract
4	pounds Alexander's pale malt extract
1	pound CaraPils malt
13	ounces 70 °L crystal malt
12	ounces Munich malt
2	ounces Bullion hop pellets, 11.1% alpha acid (60 minutes)
1	ounce Tettnang hop pellets, 4.8% alpha acid (60 minutes)
1	ounce B.C. Kent Goldings hop pellets (20 minutes)
1	ounce B.C. Kent Goldings hop pellets (5 minutes)
2/3	ounce Burton water salts
1/2	teaspoon epsom salts
	Wyeast No. 2112 California ale yeast
3/4	cup corn sugar (to prime)

Original gravity:	1.065
Final gravity:	—
Boiling time:	75 minutes
Primary fermentation:	1 month at 60 °F (16 °C) in glass
Secondary fermentation:	—
Age when judged:	3 months

Brewer's Specifics

Steep grains at 155 °F (68 °C) for 60 minutes.

Bière de Garde

Finalist, NHC, Belgian and French Ale, 1996
Aida Sulzbach, Lafayette, Louisiana
(All-Grain)

Ingredients for 5 Gallons

8	pounds pale ale malt
4 1/2	pounds Vienna malt
1	pound dark brown sugar
1/2	pound Belgian Special "B" malt
1/2	pound CaraPils malt
1/2	pound corn sugar
1	ounce Northern Brewer hop pellets, 6.9% alpha acid (45 minutes)
	Belgian ale and Belgian lager yeast (2 types)
3/4	cup corn sugar (to prime)

Original gravity:	1.092
Final gravity:	1.032
Boiling time:	120 minutes
Primary fermentation:	16 days at 60 °F (16 °C) in glass
Secondary fermentation:	—
Age when judged:	10 1/2 months

Brewer's Specifics

Mash grains at 159 °F (71 °C) for 120 minutes.

MAIBOCK

The main difference between a standard helles bock and a maibock lies in the hops. Maibock carries the distinction of being the only bock beer in which one can detect hops in the aroma, though malt should still be at the forefront. Maibock has a bit more color, in the light to medium amber range, and can be aged a little longer than helles bock. Diacetyl is acceptable for this bock in very small amounts.

Hands Offa Maibock

Gold Medal, NHC, German-Style Helles Bock, 1996
Phil Bernie, Staten Island, New York
(All-Grain)

Ingredients for 6 1/2 Gallons
12	pounds Briess pale malt
3	pounds Briess Munich malt
1 1/2	pounds Briess crystal malt
1	ounce Northern Brewer hop pellets, 8.9% alpha acid (60 minutes)
1	ounce Kent Goldings hop pellets, 4% alpha acid (60 minutes)
3/4	ounce Mt. Hood hop pellets, 4.5% alpha acid (10 minutes)
	Wyeast No. 2308 Munich lager yeast
	force-carbonate in keg

Original gravity:	1.070
Final gravity:	1.018
Boiling time:	90 minutes
Primary fermentation:	2 weeks at 50 °F (10 °C) in glass
Secondary fermentation:	6 weeks at 40 °F (4 °C) in glass
Age when judged:	7 months

Brewer's Specifics
Use the following step infusion mash schedule: 120 °F (49 °C) for 30 minutes, 150 °F (66 °C) for 60 minutes, and 168 °F (76 °C) for 5 minutes.

Judges' Comments
"Slightly fruity, which is inappropriate. Seems too bitter for the style. The balance needs to be malty."

"Malt dominates the flavor. Hop bitterness low to medium. Very good beer. Malt flavor comes through as it should. Astringency should be corrected."

"Sweet. Appropriately low hop level. The sweetness could be more malt accented. A very good beer. The only element I'm missing is a firm, big, clean, malt character."

Untitled

NHC, Maibock, 1996
Wolfram Donalies, Elgin, Illinois
(All-Grain)

Ingredients for 6 Gallons

10	pounds Belgian Pilsener malt
2	pounds German light Munich malt
1 1/2	pounds Vienna malt
1/2	pound dextrin malt
1	ounce Northern Brewer hops, 7% alpha acid (60 minutes)
2	ounces Saaz hops, 4.4% alpha acid (25 minutes)
1/2	ounce Hallertau Hersbrucker hops, 2.6% alpha acid (5 minutes)
2	teaspoons gypsum
1	teaspoon lactic acid in sparge
	Wyeast No. 2042 Danish lager yeast
	force-carbonate

Original gravity:	1.068
Final gravity:	1.018
Boiling time:	105 minutes
Primary fermentation:	8 weeks at 55 °F (13 °C) in glass
Secondary fermentation:	3 weeks at 55 °F (13 °C) in glass
Age when judged:	3 months

Brewer's Specifics

Mash grains at 124 °F (51 °C) for 30 minutes, 138 °F (59 °C) for 15 minutes, 152 °F (67 °C) for 60 minutes, 158 °F (70 °C) for 30 minutes, and 175 °F (79 °C) for 5 minutes.

Minotaur Maibock

NHC, Maibock, 1996
Rich Mansfield, San Jose, California
(All-Grain)

Ingredients for 10 Gallons

15	pounds Durst Pilsener malt
5	pounds Durst Vienna malt
5	pounds Durst Munich malt
2 1/2	ounces Mt. Hood hops, 5.4% alpha acid (60 minutes)
1 2/5	ounces Liberty hops, 2.7% alpha acid (30 minutes)
1 2/5	ounces Saaz Czech hops, 3.3% alpha acid (30 minutes)
1 1/10	ounces Liberty hops, 2.7% alpha acid (15 minutes)
1 1/10	ounces Saaz Czech hops, 3.3% alpha acid (15 minutes)
	preboiled moderately hard tap water
	Wyeast No. 2206 Bavarian lager yeast
	force-carbonate

Original gravity:	1.067
Final gravity:	1.016
Boiling time:	60 minutes
Primary fermentation:	7 days at 51 °F (11 °C) in glass
Secondary fermentation:	14 days at 40–51 °F (4–11 °C) in glass
Tertiary fermentation:	2 months at 32 °F (0 °C) in stainless steel
Age when judged:	2 months

Brewer's Specifics

Mash grains at 122 °F (50 °C) for 20 minutes, 154 °F (68 °C) for 90 minutes, and 165 °F (74 °C) for mash-out. Vorlauf 30 minutes. Sparge with 169 °F (76 °C), 5.3 pH water. Boil wort for 60 minutes. Cool to 60 °F (16 °C). Pitch 1/2 gallon yeast. Diacetyl rest is at the end of fermentation for 3 days at 57 °F (14 °C).

Untitled

NHC, Maibock, 1996
Steve Rice, Cudahy, Wisconsin
(All-Grain)

Ingredients for 6 Gallons
7	pounds DeWolf-Cosyns pale malt
6	pounds Durst Munich malt
1	pound Durst helles malt
1 1/4	ounces Perle hop pellets, 8.1% alpha acid (60 minutes)
1 1/2	ounces Hallertau hop pellets, 2.6% alpha acid (10 minutes)
	Yeast Lab® L33 Munich yeast
	counterpressure in Cornelius kegs

Original gravity:	1.070
Final gravity:	1.020
Boiling time:	90 minutes
Primary fermentation:	2 weeks at 50 °F (10 °C) in glass
Secondary fermentation:	2 weeks at 50 °F (10 °C) in glass
Tertiary fermentation:	2 months at 32 °F (0 °C) in Cornelius keg
Age when judged:	2 1/2 months

Brewer's Specifics
Mash grains at 122 °F (50 °C) for 45 minutes, 158 °F (70 °C) for 60 minutes, and 170 °F (77 °C) for 10 minutes. Sparge for 60 minutes.

Mybock-Maibock

NHC, Maibock, 1996
Steve Nance, Winston-Salem, North Carolina
(Extract/Grain)

Ingredients for 5 Gallons

8	pounds Briess two-row malt
2	pounds Briess 10 °L Munich malt
1 1/2	pounds Marie's Munich dry malt extract
3/4	pound Briess 10 °L crystal malt
1/2	pound Briess CaraPils malt
1/4	pound DeWolf-Cosyns CaraVienne malt
1 3/4	ounces Hallertau Hersbrucker hop plugs, 3.5% alpha acid (60 minutes)
1/4	ounce Hallertau Hersbrucker hop plugs, 3.5% alpha acid (15 minutes)
1/4	ounce Hallertau Hersbrucker hop plugs, 3.5% alpha acid (3 minutes)
	Wyeast No. 2206 Bavarian lager yeast
	force-carbonate in keg

Original gravity:	1.066
Final gravity:	1.017
Boiling time:	72 minutes
Primary fermentation:	14 days at 50 °F (10 °C) in glass
Secondary fermentation:	28 days at 33 °F (1 °C) in glass
Age when judged:	3 months

Brewer's Specifics

Mash grains at 154 °F (68 °C) for 60 minutes.

Get Off Maibock

NHC, Maibock, 1996
John Hanley, Seattle, Washington
(All-Grain)

Ingredients for 20 Gallons

35	pounds Gambrinus two-row malt
11	pounds Munich malt
5	pounds CaraPils malt
3	pounds honey malt
8	ounces Northern Brewer hops, 7.1% alpha acid (85 minutes)
4	ounces Hallertau hops, 4.7% alpha acid (10 minutes)
4 3/10	teaspoons gypsum per gallon added to mash water
4	milliliters lactic acid added to sparge water
	Wyeast No. 2124 Bohemian lager yeast
	force-carbonate in keg

Original gravity:	1.070
Final gravity:	1.014
Boiling time:	85 minutes
Primary fermentation:	35 days at 50 °F (10 °C) in glass
Secondary fermentation:	14 days at 50 °F (10 °C) in glass
Age when judged:	2 months

Brewer's Specifics
Mash grains at 146 °F (63 °C) for 185 minutes.

MÄRZEN/OKTOBERFEST

This style, a slightly stronger version of the Vienna style (though the terms are often used interchangeably), is a light amber to amber lager made famous by its clean balance of malty sweetness and "noble-type" variety hops. Before refrigeration, it was traditionally brewed while the weather was still cold and then stored at very cold temperatures over the summer so that it could be consumed at the start of the new brewing season. It is fairly strong (5–6 percent alcohol by volume) with no fruitiness, esters, or diacetyl. Vienna may contain trace levels of diacetyl. Brew this one early to guarantee a long cold lagering period.

Protection of the Holy Virgin

NHC, Märzen/Oktoberfest, 1996
Byron Burch and Dave Woodruff, Santa Rosa, California
(All-Grain)

Ingredients for 10 Gallons

10	pounds two-row lager malt
6	pounds German Pilsener malt
3	pounds CaraPils malt
2	pounds toasted malt
2	pounds German Munich malt
2	pounds Belgian Munich malt
1	pound 60 °L caramel malt
2	ounces 20 °L caramel malt
7/10	ounce Perle hops, for 10.64 IBU (60 minutes)
2	ounces Hallertau hops, for 7.42 IBU (30 minutes)
1 1/5	ounces Hallertau hops, for 2.23 IBU (5 minutes)
	Wyeast No. 2206 Bavarian lager yeast

Original gravity:	1.065
Final gravity:	—
Boiling time:	90 minutes
Primary fermentation:	10 days at 46 °F (8 °C) in glass
Secondary fermentation:	3 days at 60 °F (16 °C) in glass
Age when judged:	3 months

Brewer's Specifics

Employ a single decoction mash at 150 °F (66 °C) for 90 minutes.

Judges' Comments

"Rich malt character and sweetness up front. Very clean. Sweetness lingers and detracts. Alcohol is nice. Very nice clean lager. Good job. The malt character is full and rich, but the sweetness lingers too much."

"Good malty taste. This beer is a little too sweet. Very clear. Good color. Little head, undercarbonated."

Oktoberintexasfest

Gold Medal, NHC, Märzen/Oktoberfest, 1995
Todd Kellenbenz, Houston, Texas
(All-Grain)

Ingredients for 10 Gallons
16	pounds Durst Pilsener malt
7	pounds Munich malt
1 1/4	pounds 10 °L crystal malt
1 1/4	pounds 40 °L crystal malt
1 1/4	pounds 90 °L crystal malt
2	ounces Styrian Goldings hops, 5% alpha acid (45 minutes)
3	ounces Saaz hops, 3.3% alpha acid (30 minutes)
3	ounces Saaz hops, 3.3% alpha acid (10 minutes)
2	teaspoons gypsum added to mash
	Wyeast No. 2206 Bavarian lager yeast
	force-carbonate in keg

Original gravity:	1.057
Final gravity:	1.016
Boiling time:	75 minutes
Primary fermentation:	2 weeks at 48 °F (9 °C) in plastic
Secondary fermentation:	2 weeks at 48 °F (9 °C) in stainless steel
Tertiary fermentation:	3 weeks at 48 °F (9 °C) in stainless steel
Age when judged:	3 months

Brewer's Specifics
Mash grains at 152 °F (67 °C) for 60 minutes.

Judges' Comments
"Nice malt. Good toastiness. Hop bitterness a bit assertive at this point but will mellow out with age. Excellent beer. Only major problem is it seems a bit overhopped or just undermalted."

"Lacks sweet malty character in flavor profile. Too dry. Hops are at the right level, but malt does not balance it well."

"Toasted malt flavor. Low to medium bitterness. Hop flavor a tad too pronounced. Hop aroma and flavor could be cut back a little. Nice job."

OK's Toe Beer

Second Place, Club-Only Competition, Oktoberfest, 1996
Scott Day and Todd Warren, Livonia, Michigan
(All-Grain)

Ingredients for 6 Gallons

6	pounds Durst Pilsener malt
5	pounds Durst Munich malt
1	pound Durst light crystal malt
1	pound Breiss special roasted malt
1/8	pound chocolate malt
3	ounces Saaz whole hops, 2% alpha acid (60 minutes)
1/2	ounce Hallertau whole hops, 2.6% alpha acid (60 minutes)
1	ounce Saaz whole hops, 2% alpha acid (25 minutes)
1	ounce Hallertau whole hops, 2.6% alpha acid (25 minutes)
	Wyeast No. 2278 Czech Pils lager yeast
3/8	cup corn sugar (to prime)

Original gravity:	1.064
Final gravity:	1.016
Boiling time:	60 minutes
Primary fermentation:	11 days at 50 °F (10 °C) in glass
Secondary fermentation:	10 days at 42–50 °F (6–10 °C) in glass
Tertiary fermentation:	16 days at 34–42 °F (1–6 °C) in glass
Age when judged:	1 month

Brewer's Specifics

Use a double decoction mash. The rests are at: 124 °F (51 °C) for 180 minutes, 145 °F (63 °C) for 180 minutes, 155 °F (68 °C) for 180 minutes, and 170 °F (77 °C) for 180 minutes.

Milo-Märzen No. 2

Gold Medal, NHC, Märzen/Oktoberfest, 1996
George DePiro, Nyack, New York
(All-Grain)

Ingredients for 5 1/4 Gallons
5 1/2   pounds Ireks Pilsener malt
4 1/2   pounds Ireks Munich malt
1   pound CaraPils malt
3/4   pound 20 °L crystal malt
2/5   ounce Perle hop pellets, 7.3% alpha acid (39 minutes)
3/5   ounce Mittelfruh hop pellets, 3.6% alpha acid (13 minutes)
     Wyeast No. 2206 Bavarian lager yeast
     force-carbonate in keg

Original gravity:	1.062
Final gravity:	1.021
Boiling time:	140 minutes
Primary fermentation:	19 days at 46–50 °F (8–10 °C) in glass
Secondary fermentation:	45 days at 45 °F (7 °C) in glass
Tertiary fermentation:	60 days at 32 °F (0 °C) in stainless steel
Age when judged:	2 months

Brewer's Specifics
Use a double decoction mash with the following schedule: Mash-in at 95 °F (35 °C). Pull first decoction. Rest at 154 °F (68 °C) for 25 minutes. Boil 30 minutes and return to main mash raising temperature to 122 °F (50 °C). Hold for 20 minutes. Then heat mash to 151 °F (66 °C) and hold for 40 minutes. Pull second decoction and boil 30 minutes. Return to main mash, raise temperature to 159 °F (71 °C), and hold until conversion is complete. Raise temperature to 168 °F (76 °C) for mash-out. Sparge with 6 gallons of 168 °F (76 °C) (adjust water's pH to 5.8 with citric acid).

Judges' Comments
"Sweet flavor. Faint toasty tones. A bit too sweet. Needs more toast and less sweetness. Use light or no crystal malts and Munich malt to achieve this. A very nice beer. Tweak the malt profile to add toasty character. Increase hop bitterness slightly."

"Balance appropriate. Some alcohol. Smooth. Malty. Just about dead on for style."

"Sweet maltiness. Low hop. Nice balance. A very well-made interesting beer. Sweet maltiness dominates."

Scottoberfest

First Place, Club-Only Competition, Oktoberfest, 1996
Scott Bulcock, Patchogue, New York
(All-Grain)

Ingredients for 5 Gallons

6	pounds Breiss pale two-row malt
3	pounds Munton and Fison Munich malt
3/4	pound CaraPils malt
1/4	pound 40 °L crystal malt
2	ounces Hallertau hop pellets, 3.7% alpha acid (90 minutes)
1/4	ounce black patent malt
	Wyeast No. 2308 Munich lager yeast
	force-carbonate in Cornelius keg

Original gravity:	1.054
Final gravity:	1.012
Boiling time:	90 minutes
Primary fermentation:	21 days at 46 °F (8 °C) in glass
Secondary fermentation:	21 days at 46 °F (8 °C) in glass
Tertiary fermentation:	21 days at 32 °F (0 °C) in glass
Age when judged:	7 1/2 months

Brewer's Specifics
Mash grains at 154 °F (68 °C) for 70 minutes.

Oktoberfest

Finalist, NHC, Märzen/Oktoberfest, 1996
Dan Ritter, Grangeville, Idaho
(All-Grain)

Ingredients for 5 1/4 Gallons
8	pounds Belgian Pilsener malt
1/2	pound CaraPils malt
14	ounces CaraVienne malt
5	ounces Belgian Special "B" malt
1 1/4	ounces Hallertau pellet hops, 3.4% alpha acid (60 minutes)
3/4	ounce Hallertau pellet hops, 3.4% alpha acid (30 minutes)
1/2	ounce Saaz pellet hops, 3% alpha acid (10 minutes)
1/2	teaspoon 88% lactic acid added to 5 gallons sparge water
	Wyeast No. 2206 Bavarian lager yeast

Original gravity:	1.056
Final gravity:	1.016
Boiling time:	90 minutes
Primary fermentation:	20 days at 48 °F (9 °C) in glass
Secondary fermentation:	2 weeks at 46 °F (8 °C) in glass
Tertiary fermentation:	3 weeks at 34 °F (1 °C) in keg
Age when judged:	4 months

Brewer's Specifics
Mash grains at 153 °F (67 °C) for 90 minutes. Mash grains at 172 °F (78 °C) for 10 minutes.

Judges' Comments
"Smooth. Malty. Well balanced for style. Very nice. Drinkable. But a bit light overall (hops and malt)."

"A clean beer that is too caramelly for style—a decrease in this caramel character and an increase in hops would improve this beer."

Märzen

Silver Medal, NHC, Märzen/Oktoberfest, 1996
Todd Kellenbenz, Houston, Texas
(All-Grain)

Ingredients for 10 Gallons
15	pounds Pilsener two-row malt
10	pounds Vienna malt
2	pounds German light crystal malt
2	pounds German medium crystal malt
1	pound German dark crystal malt
2	ounces Williamette hops, 4.2% alpha acid (75 minutes)
1 1/2	ounces Saaz hops, 3.5% alpha acid (75 minutes)
1/2	ounce Saaz hops, 3.5% alpha acid (10 minutes)
2	teaspoons gypsum
	Wyeast No. 2206 Bavarian lager yeast

Original gravity:	1.060
Final gravity:	1.021
Boiling time:	75 minutes
Primary fermentation:	1 week at 52 °F (11 °C) in plastic
Secondary fermentation:	2 weeks at 48 °F (9 °C) in stainless steel
Tertiary fermentation:	3 weeks at 35 °F (2 °C) in stainless steel
Age when judged:	5 months

Brewer's Specifics
Mash grains at 152 °F (67 °C) for 60 minutes.

Wizard Lager

Bronze Medal, NHC, Märzen/Oktoberfest, 1995
Jeff Niggemeyer, Kent, Washington
(All-Grain)

Ingredients for 7 Gallons

11	pounds Belgian Pilsener malt
4	pounds Belgian Munich malt
3/4	pound 40 °L crystal malt
3/4	pound dextrin malt
1 2/5	ounces Hallertau hops, 4.6% alpha acid (60 minutes)
1/5	ounce Saaz hops, 5.4% alpha acid (60 minutes)
1/2	ounce Saaz hops, 5.4% alpha acid (30 minutes)
1/3	ounce Saaz hops, 5.4% alpha acid (finish)
	Wyeast No. 2278 Czech Pils lager yeast

Original gravity:	1.054
Final gravity:	1.014
Boiling time:	80 minutes
Primary fermentation:	20 days at 48 °F (9 °C) in glass
Secondary fermentation:	21 days at 38 °F (3 °C) in glass
Age when judged:	4 months

Brewer's Specifics

Mash grains for 90 minutes at 154 °F (68 °C). Use the following mash schedule: Boil 1 quart water for 5 minutes. Cool to 184 °F (84 °C). Add water to mash and stabilize temperature at 154 °F (68 °C). Allow to sit for 90 minutes. Remove 1/3 of the mash and bring to a boil. Boil for 10 minutes, remove, and add back to main mash. Stabilize temperature at 168 °F (76 °C). Allow to sit for 15 minutes. Transfer to lauter tun and sparge with 7 gallons 175 °F (79 °C) water.

Judges' Comments

"Very nice. Drinkable to slightly sweet for Vienna. Good balance."

"Subtle toasted malt character blended with low hop flavor—low to medium hop bitterness. Good conditioning—clean."

"Thick creamy head. Light copper amber color. Quite clear."

Helles Münchener

Winner, Club-Only Competition, Oktoberfest/Vienna, 1994
Tom Strand, Tacoma, Washington
(Extract/Grain)

Ingredients for 4 1/2 Gallons
  5   pounds Cooper's light malt extract syrup
  3   pounds Durst Munich malt
1 1/2 ounces Czech Saaz hops, 1.9% alpha acid (60 minutes)
  1/2 ounce Hallertau Hersbrucker hops, 3.2% alpha acid (60 minutes)
  1/2 ounce Hallertau Hersbrucker hops, 3.2% alpha acid (30 minutes)
  1/2 ounce Czech Saaz hops, 1.9% alpha acid (30 minutes)
  1/2 ounce Tettnang hops, 4.5% alpha acid (2 minutes)
  1/2 ounce Hallertau Hersbrucker hops, 3.2% alpha acid (2 minutes)
       Wyeast No. 2278 Czech Pils lager yeast
       force-carbonate keg

Original gravity:	1.058
Final gravity:	1.012
Boiling time:	90 minutes
Primary fermentation:	2 weeks at 60 °F (16 °C) in glass
Secondary fermentation:	3 weeks at 60 °F (16 °C) in glass
Age when judged:	8 months

Brewer's Specifics
Mash grains at 122 °F (50 °C) for 20 minutes (acid rest). Remove 1/3 of the mash and boil for 10 minutes. Return the decoction to the main mash, raise temperature to 155 °F (68 °C) for 30 minutes, and then raise temperature to 160 °F (71 °C) for 15 minutes or until conversion is complete. Sparge with 2 gallons of 170 °F (77 °C) water. Add malt extract to wort and boil for 90 minutes.

Judges' Comments
"Rich flavor with a nice balance of sweet malt. Some Viennalike toasted flavor. Well rounded and clean. Very good effort."

"Nice, clean, malty palate. Excellent example of style. Could use more complex malt profile. Outstanding example of style."

"Real nice maltiness. Hop flavor and bitterness comes through. Clean lager flavor."

PILSENER

This style may be subcategorized into German, Dutch/Scandinavian, or Bohemian Pilseners, but all are pale to golden with light to medium body. Pilseners have medium to high hop bitterness, and low to medium flavor and aroma. All hops used are of "noble-type" variety, classically Saaz for Bohemian styles. Low to medium maltiness is appropriate in aroma and flavor with no fruitiness or esters and very low to low diacetyl. Bohemian Pilseners differ from other varieties in intensity of all beer characteristics: bitterness, aroma, malt sweetness, color, mouthfeel, etc. German and Dutch styles are usually better attenuated and therefore dryer and paler with less bitterness than Bohemian styles. This type of beer is brewed with very soft water, as is found in its place of origin in Plzeň in the Czech Republic.

Czech Mate

Gold Medal, NHC, German Pilsener, 1995
Paul Quasarano, Franklin, Michigan
(Extract/Grain)

Ingredients for 5 Gallons

6	pounds German Pilsener malt
1	pound light dry malt extract
1/2	pound Vienna malt
1/4	pound 10 °L crystal malt
1/4	pound CaraMunich malt
1	pinch black patent malt
3	ounces Hallertau Mittelfruh hops, 4.7% alpha acid (70 minutes)
1	ounce Hallertau Mittelfruh hops, 4.7% alpha acid (20 minutes)
1/2	ounce Hallertau Mittelfruh hops, 4.7% alpha acid (10 minutes)
1/2	ounce Saaz hops, 4% alpha acid (10 minutes)
1/2	ounce Hallertau Mittelfruh hops, 4.7% alpha acid (2 minutes)
1/2	ounce Saaz hops, 4% alpha acid (2 minutes)
	Wyeast No. 2278 Czech Pils lager yeast
3/4	cup corn sugar (to prime)

Original gravity:	1.055
Final gravity:	1.014
Boiling time:	70 minutes
Primary fermentation:	10 days at 68–45 °F (20–7 °C) in glass
Secondary fermentation:	11 days at 45–25 °F (7– -4 °C) in glass
Tertiary fermentation:	15 days at 50 °F (10 °C) in glass
Age when judged:	4 months

Brewer's Specifics

Mash grains at 125 °F (52 °C) for 30 minutes. Raise temperature to 145–150 °F (63–66 °C) for 15 minutes. Remove 2 pounds of mash. Boil for 10 minutes. Add back to main mash and raise temperature to 155–160 °F (68–71 °C) for 40 minutes. Sparge with 170 °F (77 °C) water.

Judges' Comments

"Malty hoppy beer. Great effort. Clean."

"Some bite in the aftertaste. Pay attention to water treatment and pH of wort in boil. Very nice beer with just a hint of roughness."

German Pilsener

Gold Medal, NHC, German Pilsener, 1996
Jim Lopes, Fresno, California
(All-Grain)

Ingredients for 12 Gallons

- 20 pounds Durst Pilsener malt
- 3 ounces Saaz whole hop pellets, 3.2% alpha acid (90 minutes)
- 2 ounces Saaz whole hop pellets, 3.2% alpha acid (30 minutes)
- 2 ounces Saaz hops, 5.5% alpha acid (finish)
- Wyeast No. 2042 Danish lager yeast
- force-carbonate in keg

Original gravity:	1.050
Final gravity:	1.010
Boiling time:	90 minutes
Primary fermentation:	4 weeks at 47 °F (8 °C) in stainless steel
Secondary fermentation:	4 weeks at 32 °F (0 °C) in stainless steel
Age when judged:	3 months

Brewer's Specifics

Mash grains at 150 °F (66 °C) for 60 minutes.

Judges' Comments

"Good malt up front. Medium to low hop flavor. Conditioning on low side. Good balance of malt and bitterness. Lacks some freshness and hop flavor."

"Good malt. Finishing with good bitterness. True to style. Very good beer."

First Pilsener II

Gold Medal, NHC, Bohemian Pilsener, 1994
Alan Pagliere, Ann Arbor, Michigan
(All-Grain)

Ingredients for 5 Gallons
10	pounds Ireks two-row German Pilsener malt
1/2	pound CaraPils malt
1 3/5	ounces Saaz hops, 3.9% alpha acid (60 minutes)
1/4	ounce Saaz hops, 3.9% alpha acid (50 minutes)
9/10	ounce Saaz hops, 3.9% alpha acid (30 minutes)
1 1/2	ounces Saaz hops, 3.9% alpha acid (5 minutes)
	Great Western Kent Yeast Lab® No. 131 yeast
3/4	cup corn sugar (to prime)

Original gravity:	1.050
Final gravity:	1.012
Boiling time:	90 minutes
Primary fermentation:	4 days at 46–52 °F (8–11 °C) in plastic
Secondary fermentation:	23 days at 42–52 °F (6–11 °C) in glass
Age when judged:	6 months

Brewer's Specifics
Mash grains for 30 minutes at 131 °F (55 °C). Raise temperature to between 153 and 155 °F (67 and 68 °C) for 120 minutes. Raise temperature to 168 °F (76 °C) and hold for 5 minutes. Sparge with 168 °F (76 °C) water for boil volume of 4 gallons. After boil, top up to 5 gallons with preboiled water.

Judges' Comments
"Mild malt flavor finishes with nice clean hop flavor. Could use more malt and hops for style. Otherwise nicely balanced. Malt should predominate. Very nice pleasant beer but lacks that malt flavor and hoppy finish. A classic Pils. Good job."

"Lightly malty delicate palate. Good malt and hop flavor. Perhaps a tad too bitter. Some malty graininess is missing here. Nice drinking beer. Maybe just a tad hoppy and dry for style and lacking palate fullness."

"Nice hop flavor and bitterness balanced with the malt quite well. Could use a bit more maltiness but within style. Nice job. Absolutely beautiful appearance."

Pookie Pilsener

Silver Medal, NHC, German Pilsener, 1996
Richard Schwartz, Colonial Heights, Virginia
(All-Grain)

Ingredients for 5 Gallons
9	pounds Durst Pilsener malt
1 1/2	ounces Saaz pellet hops, 3.5% alpha acid (90 minutes)
1 1/2	ounces Hallertau pellet hops, 2.6% alpha acid (30 minutes)
1/4	ounce Saaz pellet hops, 3.5% alpha acid (30 minutes)
1	ounce Saaz pellet hops, 3.5% alpha acid (finish)
1/2	ounce Hallertau pellet hops, 2.6% alpha acid (finish)
2/3	ounce Hallertau pellet hops, 2.6% alpha acid added to secondary fermenter (dry)
2 1/2	gallons distilled water
2 1/2	gallons filtered tap water
	Wyeast No. 2278 Czech Pils lager yeast

Original gravity:	1.050
Final gravity:	—
Boiling time:	90 minutes
Primary fermentation:	12 days at 40 °F (4 °C) in glass
Secondary fermentation:	23 days at 35 °F (2 °C) in glass
Age when judged:	11 months

Brewer's Specifics
Employ a three-stage decoction mash.

Judges' Comments
"Nice classic Saaz hop aroma. Some apple notes from acetaldehyde but that kind of complements the hops. A nice job. Cut back a tiny bit on bitterness (my personal opinion). Watch overcarbonation. Well done."

"Hops (noble)—very nice. Has the right lager fermentation notes. Very nice beer."

Nectar of the Gods Pilsener

Gold Medal, NHC, Bohemian Pilsener, 1995
Mick and Vi Walker, Fargo, North Dakota
(All-Grain)

Ingredients for 10 Gallons
- 16 pounds German two-row malt
- 1/2 pound CaraPils malt
- 1/2 pound German caramel malt
- 2 1/2 ounces Hallertau hops, 6.3% alpha acid (60 minutes)
- 1 ounce Hallertau hops, 6.3% alpha acid (15 minutes)
- 2 ounces Saaz hops, 4.4% alpha acid (2 minutes)
- acidify sparge water to 5.7 pH
- Wyeast No. 2124 Bohemian lager yeast
- force-carbonate

Original gravity:	1.050
Final gravity:	1.015
Boiling time:	90 minutes
Primary fermentation:	15 days at 46 °F (8 °C) in glass
Secondary fermentation:	7 days at 46 °F (8 °C) in glass
Tertiary fermentation:	45 days at 32 °F (0 °C) in keg
Age when judged:	2 months

Brewer's Specifics
Employ a triple decoction mash.

Judges' Comments
"Very nice balance. Good hop flavor and bitterness. Also has a nice malt balance. Great beer. I need more! Only needs a little more hop aroma."

"Good malt, some hop flavor. Well balanced for style. Hop flavor and fermentation character are low. Very nice well-made beer."

"Rich golden color. Thick creamy head. Well-brewed beer. Good balance with emphasis on hops."

Harvest Pils

Silver Medal, NHC, Bohemian Pilsener, 1994
Mick and Vi Walker, Fargo, North Dakota
(All-Grain)

Ingredients for 10 Gallons

16 1/2   pounds two-row Pilsener malt
    1   pound CaraPils malt
4 1/2   ounces Hallertau hops, 2.9% alpha acid (60 minutes)
    1   ounce Saaz hops, 4.4% alpha acid (20 minutes)
    1   ounce Saaz hops, 4.4% alpha acid (2 minutes)
  1/2   ounce Saaz hops, 4.4% alpha acid (dry)
      Wyeast No. 2124 Bohemian lager yeast
      force-carbonate keg

Original gravity:	1.050
Final gravity:	1.015
Boiling time:	90 minutes
Primary fermentation:	21 days at 46 °F (8 °C) in glass
Secondary fermentation:	15 days at 46 °F (8 °C) in glass
Tertiary fermentation:	30 days at 32 °F (0 °C) in keg
Age when judged:	2 1/2 months

Brewer's Specifics

Mash grains at 122 °F (50 °C) for 30 minutes. Raise temperature to 150 °F (66 °C) for 90 minutes.

Judges' Comments

"Nice malt. Hop flavor and bitterness balance. Maybe a little sweet overall. Some oxidation. Nice effort overall."

"Malt flavor predominates with an intermediate hop finish. Slight fruitiness is inappropriate for style. Nice beer with clean lager flavor."

"Nice Czechlike malt flavor. Good balance and hop character. Slightly husky in background. Could use twinge of sweetness."

PORTER

Classic porter falls under the robust subcategory in the American Home-brewers Association's style guidelines. It is black without any roasted barley character—only black or chocolate malt is used. The sharp bitterness of black malt is desired for the flavor profile without burnt or charcoal flavors. A medium to full body is appropriate with a little malty sweetness evident. Hop bitterness usually ranges from medium to high. Some hop flavor and aroma are acceptable, but many porters have none at all. Fruitiness, esters, and diacetyl are acceptable in low amounts.

Jim Bob Porter

Gold Medal, NHC, Robust Porter, 1994
David Lose, Glenn Klein, and Dale Dockin,
Sebastopol, California
(Extract/Grain)

Ingredients for 5 Gallons
- 6 pounds amber malt extract
- 4 pounds dark malt extract
- 1/2 pound chocolate malt
- 1/2 pound dark caramel malt
- 2 ounces Cluster hops (45 minutes)
- 1 ounce Cascade hops (10 minutes)
- 13 small pieces of natural licorice
- Wyeast No. 1056 American ale yeast
- 3/4 cup corn sugar (to prime)

Original gravity:	—
Final gravity:	—
Boiling time:	60 minutes
Primary fermentation:	1 week in stainless steel
Secondary fermentation:	2 weeks in glass
Age when judged:	4 months

Brewer's Specifics
Steep grains for 10 minutes at the end of the boil.

Judges' Comments
"Lots of black malt. Rich flavor. Moderately high hops. Well balanced. Too much carbonation. Clean. High alcohol (try a less attenuative yeast). Slight esters with warmth. This is good beer. A real robust porter."

"A very full robust porter. Mellows as it sits in glass. Full bodied, don't add any more! A very nice drinking beer."

Prehistoric Porter

Gold Medal, NHC, Robust Porter, 1995
Fred Gibson, Pasadena, California
(All-Grain)

Ingredients for 10 Gallons
- 19 pounds Harrington two-row malt
- 2 pounds chocolate malt
- 1 1/2 pounds medium crystal malt
- 2 ounces Cluster hops, 7% alpha acid (60 minutes)
- 2 ounces Cluster hops, 7% alpha acid (30 minutes)
- 2 ounces Cascade hops, 6% alpha acid (finish)
- Wyeast No. 1056 American ale yeast
- force-carbonate in keg

Original gravity:	1.055
Final gravity:	1.014
Boiling time:	60 minutes
Primary fermentation:	5 days at 70 °F (21 °C) in stainless steel
Secondary fermentation:	14 days at 70 °F (21 °C) in stainless steel
Age when judged:	2 1/2 months

Brewer's Specifics
Mash grains at 155 °F (68 °C) for 90 minutes.

Judges' Comments
"Chocolate malt comes through—could use a little more bitterness from either black malt or bittering hops. Nice beer. A tad more black malt flavor or bittering hops would make this better."

"Very good robust flavor profile. I like the mouthfeel. Perfect balance of malt sweetness and burnt flavors. This is great porter."

"Good roast malt and hops up front. May need a bit more hop bitterness but still very good. I wouldn't change a thing except a bit more body and a touch more bitterness."

Smashing Porter

Gold Medal, NHC, Porter, 1996
Ross Frederiksen, Loomis, California
(All-Grain)

Ingredients for 5 Gallons
    8   pounds English pale ale malt
    5   pounds English brown malt
    1   pound chocolate malt
    2   ounces Fuggles hop pellets, 3.4% alpha acid (60 minutes)
    1   ounce Fuggles hop pellets, 3.4% alpha acid (45 minutes)
  1/2   ounce Fuggles hop pellets, 3.4% alpha acid (30 minutes)
  1/2   ounce Fuggles hop pellets, 3.4% alpha acid (15 minutes)
        Wyeast No. 1028 London Burton ale yeast
    4   ounces corn sugar (to prime)

Original gravity:	1.056
Final gravity:	1.014
Boiling time:	90 minutes
Primary fermentation:	5 days at 75 °F (24 °C) in glass
Secondary fermentation:	10 days at 75 °F (24 °C) in glass
Age when judged:	5 months

Brewer's Specifics
Mash grains at 154 °F (68 °C) for 60 minutes.

Judges' Comments
"Pleasant roasted malt flavor and freshness without the astringency in finish. Nice bitterness with good smooth finish. No sharp edges and perfect fullness."

"Malt and hops well balanced. Aftertaste still has roastiness. Hops are in background as they should be for this category. Aroma is very inviting. Great job."

Sarah Teall's No. 33

Silver Medal, NHC, Porter, 1996
Wendy Parker-Wood and Bev Nulman,
Albuquerque, New Mexico
(All-Grain)

Ingredients for 7 Gallons

9 1/2	pounds English two-row malt
1 1/4	pounds English 105 °L crystal malt
1	pound Hugh Baird roasted barley malt
1	pound flaked barley
1/2	pound Hugh Baird chocolate malt
1	ounce English Fuggles hop plugs, 4.3% alpha acid (60 minutes)
3/4	ounce Brewers Gold hop pellets, 7.6% alpha acid (60 minutes)
1/2	ounce East Kent Goldings hop plugs, 5.2% alpha acid (60 minutes)
1/2	ounce East Kent Goldings hop plugs, 5.2% alpha acid (30 minutes)
1/2	ounce East Kent Goldings hop plugs, 5.2% alpha acid (5 minutes)
13	tablespoons dilute lactic acid added to sparge water
1	teaspoon gypsum added to mash
	Wyeast No. 1084 Irish ale yeast
1	cup dextrose (to prime)

Original gravity:	1.060
Final gravity:	1.023
Boiling time:	75 minutes
Primary fermentation:	17 days at 72 °F (22 °C) in glass
Secondary fermentation:	8 days at 75 °F (24 °C) in glass
Age when judged:	11 months

Brewer's Specifics

Protein rest is at 128 °F (53 °C) for 30 minutes and 156 °F (69 °C) for 90 minutes. Mash-out at 168 °F (76 °C) for 10 minutes.

Judges' Comments

"Very good, rich, robust, malty flavor and very balanced in hops. Robust full body for a porter."

"Roasty bouquet. Hops in background as they should be. Very inviting. Very robust flavor. Malt and hops good, balanced. Aftertaste is pleasing. Very good beer. Almost too chewy for porter. Can't suggest anything to improve—maybe less malt!"

"Good roasted malt aroma with some fruitiness. Clean nose. Big creamy head with lots of small bubbles. Dark, rich, brown color. Good clarity. Killer porter."

Storm Peak Porter

Bronze Medal, NHC, Porter, 1995
Dave Shaffer, Lafayette, Colorado
(All-Grain)

Ingredients for 5 Gallons

8	pounds Klages malt
1	pound CaraPils malt
1	pound Munich malt
1/2	pound Ireks dark crystal malt
1/2	pound 80 °L crystal malt
1/2	pound wheat malt
1/2	pound special roasted malt
3/8	pound black patent malt
3/8	pound chocolate malt
1	ounce Perle hops, 7.5% alpha acid (63 minutes)
1	ounce Tettnang hop pellets, 4.3% alpha acid (15 minutes)
1	ounce Hallertau hop pellets, 2.6% alpha acid (15 minutes)
1	ounce Hallertau hop pellets, 2.6% alpha acid (3 minutes)
1	ounce Tettnang hop pellets, 4.3% alpha acid (3 minutes)
2	teaspoons chalk added to sparge water
	Wyeast No. 1056 American ale yeast

Original gravity:	1.056
Final gravity:	1.017
Boiling time:	78 minutes
Primary fermentation:	25 days at 62 °F (17 °C) in glass
Secondary fermentation:	2 days at 62 °F (17 °C) in glass
Age when judged:	3 months

Brewer's Specifics

Mash grains at 154 °F (68 °C) for 90 minutes. Sparge with 170 °F (77 °C) water to collect 7 1/2 gallons of wort.

Fiery Apparel Porter

Gold Medal, NHC, Robust Porter, 1993
Marvin Crippen, Seattle, Washington
(All-Grain)

Ingredients for 5 Gallons
       8   pounds two-row Klages malt
       1   pound Munich malt
    1/2   pound crystal malt
    1/2   pound chocolate malt
    1/2   pound roasted barley malt
    1/2   pound black patent malt
       1   ounce Eroica hops, 11% alpha acid (60 minutes)
    1/2   ounce Cascade hops, 6% alpha acid (15 minutes)
            Wyeast No. 1084 Irish ale yeast
       1   cup dextrose (to prime)

Original gravity:	1.065
Final gravity:	1.018
Boiling time:	120 minutes
Primary fermentation:	10 hours at 67 °F (19 °C) in glass
Secondary fermentation:	10 days at 72 °F (22 °C) in glass
Age when judged:	3 months

Brewer's Specifics
Mash grains at 153 °F (67 °C) for 120 minutes.

Judges' Comments
"Yum! Only flaw is that the degree of roasty bitterness is more appropriate for stout than porter."

"Need more malt complexity and sweetness. Overall, well balanced. Could boost chocolate and crystal."

"Fruity overtones impact this batch. Yeast could be source of fruitiness."

"Good sweetness. Nice balance. Could use more black malt."

RED ALE

This low- to medium-strength beer is malty in both aroma and flavor. Body is medium, which is fuller than expected for the beer's gravity. Bitterness is low to medium and is balanced in favor of malt with a round fruity finish and the notably buttery tones of diacetyl. This is an easy-drinking beer for Saint Patrick's day.

Joe Gillian's Red

Irish Red Ale, 1997
Amahl Turczyn, Boulder, Colorado
(All-Grain)

Ingredients for 5 Gallons

7	pounds British two-row malt
1/4	pound British 55 °L crystal malt
1/4	pound British 80 °L crystal malt
2	ounces roasted barley
1	ounce Fuggles hops, 4.4% alpha acid (60 minutes)
3/4	ounce Fuggles hops, 4.4% alpha acid (30 minutes)
3/4	ounce East Kent Goldings hops, 5.2% alpha acid (5 minutes)
1	teaspoon gypsum added to mash water
	Wyeast No. 1968 Special London ale yeast
	force-carbonate in keg

Original gravity:	1.050
Finishing gravity:	1.010
Boiling time:	60 minutes
Primary fermentation:	7 days at 68 °F (20 °C) in glass
Secondary fermentation:	7 days at 65 °F (18 °C) in glass
Tertiary fermentation:	—

Brewer's Specifics

Mash grains at 150 °F (66 °C) for 90 minutes.

Flavor Comments

This is a guess at the famous Smithwick's Irish red ale's recipe. The buttery character from the slight diacetyl left by this yeast strain complements the malty caramel tones of the crystal malt. This is a perfect session beer for Saint Patrick's Day parties, so brew a few kegs!

Kilkenny's Penny Red

NHC, Specialty Beer, 1996
Jeffrey Swearengin, Tulsa, Oklahoma
(All-Grain)

Ingredients for 4 Gallons

5	pounds Briess two-row pale malt
1	pound DeWolf-Cosyns CaraVienne 20 °L crystal malt
1/4	pound DeWolf-Cosyns Special "B" 150 °L crystal malt
2	ounces British roasted barley
3/8	ounce Bullion hop pellets, 8.5% alpha acid (90 minutes)
1/2	ounce English Bramling Cross hop pellets, 5.4% alpha acid (45 minutes)
1/2	ounce English Bramling Cross hop pellets, 5.4% alpha acid (30 minutes)
1/2	ounce English Fuggles hop plugs, 4.2% alpha acid (15 minutes)
7/8	teaspoon gypsum
1	pinch chalk
1/2	teaspoon ascorbic acid added to sparge water
1/4	teaspoon Irish moss
2	teaspoons Polyclar added to secondary
	Wyeast No. 1084 Irish ale yeast
5/8	cup dextrose (to prime)

Original gravity:	1.045
Final gravity:	1.010
Boiling time:	90 minutes
Primary fermentation:	2 days at 72–78 °F (22–26'°C) in glass
Secondary fermentation:	5 days at 64–68 °F (18–20 °C) in glass
Age when judged:	3 months

Brewer's Specifics

Use a three-step infusion. Begin with a protein rest at 95 °F (35 °C) for 30 minutes. Bring mash to 117–122 °F (47–50 °C) for 60 minutes. Bring mash to 150 °F (66 °C) for 60 minutes. Mash-out at 170 °F (77 °C) for 15 minutes.

Irish Bitter

NHC, English Bitter, 1996
James Wilts, Richmond, California
(All-Grain)

Ingredients 5 1/2 Gallons

2 1/2	pounds British two-row malt
2 1/2	pounds American two-row malt
2 1/2	pounds Belgian two-row malt
3/5	pound British 75 °L crystal malt
0.03	pound Belgian Special "B" malt
0.03	pound Belgian chocolate malt
1 1/2	ounces Goldings hops, 4.2% alpha acid (60 minutes)
1	ounce Fuggles hops, 3.5% alpha acid (30 minutes)
1/2	ounce Fuggles hops, 3.5% alpha acid (5 minutes)
1 1/10	grams epsom salts
1/2	gram salt
	Windsor ale yeast
	soft water
3/4	cup corn sugar (to prime)

Original gravity:	—
Final gravity:	—
Boiling time:	60 minutes
Primary fermentation:	18 days at 65 °F (18 °C) in glass
Secondary fermentation:	3 days at 65 °F (18 °C) in stainless steel
Age when judged:	3 months

Brewer's Specifics

Mash grains at 156 °F (69 °C) for 90 minutes.

DRY STOUT

This is the classic dry style. Made famous in Ireland, dry stout is opaque black with medium body and medium to high hop bitterness. These characteristics blend with the bitter dryness of the roasted barley. Slight malt sweetness is okay with fruit, coffee, and/or chocolate notes. No hop flavor or aroma is detectable. A slight acidity or sourness is appropriate—some commercial stout brewers add sourness to their stouts for character. Very low diacetyl is acceptable.

Deck-Head Stout

Gold Medal, NHC, Classic Dry Stout, 1995
Rob Schutte, Cincinnati, Ohio
(All-Grain)

Ingredients for 5 Gallons
8	pounds British two-row pale malt
1 1/2	pounds flaked barley
1	pound roasted barley
3/4	pound CaraPils malt
1/2	pound 40 °L crystal malt
1 1/2	ounces Kent Goldings hop plugs, 5% alpha acid (70 minutes)
1	ounce Northern Brewer hops, 6.4% alpha acid (70 minutes)
	Wyeast No. 1084 Irish ale yeast
2/3	cup corn sugar (to prime)

Original gravity:	1.054
Final gravity:	1.020
Boiling time:	70 minutes
Primary fermentation:	6 days at 63 °F (17 °C) in glass
Secondary fermentation:	9 days at 63 °F (17 °C) in glass
Age when judged:	6 months

Brewer's Specifics
Mash grains at 98 °F (37 °C) for 20 minutes. Raise temperature to 122 °F (50 °C) and hold for 20 minutes. Raise temperature to 154 °F (68 °C) for 65 minutes and 170 °F (77 °C) for 5 minutes.

Judges' Comments
"Nicely balanced beer. Some residual bitterness. Roasted barley and malt sweetness blend together well. Very good job at style. The malt profile is right on."

"Good roast and malt character. Bitterness very good. Perfect conditioning. Nice malt, roast, and bitter in finish—maybe too bitter?"

Whack That Puppy against the Wall

Finalist, World Homebrew Contest, Classic Dry Stout, 1997
Al Rose, Ann Arbor, Michigan
(All-Grain)

Ingredients for 13 1/2 Gallons

19 1/2	pounds two-row lager
6	pounds 40 °L crystal malt
1 1/2	pounds roasted barley
1 1/2	pounds flaked barley
3/4	pound black patent malt
3/4	pound chocolate malt
2 1/2	ounces Northern Brewer hops, 9.3% alpha acid (60 minutes)
	Wyeast No. 1028 London ale yeast
2/3	cup corn sugar (to prime)

Original gravity:	1.052
Final gravity:	1.012
Boiling time:	110 minutes
Primary fermentation:	18 hours at 61–63 °F (16–17 °C) in glass
Secondary fermentation:	7 days at 63–65 °F (17–18 °C) in glass
Age when brewed:	—

Brewer's Specifics

For infusion mash, hold mash temperature at 137 °F (58 °C) for 30 minutes. Bring temperature to 154 °F (68 °C) for 60 minutes.

Dave's Dry Irish Stout

Reprinted from 1996 Special Issue of *Zymurgy*
Dave Miller, Hermitage, Tennessee
(All-Grain)

Ingredients for 5 Gallons
7 1/2   pounds pale two-row malt
1   pound flaked barley
3/4   pound roasted barley
2 1/2   ounces Willamette hop pellets, 4% alpha acid (30 minutes)
   Wyeast No. 1056 American ale yeast

Original gravity:	1.052
Final gravity:	1.014
Boiling time:	90 minutes
Primary fermentation:	7 days at 65 °F (18 °C)
Secondary fermentation:	14 days at 60–65 °F (16–18 °C)
Tertiary fermentation:	—

Brewer's Specifics
Use a single infusion mash at 150 °F (66 °C) for 60 minutes. Cool and ferment around 70 °F (21 °C).

Untitled

Finalist, NHC, Classic Dry Stout, 1996
Carl Colburn, Denver, Colorado
(All-Grain)

Ingredients for 5 Gallons
- 7 pounds British pale malt
- 1 pound flaked barley
- 3/4 pound roasted barley
- 1/4 pound chocolate malt
- 2 1/2 ounces Kent Goldings hops, 5% alpha acid (80 minutes)
- 1/4 teaspoon gypsum per gallon of water
- adjust sparge water with lactic acid to 5.2 pH
- BreuTek CL-240 Irish Dry Stout yeast
- 3/4 cup corn sugar (to prime)

Original gravity:	1.048
Final gravity:	1.006
Boiling time:	90 minutes
Primary fermentation:	7 days at 68 °F (20 °C) in glass
Secondary fermentation:	12 days at 68 °F (20 °C) in glass
Age when judged:	3 months

Brewer's Specifics
Mash grains at 152 °F (67 °C) for 70 minutes. Adjust sparge water's pH to 5.2 with lactic acid and sparge with 4 gallons of water at 172 °F (78 °C).

SPRING

INDIA PALE ALE

Brewed in England for British troops stationed in India in the 18th century, this ale was made very strong and was highly hopped to preserve it through the six-month journey. It traditionally has an oaky or woody character, to mimic the barrel flavors it invariably picked up en route. Golden to deep amber or copper, India pale ale also has a medium body and maltiness. Low to medium diacetyl is acceptable for this style. Alcoholic strength is fairly high and evident. Some fruity or estery character is acceptable. The use of mineral salts in your brewing water helps give this style its sharp assertive hop character.

White Oak Ale

Finalist, NHC, India Pale Ale, 1995
Mike Harper, Oakdale, California
(Extract/Grain)

Ingredients for 5 Gallons

7	pounds American light malt extract
3	pounds Klages malt
1	pound 20 °L caramel malt
4/5	ounce Chinook hops, 12.5% alpha acid (60 minutes)
7/10	ounce Chinook hops, 12.5% alpha acid (30 minutes)
2	ounces Cascade hops, 7.8% alpha acid (dry)
	Wyeast No. 1056 American yeast
	force-carbonate in keg

Original gravity:	1.061
Final gravity:	1.020
Boiling time:	60 minutes
Primary fermentation:	1 week at 65 °F (18 °C) in glass
Secondary fermentation:	3 weeks at 65 °F (18 °C) in glass
Age when judged:	2 months

Brewer's Specifics
Steep grains at 160 °F (71 °C) for 60 minutes.

Judges' Comments
"Nice full flavor. Maltiness a bit too dominant for style. Increase hop bitterness considerably. Alcoholic strength could be more evident. Tasty beer."

"Good hop flavor and bitterness. Maltiness rounds out the palate. Alcoholic and warming but not overdone. Could use some more bitterness for this style. Reminds me of Anchor Liberty only not as bitter."

Slacker India Pale Ale

Gold Medal, NHC, India Pale Ale, 1996
Chris Neikirk, Norfolk, Virginia
(All-Grain)

Ingredients for 10 Gallons

- 18 pounds British malt
- 4 pounds U.S. two-row pale malt
- 1 pound dextrin malt
- 1 pound Munich malt
- 1 pound 60 °L crystal malt
- 3 ounces Nugget hop pellets, 11% alpha acid (60 minutes)
- 6 ounces Cascade hop pellets, 4.4% alpha acid (30 minutes)
- 2 ounces Kent Goldings hops, 4.2% alpha acid (dry, 1 week)
  Wyeast No. 1028 London ale yeast
- 1 cup corn sugar (to prime)

Original gravity:	1.062
Final gravity:	1.014
Boiling time:	85 minutes
Primary fermentation:	6 days at 63 °F (17 °C) in plastic
Secondary fermentation:	10 days at 63 °F (17 °C) in glass
Age when judged:	3 1/2 months

Brewer's Specifics
Mash grains at 130 °F (54 °C) for 30 minutes and 153 °F (67 °C) for 75 minutes.

Judges' Comments
"Long on bitterness. Long on hop flavor. Malt is well balanced. Clean beer. Very tasty."

"Malty, but slight hop aftertaste fades fast. Slight diacetyl. Some apple. Add more hops late in boil."

Ugly Stepsister Star of the Sun

Bronze Medal, NHC, India Pale Ale, 1996
Nate Kowash, Portland, Oregon
(All-Grain)

Ingredients for 5 Gallons

13	pounds Telford's pale malt
1/2	pound toasted pale malt
1/4	pound 120 °L crystal malt
1/4	pound malted wheat
2	ounces Columbus hop pellets, 15% alpha acid (60 minutes)
2	ounces Kent Goldings hop pellets, 5% alpha acid (15 minutes)
2	ounces Willamette hop pellets, 4.9% alpha acid (finish)
1/2	teaspoon per gallon gypsum
1/2	teaspoon per gallon epsom salts
1/4	teaspoon per gallon chalk
	Wyeast No. 1318 London III ale yeast
3/4	cup corn sugar (to prime)

Original gravity:	1.050
Final gravity:	1.010
Boiling time:	90 minutes
Primary fermentation:	5 days at 60–65 °F (16–18 °C) in plastic
Secondary fermentation:	2 weeks at 55–60 °F (13–16 °C) in glass
Age when judged:	4 months

Brewer's Specifics

Mash grains at 156 °F (69 °C) for 60 minutes.

Judges' Comments

"Hop and malt well balanced but light."

"Solid hop aroma. Nice fruitiness, too. Bitterness dominates only slightly. Very tasty beer. Clear."

Champion Reserve India Ale

Reprinted from 1996 Special Issue of *Zymurgy*
Greg Noonan, West Lebanon, New Hampshire
(Extract/Grain)

Ingredients for 5 Gallons
7	pounds light dry malt extract
3/4	pound CaraPils malt
1/2	pound crystal malt
2 1/2	AAU Cascade hops (45 minutes)
3 1/2	AAU Cascade hops (45 minutes)
6	AAU Cascade hops (30 minutes)
2 1/4	ounces Perle hops (finish)
1	ounce Cascade hop pellets added to secondary fermentation (dry)
2	teaspoons gypsum
1 1/2	teaspoons epsom salts
1/4	teaspoon kosher salt
1/4–1/3	ounce fruity estery ale yeast slurry
	[*I suggest Wyeast No. 1098 or No. 1335.—Ed.*]
3/4	cup corn sugar (to prime)

Original gravity:	1.052
Final gravity:	1.014
Boiling time:	45 minutes
Primary fermentation:	7 days at 70 °F (21 °C)
Secondary fermentation:	14 days at 68 °F (20 °C)
Tertiary fermentation:	—

Brewer's Specifics
Mash grains at 153 °F (67 °C) for 60 minutes. Sparge.

Dances with Humulus Lupulus

Gold Medal, NHC, India Pale Ale, 1993
Kelly Dunham, Pacifica, California
(Extract/Grain)

Ingredients for 5 Gallons

6	pounds light dry malt extract
1 1/2	pounds 20 °L crystal malt
1	pound dry wheat malt extract
1/2	pound 40 °L crystal malt
1/2	pound wheat malt
1/4	pound flaked barley
1/8	pound chocolate malt
1	ounce Chinook hops, 12.8% alpha acid (75 minutes)
1/2	ounce Centennial hops, 10.9% alpha acid (45 minutes)
1/2	ounce Goldings hops, 4.7% alpha acid (45 minutes)
1	ounce Centennial hops, 10.9% alpha acid (20 minutes)
1/2	ounce Goldings hops, 4.7% alpha acid (20 minutes)
1	ounce Centennial hops, 10.9% alpha acid (5 minutes)
1/2	ounce Centennial hops, 10.9% alpha acid (dry)
1/2	ounce Goldings hops, 4.7% alpha acid (dry)
	Sierra Nevada ale yeast (or Wyeast No. 1056 American ale yeast)
1	cup corn sugar (to prime)

Original gravity:	1.068
Final gravity:	1.024
Boiling time:	75 minutes
Primary fermentation:	28 days at 60 °F (16 °C) in glass
Secondary fermentation:	—
Age when judged:	5 months

Brewer's Specifics

Bring wort and grains to boil. Remove grains at 180 °F (82 °C).

Judges' Comments

"Well-balanced flavor. Nice, proper, lingering, clean, hop astringency."

"High hop flavor and bitterness. Medium maltiness. Excellent beer!"

"Aftertaste lingers a little long. Great floral aroma."

"Good bitterness. Alcohol noticeable but could be a little more pronounced. Good clean taste. Hop flavor could be greater. Well-made beer."

Jim's IPA

Third Place, Club-Only Competition, India Pale Ale, 1996
James Berdan, Sacramento, California
(All-Grain)

Ingredients for 5 Gallons
- 10 pounds pale ale malt
- 1 pound 95 °L crystal malt
- 1 ounce Columbus hop pellets, 13% alpha acid (60 minutes)
- 1 ounce Kent Goldings hop pellets, 5.2% alpha acid (15 minutes)
- 1/4 ounce Kent Goldings hop pellets, 6% alpha acid (15 minutes)
- 1 ounce Cascade hop pellets, 4.1% alpha acid (dry)
- Wyeast No. 1056 American ale yeast
- force-carbonate in keg

Original gravity:	1.058
Final gravity:	1.013
Boiling time:	75 minutes
Primary fermentation:	6 days at 68 °F (20 °C) in glass
Secondary fermentation:	12 days at 45 °F (7 °C) in glass
Age when judged:	2 months

Brewer's Specifics
Mash grains at 153 °F (67 °C) for 90 minutes.

B3

Second Place, Club-Only Competition, 1996
Kevin Day and Todd Nelson, Long Beach, California
(All-Grain)

Ingredients for 10 Gallons
12 1/2 pounds Klages malt
1 1/2 pounds Munich malt
1 1/2 pounds torrefied wheat
1 pound 35 °L crystal malt
1 ounce Cascade hops, 4.2% alpha acid (60 minutes)
1 ounce Centennial hops, 8.8% alpha acid (30 minutes)
1 ounce Cascade hops, 4.2% alpha acid (8 minutes)
1/2 ounce Centennial hops, 8.8% alpha acid (5 minutes)
1 ounce Cascade hops, 4.2% alpha acid (3 minutes)
1 ounce Centennial hops, 8.8% alpha acid (3 minutes)

Original gravity:	1.070
Final gravity:	1.018
Boiling time:	75 minutes
Primary fermentation:	—
Secondary fermentation:	—
Age when judged:	—

Impale Ale

India Pale Ale, 1996
Amahl Turczyn, Boulder, Colorado
(All-Grain)

Ingredients for 10 Gallons
    15 pounds Hugh Baird pale malt
     3 pounds Hugh Baird 30 °L crystal malt
     2 pounds honey malt
     2 ounces Kent Goldings hop pellets, 5.7% alpha acid (60 minutes)
     2 ounces Kent Goldings hop pellets, 5.7% alpha acid (30 minutes)
     1 ounce Kent Goldings hop pellets, 5.7% alpha acid (15 minutes)
     3 ounces Mt. Hood hop pellets, 4.0% alpha acid (1 minute)
     2 ounces Mt. Hood hop pellets, 4.0% alpha acid (dry, 1 week)
        Wyeast No. 1056 American ale yeast

Original gravity:	1.065
Final gravity:	1.012
Boiling time:	90 minutes
Primary fermentation:	2 weeks at 65 °F (18 °C)
Secondary fermentation:	2 months at 60–65 °F (16–18 °C)
Tertiary fermentation:	—

Brewer's Specifics
Mash grains at 150 °F (66 °C) for 60 minutes. Fine with gelatin in the secondary fermenter.

Flavor Comments
This is a high-powered pale ale and is best served at 55 °F (13 °C) from a keg. Splash it into the pint glass—the aeration tends to give British ales a wonderful mellow smoothness. The liberal use of hops in the kettle and in the conditioning vessel give this brew a huge floral spicy character and a dry finish. A hop head's paradise!

KÖLSCH

Originally brewed in Cologne (or Köln in German), this distinctive ale style is light in alcoholic strength (under 5 percent by volume) and in its golden color. It is a very well-attenuated beer and is made with a special yeast that displays characteristics of both top- and bottom-fermenting strains. It can be faintly fruity and usually has a well-balanced neutral finish. Wheat is sometimes used in the all-malt grist but usually not in quantities of more than 15 percent. Both body and maltiness are light. There is little or no diacetyl.

Cowabunga Kölsch

Winner, Club-Only Competition, Kölsch, 1996
Jack Kinsman, Bartlett, Illinois
(All-Grain)

Ingredients for 10 Gallons
14	pounds German Pilsener malt
1	pound American two-row malt
1	pound malted wheat
1/2	pound CaraPils malt
2 1/5	ounces Perle hops, 4.8% alpha acid (60 minutes)
1 4/5	ounces Perle hops, 4.8% alpha acid (20 minutes)
1	ounce Saaz hop plugs, 3.1% alpha acid (2 minutes)
	Wyeast No. 2565 Kölsch yeast
	force-carbonate in keg

Original gravity:	1.042
Final gravity:	1.012
Boiling time:	90 minutes
Primary fermentation:	1 week at 70 °F (21 °C) in glass
Secondary fermentation:	2 weeks at 50 °F (10 °C) in glass
Tertiary fermentation:	4 weeks at 35 °F (2 °C) in stainless steel
Age when judged:	3 months

Brewer's Specifics
Mash grains at 128 °F (53 °C) for 30 minutes. Raise temperature to 154 °F (68 °C) for 60 minutes and 165 °F (74 °C) for 5 minutes.

Judges' Comments
"Very nice, light, crisp flavor. Well balanced. Very nice conditioning. Light malt fades to nice hop flavor."

"Good malty flavor. No off-flavors noted. Dryness about right."

"Slightly 'corny' taste. A bit of vegetable. Hops are very restrained. A bit too estery. Maltiness not pronounced sufficiently."

Kölsch #4

Gold Medal, NHC, Kölsch, 1995
Bennett Dawson, St. Albans, Vermont
(All-Grain)

Ingredients for 5 Gallons

3	pounds two-row malt
3	pounds DeWolf-Cosyns Pilsener malt
4	ounces DeWolf-Cosyns CaraVienne malt
4	ounces DeWolf-Cosyns CaraPils malt
4	ounces DeWolf-Cosyns wheat malt
1 1/2	ounces Hallertau Hersbrucker hops, 3.5% alpha acid (75 minutes)
1/2	ounce Hallertau Hersbrucker hops, 3.5% alpha acid (15 minutes)
1/2	ounce Czech Saaz hops, 3.1% alpha acid (5 minutes)
	Wyeast No. 2565 Kölsch yeast
	force-carbonate in keg

Original gravity:	1.046
Final gravity:	1.006
Boiling time:	90 minutes
Primary fermentation:	7 days at 55 °F (13 °C) in glass
Secondary fermentation:	12 days at 55 °F (13 °C) in glass
Age when judged:	3 months

Brewer's Specifics

Mash grains at 122 °F (50 °C) for 30 minutes. Raise temperature to 146 °F (63 °C) for 90 minutes, 152 °F (67 °C) for 30 minutes, and 158 °F (70 °C) for 15 minutes. Mash-out at 170 °F (77 °C). Sparge with 5 gallons of 170 °F (77 °C) water.

Judges' Comments

"A good dry flavor. Some malt sweetness evident. Hop-malt balance good for style. A drinkable beer."

"Initial delicate malty sweetness. Hop bitterness is acceptable but could be higher to offset sweet character. I would love to have a basement full of this beer!"

Kölsch 45

Finalist, NHC, Kölsch, 1995
Bill Murphy, Brookline, Massachusetts
(All-Grain)

Ingredients for 3 Gallons

5	pounds Belgian Pilsener malt
1/2	pound wheat malt
1	ounce Hallertau hops, 4% alpha acid (45 minutes)
1/4	ounce Hallertau hops, 3% alpha acid (15 minutes)
1/6	ounce Hallertau hops, 3% alpha acid (5 minutes)
	German alt yeast
2 3/4	ounces dextrose (to prime)

Original gravity:	1.045
Final gravity:	1.010
Boiling time:	90 minutes
Primary fermentation:	2 weeks at 60 °F (16 °C) in glass
Secondary fermentation:	2 weeks at 60 °F (16 °C) in glass
Age when judged:	3 months

Brewer's Specifics

Mash grains at 125–130 °F (52–54 °C) for 25 minutes. Raise temperature to 150 °F (66 °C) for 75 minutes and then to 165–170 °F (74–77 °C) for 10 minutes.

Judges' Comments

"Slightly fruity. Very clean. Flavor of hops lingers nicely. Very subtle maltiness. Could be a little fresher but understandably so. This is very well made and appropriate in all aspects of the style. Well done."

"Good restrained fruitiness. Good effort."

Köln Ale

Silver Medal, NHC, Kölsch, 1996
Mark Bayer, St. Charles, Missouri
(All-Grain)

Ingredients for 5 Gallons

6	pounds DeWolf-Cosyns Pilsener malt
3/4	pound DeWolf-Cosyns wheat malt
3/8	pound DeWolf-Cosyns CaraVienne malt
3/8	pound Briess CaraPils malt
1	ounce Perle hops, 9.5% alpha acid (60 minutes)
1/2	ounce Tettnang hops, 4.5% alpha acid (15 minutes)
1/2	ounce Liberty hops (5 minutes)
1/2	teaspoon chalk added to mash
	sparge water acidified with lactic acid
	Wyeast No. 2565 Kölsch yeast
3/5	cup corn sugar (to prime)

Original gravity:	1.042
Final gravity:	1.010
Boiling time:	90 minutes
Primary fermentation:	30 days at 62–66 °F (17–19 °C) in glass
Secondary fermentation:	7 days at 62–66 °F (17–19 °C) in glass
Age when judged:	4 months

Brewer's Specifics

Mash grains at 142–152 °F (61–67 °C) for 135 minutes.

Judges' Comments

"Straw golden [color for] style [is] appropriate. Slight haze—okay. Chill. Great head—tight bead. Lace—lasts. Effervescent on the tongue. Sweet presentation. Finishes dry. Medium bitterness. Good balance. Great job!"

"Good color and clarity. Excellent head retention. Very good example of style but needs lower hop bitterness for better balance."

"I picked up a very slight wine aroma. Excellent brew for style."

"One of the better beers today. Very good balance. Fine example."

LAMBIC

This highly unusual Belgian style traditionally uses spontaneous fermentation with wild yeasts to produce a tart winelike ale. Fruit is often added. This beer is made from 30–40 percent wheat and is of light strength, color, and body. Lambic is hopped with aged hops, resulting in very low bitterness and very little or no hop aroma and it usually takes longer than a year to age properly.

Gueuze is the name for plain lambic, though with the explosion of flavors and aromas from a classic gueuze, there is nothing plain about it. Cherries, raspberries, and peaches are added to produce kriek, framboise, and pêche, respectively.

Emulating this style requires great patience and dedication, though many homebrewers take on the challenge with impressive results. If you wish to pursue this style, here are some tips: (1) The various microflora necessary to reproduce a true lambic completely ruins other styles of beer, so take careful precautions to avoid cross-contamination of your equipment. (2) An easy way to sour your beer is to add a half pound or so of crushed, pale, two-row malt to your batch of wort and let it sit overnight to encourage the production of *Lactobacillus* and *Pediococcus* bacteria, which occurs naturally on barley. You may get more sourness than you want. However, there are other strains of bacteria present in real lambic, which give a greater depth of flavor than just sourness.

Up the Kriek

Silver Medal, NHC, Belgian-Style Lambic, 1996
Paul Edwards, Indianapolis, Indiana
(All-Grain)

Ingredients for 4 Gallons

7 3/4	pounds Munton and Fison pale malt
2	pounds torrefied wheat
1/2	pound DeWolf-Cosyns CaraPils malt
1	ounce Hallertau whole hops, 1% alpha acid (120 minutes)
	Wyeast *Brettanomyces* yeast and sediment from 3 bottles of Frank Boon Gueuze
1	gallon sour cherry juice added to secondary
3/4	cup corn sugar (to prime)

Original gravity:	1.050
Final gravity:	—
Boiling time:	120 minutes
Primary fermentation:	2 months at 65 °F (18 °C) in glass
Secondary fermentation:	2 years at 65 °F (18 °C) in glass
Age when judged:	—

Brewer's Specifics

Mash grains at 158 °F (70 °C) for 60 minutes. Sparge to collect 6 gallons of wort. Boil down to 4 gallons. Add 1 gallon sour cherry juice to secondary to bring final volume to 5 gallons.

Judges' Comments

"Cherry sourness and taste. Sour lactic complexity with a lingering cherry sourness. *Brettanomyces* character in nose could be increased. Good cherry flavor and nice sourness."

"Oily mouthfeel. Good intense sourness lasts. Needs more complexity. Good kriek, perhaps not as wild as some would like, but better than most commercially available."

Lamp Lighter Lambic

Finalist, NHC, Belgian Lambic, 1996
Chuck Allen, Westminster, Colorado
(Extract/Grain)

Ingredients for 5 Gallons
- 4 pounds Dutch extra light dry malt extract
- 3 pounds Belgian pale malt
- 1 pound Belgian wheat
- 1 pound Belgian CaraVienne 24 °L malt
- 1 ounce Styrian Goldings hops, 5.0% alpha acid (60 minutes)
- Yeast Lab® *Pediococcus cerevisiae* bacteria
- Yeast Lab Belgian Trappist yeast A08
- Yeast Lab *Brettanomyces lambicus* yeast

Original gravity:	1.063
Final gravity:	1.021
Boiling time:	60 minutes
Primary fermentation:	7 days at 68–70 °F (20–21 °C)
Secondary fermentation:	7 days at 68–70 °F (20–21 °C)
Tertiary fermentation:	22 days at 68–70 °F (20–21 °C)
Final fermentation:	6 days at 68–70 °F (20–21 °C)
Age when judged:	4 months

Brewer's Specifics
Add 4 quarts of water to brew pot and bring to 135 °F (57 °C). Add all pale and wheat grains and stabilize at 124 °F (51 °C). Let stand with no heat for 30 minutes. Bring 2 quarts plus 1 pint of water to boil and add to mash, bringing temperature to 145 °F (75 °C). Raise heat to 156 °F (69 °C). Add specialty grains and let stand for 30 minutes. Remove grains and sparge with 1 gallon of 170°F (77 °C) water.

Cherries Jubilee

Gold Medal, NHC, Fruit Lambic, 1995
Gregg Rentko, Madison, New Jersey
(Extract/Grain)

Ingredients for 5 Gallons
10	pounds Washington State cherries with stems removed
5	pounds light dry malt extract
2	pounds unmalted wheat berries
1 1/2	pounds two-row pale malt
1	pound light dry malt extract
1	ounce Saaz hops, 2.8% alpha acid,
	crushed and aged for 4 to 6 weeks (15 minutes)
	Wyeast *Brettanomyces bruxellensis* culture
	Whitbread English ale yeast culture
	Brettanomyces lambicus culture in 1 quart starter
	Pediococcus culture in 1 quart starter
3/4	cup dextrose (to prime)

Original gravity:	—
Final gravity:	1.011
Boiling time:	45 minutes
Primary fermentation:	4 weeks at 65–70 °F (18–21 °C) in glass
Secondary fermentation:	8 weeks at 65–70 °F (18–21 °C) in glass
Tertiary fermentation:	4 week at 65 °F (18 °C) in glass
Age when judged:	9 months

Brewer's Specifics
Cook cracked wheat berries in 6 quarts boiling water for 30 minutes. Cool to 145 °F (63 °C) and add malt. Rest at 120 °F (49 °C) for 30 minutes. Raise temperature to 130 °F (54 °C) and add 1 quart of boiling water. Raise temperature to 150 °F (66 °C) for 10 minutes and then to 158 °F (70 °C) for 20 minutes. Sparge with 2 quarts of 170 °F (77 °C) water. Boil wort with malt extract. Cool and pitch *B. bruxellensis* and Whitbread yeast. After 4 weeks, soak cherries in 180 °F (82 °C) water for 15 minutes and boil 1 pound of dry malt extract in 1 quart of water for 15 minutes. Add cherries to secondary fermenter. Add the rest of the malt extract and starters of *B. lambicus* and *Pediococcus* cultures.

Judges' Comments
"Sour. Very acetic. Not much fruit contribution. Dry and sour aftertaste. Needs more *Brettanomyces* character. Good overall balance and a good effort."

Diablo Rouge

Silver Medal, NHC, Belgian-Style Lambic, 1995
Walter Dobrowney, Saskatoon, Saskatchewan, Canada
(All-Grain)

Ingredients for 5 1/2 Gallons

8	pounds raspberries
7	pounds two-row Harrington malt
3 1/2	pounds unmalted wheat
1/2	pound carastan malt
1 4/5	ounces mixed 3-year-old hops, 2% alpha acid (70 minutes)
	Brettanomyces lambicus yeast
	Pediococcus damnosus culture
	Wyeast No. 1056 American ale yeast
1	cup corn sugar (to prime)

Original gravity:	1.052
Final gravity:	1.008
Boiling time:	90 minutes
Primary fermentation:	450 days at 60–70 °F (16–21 °C) in oak
Secondary fermentation:	—
Age when judged:	3 months

Brewer's Specifics
Mash grains at 156 °F (69 °C) for 30 minutes.

Judges' Comments
"Balance is okay, just *Brettanomyces* is too light. Nice sour aftertaste. Needs more *Brettanomyces* flavor. Overall quite nice though."

"Nice lambic aroma with esters, *Brettanomyces*, and raspberries. Hard to find fault here. There may be a hint of phenol. Slight haze. Pink body. Good carbonation. Great head retention. I'd like to try this in 6 months."

Belgian-Style Lambic

Gold Medal, NHC, Belgian-Style Lambic, 1996
Ron Raike, Orlando, Florida
(All-Grain)

Ingredients for 15 1/2 Gallons
9	pounds DeWolf-Cosyns two-row pale malt
7 3/4	pounds raw wheat
4	pounds flaked wheat
1 1/2	pounds DeWolf-Cosyns CaraVienne malt
4	ounces Cascade hops, two years old (150 minutes)
6 4/5	ounces Headstart *Brettanomyces bruxellensis* starter
6 4/5	ounces Headstart *Brettanomyces lambicus* starter
6 4/5	ounces Headstart *Kloeckera apiculata* starter
6 4/5	ounces Headstart *Candida lambicus* starter
6 4/5	ounces Boon Gueuze dregs (3-year-old bottle) starter
6 4/5	ounces starter made from dregs of previous lambic-style batch
6 4/5	ounces Wyeast No. 1056 American ale liquid yeast starter (pitched after 2 weeks)
6 4/5	ounces Headstart *Pediococcus damnosus* starter (pitched after 3 months)
1/2	cup corn sugar (to prime)

Original gravity:	1.058
Final gravity:	—
Boiling time:	150 minutes
Primary fermentation:	12 months at 68–78 °F (20–26 °C) in stainless steel
Secondary fermentation:	—
Age when judged:	3 months

Brewer's Specifics
Dough-in with 155 °F (68 °C) water. Rest at 113 °F (45 °C). Use the following 240-minute turbidish triple decoction mash schedule. First decoction is thick but milky, second is similar, third is 98% liquid. Each decoction is 4 to 5 quarts. Rest for 30 minutes between each decoction at 140 °F (60 °C) and 158 °F (70 °C). Heat sparge water to 176–194 °F (80–90 °C). Lauter for 150 minutes. First runnings are 1.051. Collect 17 gallons. Boil for 150 minutes. Chill 13 gallons and pitch yeast and bacteria according to above schedule.

Judges' Comments
"Somewhat sweet. Oily mouthfeel, very good. Lactic sourness could be more intense. *Brettanomyces* taste faint. In style, very good beer. Mouthfeel dead on, but residual sweetness is perhaps cloying."

Red Son

Bronze Medal, NHC, Belgian-Style Lambic, 1996
Walter Dobrowney, Saskatoon, Saskatchewan, Canada
(All-Grain)

Ingredients for 6 Gallons

10	pounds raspberries added 1 month before bottling
8	pounds two-row Harrington malt
3 1/2	pounds unmalted wheat
1/2	pound DeWolf-Cosyns CaraVienne malt
1 1/2	ounces mixed 3-year-old hops (90 minutes)
	Brettanomyces lambicus added 2 weeks after pitching
	Wyeast No. 1056 American ale yeast
	Pediococcus damnosus added 2 weeks after pitching
	Wyeast No. 1056 American ale yeast
	Wyeast No. 1056 American ale yeast
3/4	cup dextrose (to prime)

Original gravity:	1.052
Final gravity:	1.000
Boiling time:	120 minutes
Primary fermentation:	14 months at 58–68 °F (14–20 °C) in oak
Secondary fermentation:	—
Age when judged:	8 months

Brewer's Specifics

Mash grains at 156 °F (69 °C) for 60 minutes.

PALE ALE

This very wide category includes both English- and American-style pale ales. The main difference is hop choice. English hops have a slightly more floral grassy aroma, whereas American varieties are a bit more pungent, citrusy, and spicy. This is perhaps the most basic style and the easiest to brew. It can be made year-round, though March and May brewing ensure a good supply throughout spring and summer. In England, the term pale ale is misleading, as it refers to a wider variety of ales than in the United States. Bitter, for example, while in a category by itself, might be called a pale ale simply to differentiate it from browns and stouts. To avoid confusion, we'll say pale ale has a pale golden to copper color; low to medium maltiness; and high hop bitterness, flavor, and aroma. Low-alpha hops, British or American, are preferred. Most pale ales have a light to medium body, fruity or estery flavors, and low levels of diacetyl.

IBU Who?

Gold Medal, NHC, American Pale Ale, 1996
John Allen, Alpharetta, Georgia
(Extract/Grain)

Ingredients for 5 Gallons

9	pounds Superbrau pale malt extract
1	pound Hugh Baird 13–17 °L crystal malt
1/2	pound DeWolf-Cosyns biscuit malt
1/2	pound DeWolf-Cosyns aromatic malt
1/4	pound DeWolf-Cosyns CaraVienne malt
2	ounces Columbus hops, 15% alpha acid (60 minutes)
1	ounce Perle hops, 8.4% alpha acid (60 minutes)
1	ounce Columbus hops, 15% alpha acid (10 minutes)
1	ounce Columbus hops, 15% alpha acid (5 minutes)
2	ounces Cascade hops, 5.8% alpha acid (dry, 4 days)
	Wyeast No. 1056 American ale yeast
3/4	cup corn sugar (to prime)

Original gravity:	1.066
Final gravity:	1.020
Boiling time:	60 minutes
Primary fermentation:	7 days at 68 °F (20 °C) in glass
Secondary fermentation:	4 days at 38 °F (3 °C) in glass
Age when judged:	3 1/2 months

Brewer's Specifics

Steep grains at 155 °F (68 °C) for 30 minutes.

Judges' Comments

"Slight malt sweetness with a bitter finish—good. Hop flavor is apparent. Some fruitiness, which is okay. The bitterness is at the high end."

"Hop bitterness is robust and very appropriate for style requirements. Some additional maltiness would improve flavor. Also, additional fruity estery content would help."

"Puckering bitterness overwhelms. Grapefruit and lime. Slight diacetyl. May have oversparged. Reduce hops a little. Increase maltiness."

Ian's Ale

Gold Medal, NHC, American Pale Ale, 1995
John Arends, Calistoga, California
(All-Grain)

Ingredients for 10 Gallons

18	pounds two-row malt
1	pound 40 °L crystal malt
1	pound 20 °L crystal malt
1	pound Munich 10 °L malt
1	pound wheat malt
1/2	ounce Chinook hop pellets, 11.3% alpha acid (60 minutes)
1/2	ounce Chinook hop pellets, 11.3% alpha acid (30 minutes)
3	ounces Cascade hop pellets, 6% alpha acid (30 minutes)
2	ounces Cascade hop pellets, 6% alpha acid (2 minutes)
3	ounces Cascade hop pellets, 6% alpha acid (dry)
	Wyeast No. 1056 American ale yeast
3/4	cup corn sugar (to prime)

Original gravity:	1.054
Final gravity:	1.010
Boiling time:	75 minutes
Primary fermentation:	13 days at 66 °F (19 °C) in glass
Secondary fermentation:	10 days at 66 °F (19 °C) in glass
Age when judged:	3 months

Brewer's Specifics
Mash grains at 154 °F (68 °C) for 75 minutes.

Judges' Comments
"Caramel sweetness. Hop bitterness on the low side of high but is a smooth bitterness. An excellent beer! A touch more bittering hops would be truer to style."

"Excellent balance of hops and malt. Slightly overcarbonated. Very good beer. A little more finishing hops would really put this over the edge."

Vince's Pale

Gold Medal, NHC, American Pale Ale, 1994
John Arends, Calistoga, California
(All-Grain)

Ingredients for 10 Gallons

10	pounds two-row malt
1	pound British 30–37 °L crystal malt
1	pound 20 °L crystal malt
1	pound Munich 10 °L malt
1	pound red wheat malt
1/2	ounce Chinook hops, 11.3% alpha acid (60 minutes)
1	ounce Cascade hops, 6% alpha acid (30 minutes)
1/2	ounce Chinook hops, 11.3% alpha acid (30 minutes)
2	ounces Cascade hops, 6% alpha acid (2 minutes)
3	ounces Cascade hops, 6% alpha acid (dry)
	Wyeast No. 1056 American ale yeast
3/4	cup corn sugar (to prime)

Original gravity:	1.054
Final gravity:	1.010
Boiling time:	75 minutes
Primary fermentation:	14 days at 68 °F (20 °C) in glass
Secondary fermentation:	8 days at 68 °F (20 °C) in glass
Age when judged:	—

Brewer's Specifics
Mash grains at 154 °F (68 °C) for 75 minutes. Sparge with 180 °F (82 °C) water.

Judges' Comments
"Hops and malt tumble together on palate to really come alive and explode. Good balance. Good conditioning. Very drinkable."

"Appropriate hop bitterness. Blends nicely with malt. Slight oxidation gives a little harshness to bittering hops. Clean, crisp, and satisfying. Hops are perfect. Slight oxidation, but otherwise look out Sierra Nevada."

Mullethead Ale

Gold Medal, NHC, Classic English Pale Ale, 1995
Dave Shaffer, Lafayette, Colorado
(All-Grain)

Ingredients for 10 Gallons

16	pounds Klages malt
1	pound Ireks dark crystal malt
1	pound 35 °L crystal malt
1	pound special roasted malt
1	pound Victory malt
1	pound Munich malt
1	pound CaraPils malt
1	pound wheat malt
1	ounce Perle hops, 7.5% alpha acid (80 minutes)
1	ounce U.S. Hallertau hops, 5.2% alpha acid (80 minutes)
1 1/2	ounces Saaz hop pellets, 3.6% alpha acid (12 minutes)
1 1/2	ounces Hallertau Hersbrucker hop pellets, 2.6% alpha acid (12 minutes)
1 1/2	ounces Hallertau Hersbrucker hop pellets, 2.6% alpha acid (3 minutes)
1	ounce Tettnang hop pellets, 4.3% alpha acid (3 minutes)
1 1/2	ounces Hallertau hop pellets, 5.2% alpha acid (dry)
1 1/2	ounces Saaz hop pellets, 3.6% alpha acid (dry)
	Wyeast No. 1056 American ale yeast
3/4	cup dextrose (to prime)

Original gravity:	1.054
Final gravity:	1.013
Boiling time:	90 minutes
Primary fermentation:	23 days at 63 °F (17 °C) in glass
Secondary fermentation:	16 days at 63 °F (17 °C) in glass
Age when judged:	3 months

Brewer's Specifics

Mash grains at 132 °F (56 °C) for 31 minutes. Raise temperature to 154 °F (68 °C) for 70 minutes. Sparge with 170 °F (77 °C) water to collect 13 1/2 gallons of wort.

Judges' Comments

"Slight malt character with lingering hop finish. Slight woody character adds complexity. Could use more bittering hops. Nice British character."

Red, White, and Blue Ale

Bronze Medal, NHC, American Pale Ale, 1996
Walter Dobrowney, Saskatoon, Saskatchewan, Canada
(All-Grain)

Ingredients for 5 Gallons

8 3/4 pounds two-row Harrington malt
1/2 pound Munich malt
1/2 pound DeWolf-Cosyns aromatic malt
1/4 pound DeWolf-Cosyns biscuit malt
1/4 pound DeWolf-Cosyns CaraVienne malt
1 ounce Northern Brewer hop plugs, 7.8% alpha acid (60 minutes)
1/2 ounce Cascade hops, 7.4% alpha acid (30 minutes)
1 ounce Cascade hops, 7.4% alpha acid (2 minutes)
Wyeast No. 1056 American ale yeast
force-carbonate

Original gravity:	1.049
Final gravity:	1.008
Boiling time:	60 minutes
Primary fermentation:	8 days at 66 °F (19 °C) in glass
Secondary fermentation:	6 days at 50 °F (10 °C) in glass
Age when judged:	4 months

Brewer's Specifics

Mash grains at 157 °F (69 °C) for 60 minutes.

Ridgewood Pale Ale

Silver Medal, NHC, American Pale Ale, 1995
Ken Brown, Fremont, California
(All-Grain)

Ingredients for 5 Gallons
9 1/2	pounds domestic two-row malt
1	pound 10 °L crystal malt
1/2	pound 20 °L crystal malt
1/2	pound light Munich malt
3/4	ounce Cascade hops, 5.5% alpha acid (60 minutes)
1	ounce Cascade hops, 5.5% alpha acid (20 minutes)
1	ounce Willamette hops, 5.2% alpha acid (20 minutes)
1	ounce Cascade hops, 5.5% alpha acid (dry)
2	teaspoons gypsum added to 11 quarts of water for protein rest
2	teaspoons gypsum added to 6 1/2 quarts of water for sparge
	Wyeast No. 1056 American ale yeast
1/2	cup corn sugar (to prime)

Original gravity:	1.052
Final gravity:	1.013
Boiling time:	60 minutes
Primary fermentation:	10 days at 60 °F (16 °C) in glass
Secondary fermentation:	7 days at 60 °F (60 °C) in glass
Age when judged:	3 months

Brewer's Specifics
Mash grains at 122 °F (50 °C) for 30 minutes and 157 °F (69 °C) for 60 minutes.

Judges' Comments
"Light amber color and clarity very good. This beer is growing on me. The hops are overpowering at first, but as your mouth adjusts it's quite enjoyable."

"Overall a wonderful beer. I'll take a case. Lacks much of any nose. Could use more maltiness in palate (slight)."

Stone Chimney Pale Ale

**Second Place, Club-Only Competition,
American Pale Ale, 1997
Andy Widger, Salamanca, New York
(Extract/Grain)**

Ingredients for 5 Gallons
6	pounds Munton and Fison light dried malt extract
1/2	pound crystal malt
1 1/10	ounces Chinook hops, 12.7% alpha acid (60 minutes)
1/2	ounce Chinook hops, 12.7% alpha acid (2 minutes)
2	ounces Cascade hops, 6.5% alpha acid (2 minutes)
	Wyeast No. 1056 American ale yeast
2/3	cup corn sugar (to prime)

Original gravity:	1.048
Final gravity:	1.008
Boiling time:	60 minutes
Primary fermentation:	7 days at 65 °F (18 °C) in glass
Secondary fermentation:	7 days at 65 °F (18 °C) in glass
Age when judged:	3 months

Brewer's Specifics
Steep grains for 10–15 minutes.

Clowning Around Ale

Winner, Club-Only Competition, American Pale Ale, 1996
Duane Maki, Cedar Rapids, Iowa
(All-Grain)

Ingredients for 5 Gallons

7	pounds Briess two-row malt
3	pounds Munich light malt
1	pound Vienna malt
1/4	pound 80 °L crystal malt
1/4	pound six-row CaraPils malt
1 3/4	ounces Cascade hop pellets, 4.9% alpha acid (60 minutes)
1/2	ounce Cascade hop pellets, 4.9% alpha acid (45 minutes)
1/2	ounce Cascade hop pellets, 4.9% alpha acid (30 minutes)
1 1/2	ounces Cascade hop pellets, 4.9% alpha acid (15 minutes)
1	ounce East Kent Goldings hop pellets, 4.9% alpha acid (15 minutes)
1	ounce Cascade hop pellets, 4.9% alpha acid (dry, 4 days)
1/2	ounce East Kent Goldings hop pellets, 4.9% alpha acid (dry, 4 days)
	Wyeast No. 1056 American ale yeast
2/3	cup dextrose (to prime)

Original gravity:	1.050
Final gravity:	1.009
Boiling time:	90 minutes
Primary fermentation:	4 days at 68 °F (20 °C) in plastic
Secondary fermentation:	13 days at 62–68 °F (17–20 °C) in plastic
Age when judged:	10 months

Brewer's Specifics

Mash grains at 154 °F (68 °C) for 90 minutes.

Judges' Comments

"High hop bitterness balances initial sweetness. Hop flavor evident. Fruity diacetyl detectable. A nice beer. Good use of flavor hops."

"Very nice citrusy hop flavor. Nice clean bitterness in the finish. Light malt note in background. Clean crisp hop flavor and a nice lingering bitterness."

American-Ind. Ale

First Place, Club-Only Competition, American Pale Ale, 1997
Shekhar and Paula Nimkar, Lynn, Massachusetts
(All-Grain)

Ingredients for 10 Gallons
19	pounds Munton and Fison pale malt
1 1/2	pounds Hugh Baird crystal malt
10	AAU Perle hops (70 minutes)
8	AAU Mt. Hood hops (70 minutes)
8	AAU Mt. Hood hops (10 minutes)
2	ounces Cascade hops (finish)
1 1/2	ounces Cascade hops (dry, 2 weeks)
	Wyeast No. 1056 American ale yeast
	force-carbonate

Original gravity:	1.048
Final gravity:	—
Boiling time:	90 minutes
Primary fermentation:	10 days at 65 °F (18 °C) in glass
Secondary fermentation:	2 weeks at 65 °F (18 °C) in glass
Age when judged:	6 months

Brewer's Specifics
Use a single infusion mash at 150 °F (66 °C) for 120 minutes.

DUNKELWEIZEN

A darker version of weisse beer, dunkelweizen is brewed with up to 70 percent wheat and has a malty, complex, breadlike aroma. It can be fermented at warmer temperatures to bring out the estery phenolic character of the yeast. This darker version's spicy and fruity tones are masked somewhat by the darker malts employed. Decoction mashes are also traditional for this style to bring out malt characteristics. Deep copper to brown in color, dunkelweizens have very low levels of hop bitterness, aroma, and flavor. The mouthfeel is moderate from fairly low finishing gravities, and there shouldn't be detectable levels of diacetyl. The style is made to a moderate strength from original gravities of 1.045–1.054 (11.5–13.5 °Plato).

Dinkely Dunkely Weissely Weissely Do

Bronze Medal, NHC, Dunkelweizen, 1996
Kelly Robinson, Ceres, California
(All-Grain)

Ingredients for 6 Gallons

- 7 pounds DeWolf-Cosyns Belgian wheat malt
- 4 pounds Durst Munich malt
- 1/2 pound Great Western 90 °L caramel malt
- 2 ounces Weyermann roasted wheat malt
- 3/4 ounce Hallertau hop pellets, 4.8% alpha acid (60 minutes)
- Brewers Resource CL-920 yeast
- force-carbonate in keg

Original gravity:	1.047
Final gravity:	1.012
Boiling time:	90 minutes
Primary fermentation:	5 days at 68 °F (20 °C) in glass
Secondary fermentation:	14 days at 37 °F (3 °C) in glass
Age when judged:	—

Brewer's Specifics

Employ a double decoction mash with rest mash temperatures of 124 °F (51 °C), 140 °F (60 °C), and 158 °F (70 °C). Sparge with 170 °F (77 °C) water.

Judges' Comments

"The dark malts are too strong—they detract from the estery phenolic character that seems a little subtle."

"Roasty CaraMunich-type maltiness dominates over phenolic characteristics. Use less CaraMunich, crystal, or roasted-type malts to allow more of the phenols to balance out the beer."

The Brews Brothers Palousen Dunkelweizen

First Place, Club-Only Competition, Dunkelweizen, 1995
Rob Nelson, Duvall, Washington
(All-Grain)

Ingredients for 5 Gallons
- 5 pounds wheat malt
- 4 pounds Pilsener malt
- 4 ounces chocolate malt
- 3 ounces Belgian aromatic malt
- 3 ounces Belgian biscuit malt
- 3 ounces Victory malt
- 3 ounces CaraPils malt
- 3/4 ounce Tettnang hops, 6.2% alpha acid (60 minutes)
  Wyeast No. 3068 Weihenstephan Wheat ale yeast
- 1 cup corn sugar (to prime)

Original gravity:	1.056
Final gravity:	1.015
Boiling time:	60 minutes
Primary fermentation:	6 days at 76 °F (24 °C) in glass
Secondary fermentation:	—
Age when judged:	2 months

Brewer's Specifics
Dough-in grains with 2 7/10 gallons of 120 °F (49 °C) water and let sit for 20 minutes. Raise the temperature slowly to 122 °F (50 °C) and hold for 30 minutes. Remove about 1 gallon of the stiff part of the mash and put it into another pot. Raise temperature to 140 °F (60 °C) and hold for 15 minutes. Raise temperature to 158 °F (70 °C) and hold for 15 minutes. Raise temperature to boiling for 15 minutes. Return this to the mash (mash temperature should be about 138 °F [59 °C]). Pull another gallon and repeat the process (main mash temperature should be about 151 °F [66 °C]). Hold this temperature for 45 minutes until iodine tests negative for starch. Pull 1 gallon, boil, and return to main mash to hit mash-out temperature of 168 °F (76 °C). You may need a heat source to maintain the main mash temperature. If you have the equipment, pull 40% for the first decoction and skip the third decoction.

Judges' Comments
"Malty with clove and banana prominent. Very nice brew."

Untitled

NHC, German-Style Dunkelweizen, 1996
Paul Hale, Burlington, Vermont
(All-Grain)

Ingredients for 11 Gallons
10	pounds Harrington pale malt
10	pounds Harrington wheat malt
2 1/2	pounds German dark crystal malt
1	pound German light crystal malt
1/2	pound chocolate malt
2	ounces Hallertau hop pellets, 3% alpha acid (60 minutes)
	Yeast Lab® W51 yeast

Original gravity:	1.056
Final gravity:	—
Boiling time:	90 minutes
Primary fermentation:	2 weeks at 60 °F (16 °C) in glass
Secondary fermentation:	6 weeks at 45 °F (7 °C) in glass
Age when judged:	3 months

Brewer's Specifics
Use a single decoction mash.

Steiner Weizen

NHC, German-Style Dunkelweizen, 1996
Martin Rapnicki, Redford, Michigan
(All-Grain)

Ingredients for 5 Gallons

7	pounds Belgian wheat malt
7	pounds Belgian Munich malt
1/2	pound British chocolate malt
2	ounces Saaz hops, 2% alpha acid (60 minutes)
1 1/2	ounces Saaz hops, 2% alpha acid (30 minutes)
1/2	ounce Saaz hops, 2% alpha acid (5 minutes)
	Wyeast No. 3068 Weihenstephan Wheat ale yeast
1	cup corn sugar (to prime)

Original gravity:	1.044
Final gravity:	1.014
Boiling time:	60 minutes
Primary fermentation:	4 days at 66 °F (19 °C) in glass
Secondary fermentation:	10 days at 66 °F (19 °C) in glass
Age when judged:	3 1/2 months

Brewer's Specifics

Boil all grains in 3 1/2 gallons of 130 °F (54 °C) water. Hold at 122 °F (50 °C) for 30 minutes. Raise temperature to 158 °F (70 °C) for 45 minutes. Sparge with 4 gallons of 170 °F (77 °C) water.

Untitled

Finalist, NHC, German-Style Dunkelweizen, 1996
Mark Zeltan, Green Bay, Wisconsin
(All-Grain)

Ingredients for 5 Gallons

4	pounds Briess two-row malt
2 1/2	pounds rice
1 1/2	pounds Briess wheat malt
1	pound 80 °L crystal malt
1/2	pound chocolate malt
1	ounce East Kent Goldings hop pellets, 5.8% alpha acid (60 minutes)
1/4	ounce Northern Brewer hop pellets, 8.2% alpha acid (60 minutes)
	Wyeast No. 3068 Weihenstephan Wheat ale yeast

Original gravity:	1.042
Final gravity:	1.018
Boiling time:	60 minutes
Primary fermentation:	4 days at 68 °F (20 °C) in stainless steel
Secondary fermentation:	9 days at 68 °F (20 °C) in glass
Age when judged:	4 months

Brewer's Specifics
Mash grains at 122–149 °F (50–65 °C) for 4 hours.

FESTBIER

It is hard to pin down an accurate description of this style, as it tends to vary quite a bit. The term usually refers to a lager similar to Märzen/Oktoberfest but of a lighter color. A popular example of Bavarian festbier is full golden in color, with malt flavors dominant, but without the sweetness of a helles bock. Generally no hop aroma is acceptable with low to medium bitterness from "noble-type" German hop varieties. No fruitiness, esters, and diacetyl are allowed for the style. Moderate to high strength, festbier's original gravity is 1.055–1.061 (13–15 °Plato). In southern Germany, many breweries come out with a strong version of their own specialty to serve at summer celebrations.

Polska Fest Beer

Festbier, 1996
Amahl Turczyn, Boulder, Colorado
(All-Grain)

Ingredients for 10 Gallons
- 10 pounds Belgian Pilsener malt
- 5 pounds German Munich malt
- 1/2 pound Belgian CaraPils malt
- 2 ounces Tettnang hop pellets, 4.4% alpha acid (60 minutes)
- 2 ounces Tettnang hop pellets, 4.4% alpha acid (30 minutes)
- 1 ounce Polish Lublin hop pellets, 3.7% alpha acid (15 minutes)
- 1 teaspoon gypsum added to mash water
- Wyeast No. 2278 Czech Pils lager yeast
- force-carbonate in keg

Original gravity:	1.046
Final gravity:	1.010
Boiling time:	120 minutes
Primary fermentation:	1 week at 50 °F (10 °C) in glass
Secondary fermentation:	3 weeks at 40 °F (4 °C) in glass
Tertiary fermentation:	2 weeks at 35 °F (2 °C) in stainless steel

Brewer's Specifics
Mash grains at 140 °F (60 °C) for 15 minutes. Add boiling water to mash to bring temperature to 151 °F (66 °C) and hold for 60 minutes. Recirculate runoff for clarity and sparge into kettle with 170 °F (77 °C) water.

Flavor Comments
This is a deliciously well-balanced golden lager, strong enough for celebrations, and light enough to keep celebrating. Polish hops give this beer its name as well as an unusual herbal spiciness. Nazdrowie!

SuperFest Lager

Festbier, 1997
Charlie Papazian, Boulder, Colorado
(Extract/Grain)

Ingredients for 5 Gallons
3 1/3   pounds German amber malt extract
2 1/2   pounds two-row pale malt
2 1/2   pounds Munich malt
   2   pounds Vienna malt
 1/2   pound Victory (or other aromatic) malt
 1/2   pound Belgian CaraMunich malt
   6   HBU Czech Saaz hops (60 minutes)
   6   HBU German Hallertau hops (30 minutes)
   1   ounce American Mt. Hood hops (1–3 minutes)
 1/4   teaspoon Irish moss
     Wyeast No. 2206 Bavarian lager yeast
 3/4   cup corn sugar (to prime)

Original gravity:	1.067
Final gravity:	1.018
Boiling time:	60 minutes
Primary fermentation:	4–6 days at 60 °F (16 °C)
Secondary fermentation:	2 weeks at 50 °F (10 °C)
Tertiary fermentation:	2 weeks at 40 °F (4 °C)

Brewers' Specifics

Employ a step infusion mash to mash the grains. Add 8 quarts (7.6 liters) of 143 °F (62 °C) water to the crushed grain, stir, stabilize, and hold the temperature at 133 °F (56 °C) for 30 minutes. Add 4 quarts (3.8 liters) of boiling water. Add heat to bring temperature up to 152 °F (66.7 °C). Hold for about 60 minutes. After conversion, raise temperature to 167 °F (75 °C), lauter, and sparge with 4 gallons (15.2 liters) of 170 °F (77 °C) water. Collect about 5.5 gallons (21 liters) of runoff, add bittering hops, and bring to a full and vigorous boil.

The total boil time is 60 minutes. When 20 minutes remain, add flavor hops. When 10 minutes remain, add Irish moss. After a total wort boil of 60 minutes, turn off the heat, add aroma hops, and let steep 1–3 minutes. Then separate or strain out and sparge hops. Chill the wort to 60 °F (15.6 °C) and direct into a sanitized fermenter. Aerate the cooled wort well. Add active yeast and ferment for 4–6 days in the primary. Then transfer into a secondary fermenter, chill to 50 °F (10 °C), and allow to age for 2 weeks or more. Then drop temperature to 40 °F (4.4 °C) and lager for an additional 2 weeks.

When secondary aging is complete, prime with sugar, and bottle or keg. Let condition at temperatures above 60 °F (15.6 °C) until clear and carbonated.

Flavor Comments

"Noble-type" hop bitterness accents a smooth mellow maltiness—not excessively bitter. A light to medium amber color portrays the rich blend of flavor malts. Attention to temperature controls minimizes esters and produces a well-rounded easy-drinking beer that is enhanced with a bit more alcohol than many amber lagers. Great for toasting the beginning of the holiday season.

Scott's Springfest Lager

NHC, Festbier, 1996
Mike Brennan, Justice, Illinois
(Extract/Grain)

Ingredients for 5 Gallons

15	pounds CaraMunich malt
5	pounds Munich malt
3 3/10	pounds Munton and Fison light malt extract
2	pounds Belgian pale two-row malt
1	pound CaraVienne malt
1 1/2	ounces Hallertau Hersbrucker hop pellets, 4% alpha acid (60 minutes)
1 1/2	ounces Hallertau Hersbrucker hop pellets, 4% alpha acid (25 minutes)
1/2	teaspoon calcium chloride
1/2	teaspoon gypsum
1/4	teaspoon phosphoric acid
	Wyeast No. 2124 Bohemian lager yeast
3/4	cup corn sugar (to prime)

Original gravity:	1.052
Final gravity:	1.011
Boiling time:	75 minutes
Primary fermentation:	7 days at 53 °F (12 °C) in plastic
Secondary fermentation:	12 days at 52 °F (11 °C) in glass
Tertiary fermentation:	7 days at 40 °F (4 °C) in glass
Age when judged:	3 months

Brewer's Specifics

Mash grains at 155 °F (68 °C) for 90 minutes. Mash-out at 165 °F (74 °C) for 30 minutes.

LAGER, UNITED STATES

This style is so popular worldwide, one would think it would be relatively easy to brew. However, it is one of the most difficult. The light color and body require very pale varieties of malt with a careful boil. The subtle flavors demand extra care and attention to sanitation and yeast management, as well as carefully controlled temperatures in fermentation and lagering. Many homebrewers rise successfully to the challenge, proving that the industry giants don't have a monopoly on this beer. American standard, premium, and dry lager styles are all very pale in color, with light body, low to medium bitterness, and low hop aroma and flavor. Fruitiness, esters, and diacetyl are inappropriate to the style, unless you are brewing a cream ale or cream lager. This is definitely a hot weather thirst-quencher.

Export—Not!

Gold Medal, NHC, Premium Lager, 1996
David Stone, Farmington Hills, Michigan
(Extract/Grain)

Ingredients for 5 Gallons
5	pounds American two-row malt
3	pounds dry light malt extract
1/2	pound German light crystal malt
1/2	pound Munich malt
1/2	pound CaraPils malt
1/2	ounce Perle hops, 7.4% alpha acid (60 minutes)
1	ounce Tettnang hops, 5.2% alpha acid (30 minutes)
1/2	ounce Tettnang hops, 5.2% alpha acid (15 minutes)
1/2	ounce Tettnang hops, 5.2% alpha acid (3 minutes)
	Wyeast No. 2007 Pilsen lager yeast
3/4	cup corn sugar (to prime)

Original gravity:	1.042
Final gravity:	1.013
Boiling time:	60 minutes
Primary fermentation:	14 days at 60 °F (16 °C) in glass
Secondary fermentation:	34 days at 35 °F (2 °C) in glass
Age when judged:	3 months

Brewer's Specifics
Mash grains at 155 °F (68 °C) for 60 minutes.

Judges' Comments
"Well-made beer. Very clean. Well balanced."

"Very clean and well balanced. Good hop in aftertaste. Dark for category."

"Full lager flavor. Slight hop flavor, okay. Good golden color."

Sunrise Lager

Gold Medal, NHC, American Standard, 1995
Arthur Metzner, Fort Washington, Maryland
(Extract/Grain)

Ingredients for 5 Gallons
- 5 pounds two-row lager malt
- 2 pounds flaked barley
- 1 pound flaked maize
- 1/2 pound CaraPils dextrin malt
- 1/2 pound extra light dry malt extract
- 2 ounces crystal malt
- 3/5 ounce Cascade hops, 6.1% alpha acid (45 minutes)
- 2/5 ounce Cascade hops, 6.1% alpha acid (33 minutes)
- Wyeast No. 2007 Pilsen lager yeast
- 7/8 cup corn sugar (to prime)

Original gravity:	1.040
Final gravity:	—
Boiling time:	55 minutes
Primary fermentation:	15 days at 50 °F (10 °C) in plastic
Secondary fermentation:	6 days at 50 °F (10 °C) in glass
Age when judged:	5 months

Brewer's Specifics
Mash grains at 115 °F (46 °C) for 60 minutes. Remove and boil enough of the mash so that the temperature stabilizes at 145–150 °F (65–66 °C) when you add it back to the main mash. Let sit for 60–90 minutes. Again, remove and boil enough of the mash so that the temperature stabilizes at 160 °F (71 °C) when you add it back to the main mash.

Judges' Comments
"Malty with just the kiss of the hops. Carbonation high but appropriate. Very good beer. Very close to commercial standards."

"Grainy flavor up front. Low malt and hop flavor. Tastes like Michelob. Really well done."

"Clean flavor. Good balance. A bit too much corn and grain flavors."

Clarabelle's Cream Ale

Gold Medal, NHC, Cream Ale, 1994
Jeffrey Cypert, Ross, Texas
(Extract/Grain)

Ingredients for 6 Gallons

- 6 pounds Alexander's pale malt extract syrup
- 1 1/2 pounds Briess pale malt
- 1 pound flaked maize
- 1/2 pound Belgian biscuit malt
- 1 ounce Hallertau hops, 4.2% alpha acid (60 minutes)
- Wyeast No. 1056 American ale yeast
- force-carbonate in keg

Original gravity:	1.050
Final gravity:	1.010
Boiling time:	75 minutes
Primary fermentation:	7 days at 58 °F (14 °C) in glass
Secondary fermentation:	7 days at 65 °F (18 °C) in glass
Tertiary fermentation:	14 days at 36 °F (2 °C) in stainless steel
Age when judged:	3 months

Brewer's Specifics

Mash grains at 120 °F (49 °C) for 60 minutes. Raise temperature to 148 °F (64 °C) for 15 minutes.

Judges' Comments

"Light malt flavor. Little hop flavor but clean. No off-tastes. Very clean. Delicate effort. No obvious faults. Could use a touch more hops in boil to balance."

"Creamy. Very sweet. Need to balance with more hops. Good finish. Very candy sweet. Adjust the hopping rate."

Untitled

Bronze Medal, NHC, American Lager, 1996
Billy Graham, Pasadena, Maryland
(All-Grain)

Ingredients for 5 Gallons
8   pounds six-row malt
1   ounce Cluster hops, 8.1% alpha acid (60 minutes)
1/4   ounce Kent Goldings hops, 5.1% alpha acid (15 minutes)
1/4   ounce Kent Goldings hops, 5.1% alpha acid (dry)
    Wyeast No. 2007 Pilsen lager yeast
3/4   cup dextrose (to prime)

Original gravity:	1.048
Final gravity:	1.010
Boiling time:	105 minutes
Primary fermentation:	1 day at 58–60 °F (14–16 °C)
Secondary fermentation:	18 days at 55 °F (13 °C)
Age when judged:	4 months

Brewer's Specifics
Use a three stage decoction mash for a total time of 120 minutes.

Judges' Comments
"Nice malt-hop balance. Good sweet malt start with crisp hop finish. Excellent—a well-made beer. Nice dry finish. Clean."

"Very clean. Well balanced. Excellent example of the style. Well made."

Light Lager

Silver Medal, NHC, American Standard Lager, 1995
Ron Brooks, St. Louis, Missouri
(All-Grain)

Ingredients for 5 1/4 Gallons
2 1/2 pounds German Pilsener malt
2 1/2 pounds North American six-row pale malt
2 pounds short grain brown rice
3/4 ounce Cluster hop pellets, 7.6% alpha acid (60 minutes)
1/4 ounce Cluster hop pellets, 7.6% alpha acid (finish)
1 1/2 teaspoons gypsum added to boil
Wyeast No. 2007 Pilsen lager yeast
1/3 cup corn sugar (to prime)

Original gravity:	1.040
Final gravity:	1.013
Boiling time:	75 minutes
Primary fermentation:	8 days at 50 °F (10 °C) in glass
Secondary fermentation:	4 days at 58 °F (14 °C) in glass
Age when judged:	7 months

Brewer's Specifics
Boil rice for 45 minutes. Dough-in at 125 °F (52 °C) for 50 minutes. Add rice. Raise temperature to 145 °F (63 °C) for 50 minutes, 155 °F (68 °C) for 20 minutes, and 168 °F (76 °C) for 5 minutes. Sparge with 4 1/2 gallons of 170 °F (77 °C) water for 60 minutes.

Judges' Comments
"Good effort on a difficult style."

"Color very pale. Brilliant clarity. Large head. Malt light—appropriate. Very good effort for style."

"Clean light flavor—good. Could be too much bittering hops."

SCOTCH ALE

This unique style, like its English counterpart barley wine, requires lengthy fermentation and conditioning because of its strength. Scotch ales are stronger than Scottish ales, ranging from an original gravity of 1.070–1.110 (17–27 °Plato). Unlike barley wines, Scotch ales are fermented at relatively cold temperatures (58–64 °F [14–18 °C]) for ale yeasts, discouraging fruity estery flavors that are characteristic of ales, and encouraging alcohol production. Their color ranges from gold to amber to dark brown. With relatively high finishing gravities, Scotch ales retain a full silky mouthfeel and sturdy head retention. Hop bitterness is very low—just enough to partially counter the sweetness of the malt. Scottish brewers traditionally used aged hops, so no hop flavor or aroma is appropriate for this style. Low levels of diacetyl are acceptable. Overpitching a sturdy British yeast strain with only moderate aeration will help the fermentation of this colossal brew.

Nessie

Gold Medal, NHC, Strong Scotch Ale, 1995
Grant Heath, Huntsville, Alabama
(Extract/Grain)

Ingredients for 15 Gallons

21	pounds Belgian Pilsener malt
7	pounds British pale ale malt
6 1/4	pounds amber dried malt extract
2	pounds CaraVienne malt
2	pounds German dark crystal malt
1	pound Belgian Special "B" malt
1 1/2	ounces Kent Goldings hops, 5.2% alpha acid (60 minutes)
1/2	ounce Kent Goldings hops, 5.2% alpha acid (30 minutes)
	Wyeast No. 1728 Scottish ale yeast
	force-carbonate in keg

Original gravity:	1.085
Final gravity:	1.030
Boiling time:	90 minutes
Primary fermentation:	8 days at 60 °F (16 °C) in glass
Secondary fermentation:	15 days at 60 °F (16 °C) in glass
Tertiary fermentation:	2 weeks at 32 °F (0 °C) in stainless steel
Age when judged:	6 1/2 months

Brewer's Specifics
Mash grains at 156 °F (69 °C) for 60 minutes.

Judges' Comments
"Nice malt. Slight astringency and a bit overcarbonated. Alcohol balances with malt."

"Little fruitiness detected in taste. Also picking up some esters after fruit fades. Great balance with malt [and] alcohol. Back down on fruitiness and esters."

Hilter Kilter
Wee Heavy Scotch Ale

Gold Medal, NHC, Strong Scotch Ale, 1996
Loren Claypool and Jeff Boggess, Scott Depot, West Virginia
(Extract/Grain)

Ingredients for 5 Gallons

6 2/3	pounds Glenbrew light malt extract
6	pounds pale ale malt
2	pounds Klages malt
2	pounds CaraPils malt
1/2	pound Laaglander dry malt extract
2	ounces roasted barley
2 1/2	ounces East Kent Goldings hop pellets, 4.6% alpha acid (60 minutes)
1	teaspoon Irish moss (15 minutes)
	Wyeast No. 1728 Scottish ale yeast
2/3	cup corn sugar (to prime)

Original gravity:	1.094
Final gravity:	1.019
Boiling time:	90 minutes
Primary fermentation:	22 days at 65 °F (18 °C) in glass
Secondary fermentation:	—
Age when judged:	18 months

Brewer's Specifics

Mash grains in 3 gallons of filtered tap water at 153 °F (67 °C) for 90 minutes. Sparge with 5 gallons of 165 °F (74 °C) filtered tap water.

Judges' Comments

"Big malt taste up front with strong alcohol end. Good hop finish."

"Intense malt flavor balanced with high alcohol."

"Very nice beer. Everything blends together well."

"Pronounced hop bitterness. Licoricelike flavor predominates."

Wee Heavier

Bronze Medal, NHC, Strong Scotch Ale, 1996
Alan Moore, Toronto, Ontario, Canada
(Extract/Grain)

Ingredients for 5 Gallons

6 1/5	pounds Edme ale malt extract
5 1/2	pounds Munton and Fison pale malt
5 1/2	pounds Hugh Baird pale malt
10	ounces Hugh Baird roasted barley
1	ounce Kent Goldings hop pellets, 4.2% alpha acid (75 minutes)
1/2	ounce Northern Brewer hop pellets, 7% alpha acid (75 minutes)
1	teaspoon gypsum added to 9 gallons of water
	Wyeast No. 1728 Scottish ale yeast
5	ounces corn sugar (to prime)

Original gravity:	1.100
Final gravity:	1.026
Boiling time:	120 minutes
Primary fermentation:	5 days at 62–70 °F (17–21 °C) in plastic
Secondary fermentation:	12 days at 62 °F (17 °C) in glass
Tertiary fermentation:	40 days at 34 °F (1 °C) in glass
Age when judged:	6 months

Brewer's Specifics

Mash grains at 156 °F (69 °C) for 90 minutes.

MacGregor's Fist

Scotch Ale, 1997
Amahl Turczyn, Boulder, Colorado
(All-Grain)

Ingredients for 10 Gallons

30	pounds Scottish pale malt
10	ounces 120 °L crystal malt
6	ounces roasted barley
1 1/2	ounces Northern Brewer hop pellets, 6.9% alpha acid (120 minutes)
1	ounce Columbus hop pellets, 13.5% alpha acid (120 minutes)
1	ounce Kent Goldings hop pellets, 5.8% alpha acid (120 minutes)
	Wyeast No. 1728 Scottish ale yeast
	force-carbonate in keg

Original gravity:	1.096
Final gravity:	1.036
Boiling time:	120 minutes
Primary fermentation:	2 weeks at 60 °F (16 °C) in glass
Secondary fermentation:	4 weeks at 62 °F (17 °C) in glass
Tertiary fermentation:	6 months at 50 °F (10 °C) in stainless steel

Brewer's Specifics

Mash grains at 150 °F (66 °C) for 60 minutes.

Flavor Comments

MacGregor's Fist is a quintessentially malty, yet balanced, wee heavy. The cool fermentation temperature and extensive cellaring prevent off-flavors and encourage diacetyl reduction, leaving only the aroma of malt and just enough hop balance to keep it from being cloyingly sweet. MacGregor's Fist will continue to improve for years after you bottle it, taking on port- and sherrylike characteristics as it dries out in the bottle; therefore, it's an ideal choice to savor only on special occasions.

MacLaren's Argull Ale

Bronze Medal, NHC, Strong Scotch Ale, 1995
Ross Hastings, Edmonton, Alberta, Canada
(All-Grain)

Ingredients for 3 1/2 Gallons

11 1/2	pounds two-row malt
2	pounds 12 °L Munich crystal malt
5	ounces Hugh Baird 75 °L crystal malt
5	ounces CaraMunich malt
3	ounces roasted barley
7/10	ounce Kent Goldings hops, 5% alpha acid (45 minutes)
2/5	ounce Fuggles hops, 4.2% alpha acid (45 minutes)
	filtered and preboiled water
	Wyeast No. 1728 Scottish ale yeast
1/3	cup corn sugar (to prime)

Original gravity:	1.084
Final gravity:	1.022
Boiling time:	90 minutes
Primary fermentation:	13 days at 59 °F (15 °C) in glass
Secondary fermentation:	23 days at 57 °F (14 °C) in glass
Age when judged:	6 months

Brewer's Specifics

Use a single decoction mash. Boil 17 1/2 quarts water at 138 °F (59 °C). Hold main mash at 125 °F (52 °C) for 60 minutes. One-third dense mash-out at 20 minutes. Raise the temperature of the decoction mash to 155 °F (68 °C) for 10 minutes and boil. Add back to main mash and raise temperature to 155 °F (68 °C) for 80 minutes. Mash-out at 180 °F (82 °C). Sparge at 180 °F (82 °C).

Judges' Comments

"Malt predominates. Some alcohol. Some butter. Nice head. Very slight haze. Good beer. Few problems."

"Alcoholic nose. Nice and clear—good color. Very good—maybe could use more body to balance malt and alcohol."

Mason Is Wee Heavy

Gold Medal, NHC, English and Scottish Strong Ale, 1993
Ray Call, Stockton, California
(All-Grain)

Ingredients for 5 Gallons
14	pounds pale malt
4	pounds British crystal malt
2 1/4	pounds toasted malt
2	pounds Munich malt
1/4	pound Special "B" malt
1 1/4	ounces Saaz hops, 4.9% alpha acid (60 minutes)
1	ounce Northern Brewer hops, 7.1% alpha acid (60 minutes)
1/2	ounce Cascade hops, 6.7% alpha acid (60 minutes)
1/2	ounce Tettnang hops, 4.5% alpha acid (15 minutes)
	Wyeast No. 1056 American ale yeast

Original gravity:	1.085
Final gravity:	—
Boiling time:	90 minutes
Primary fermentation:	9 days at 70 °F (21 °C) in glass
Secondary fermentation:	7 days at 70 °F (21 °C) in glass
Age when judged:	9 months

Brewer's Specifics
Mash grains at 155 °F (68 °C) for 75 minutes.

Judges' Comments
"Wow! Very rich. Almost berrylike. Blackberries. Dark cherries. This is very well made."

"Sweet malt dominates. Good balance. Alcohol evident. Slightly coarse roast character on the perceptible edge. This beer could be balanced by a bit more bitterness."

"Clean. Smooth with malt dominating. Nice low carbonation. Pleasant lingering aftertaste. Diacetyl comes through ever so slightly."

"Malty rich. Nice alcohol presence. The hop is there but it shows late as is appropriate."

FRUIT BEER

This is another fairly open category, limited only by the availability of fruit used. Any strain of lager or ale yeast is acceptable, though it's important to note that fruit sugars are very fermentable by yeast and often lower your finishing gravity considerably. Also, hop bitterness doesn't go with many fruit flavors, so as a rule of thumb, go easy on bittering hops (although "noble-type" varieties like Saaz and Tettnang add a wonderful complexity when used sparingly for aroma). Mash at fairly high temperatures or use malt extract to provide a balancing malt sweetness. Otherwise, you'll end up with a dry alcoholic finish to your beer, depending on how much fruit you use. Other heavier flavors often overpower delicately flavored fruit, like blueberries, so don't use a yeast with a lot of flavorful character. It's a good idea to use wheat malt to lighten the beer in color and flavor as well as to bring out the fruit. More experienced brewers add puréed fruit at racking time rather than in the boil. This practice helps prevent a mean chill haze from the fruit pectin and allows the fruit's more delicate aromatic qualities to stay in the beer instead of being cooked out. Make sure your fruit is fresh and clean and be sure to minimize oxygen uptake when adding the purée, even though the secondary fermentation of fruit sugars should metabolize most of it. Good bets for fruit beers include boysenberries, raspberries, blackberries, marionberries, chokecherries, cherries (especially sour cherries), and blueberries. Several excellent fruit extracts are also available, and while many don't retain quite the same flavors as fresh fruit, they are much more convenient and sanitary to use. It's a style worth experimenting with in the summer months.

Beaver Creek™ Strawberry Ale

Gold Medal, NHC, Strawberry Ale, 1996
Tom Bergman and Chas Peterson, Jefferson, Maryland
(Extract/Grain)

Ingredients for 6 Gallons

10	pounds puréed frozen strawberries added to secondary fermenter
2 1/2	pounds pale malt
1 1/2	pounds clover honey
1 1/2	pounds Pilsener malt
1	pound Klages malt
1	pound light dry malt extract
1	pound flaked corn
1/2	pound biscuit malt
1/2	pound CaraPils malt
1 1/2	ounces strawberry extract
1	ounce Willamette hops, 4.9% alpha acid (60 minutes)
	Wyeast No. 1056 American ale yeast
3/4	cup corn sugar (to prime)

Original gravity:	1.049
Final gravity:	0.999
Boiling time:	60 minutes
Primary fermentation:	7 days at 63 °F (17 °C) in glass
Secondary fermentation:	14 days at 65 °F (18 °C) in plastic
Tertiary fermentation:	35 days at 65 °F (18 °C) in glass
Age when judged:	12 months

Brewer's Specifics

Mash grains at 126 °F (52 °C) for 30 minutes. Raise temperature to 153 °F (67 °C) for 40 minutes and 156 °F (69 °C) for 50 minutes.

Judges' Comments

"Tartness from fruit as expected. Flavor very low—strawberries difficult to work with. Astringent finish. Somewhat one dimensional in flavor. Dry and sour and tart. Needs some balancing sweetness and fruit flavor."

"Very astringent and somewhat sour taste."

"Lighter strawberry flavor than aroma but very pleasant flavor. Good conditioning—no whopper flaws. Nice summer beer. Fine job."

Susie's Belgian Pêchebier

Gold Medal, NHC, Fruit Beer, 1995
Russ Bee, Rockwall, Texas
(Extract/Grain)

Ingredients for 5 Gallons

7 1/4	pounds pale malt extract
1 1/2	pounds 20 °L American crystal malt
1	pound American two-row pale malt
4	ounces natural peach extract
3/4	ounce Hallertau hops, 7.5% alpha acid (45 minutes)
	Wyeast No. 1056 American ale yeast
3/4	cup corn sugar (to prime)

Original gravity:	1.056
Final gravity:	1.012
Boiling time:	60 minutes
Primary fermentation:	6 days at 72 °F (22 °C) in glass
Secondary fermentation:	5 days at 72 °F (22 °C) in glass
Age when judged:	7 1/2 months

Brewer's Specifics

Mash grains at 151 °F (66 °C) for 60 minutes. Add peach extract at bottling with priming sugar.

Judges' Comments

"Strong peach bouquet. Very pleasing. Alcoholic aftertaste. Fine and tasty. Carbonation is excellent. Aftertaste is only drawback."

"Peach is up front. Slight astringency is evident. A fine effort. Next time be a little more careful with wort transfer methods."

"Peach, caramel malt, hops all balanced. Slight metallic aftertaste. A little bitter [and] astringent. Great dessert fruit beer."

Raspberry Nightmare

Bronze Medal, NHC, Fruit Beer, 1996
Suzette Smith, Madison, New Jersey
(Extract)

Ingredients for 5 Gallons
- 2 cans John Bull Barleywine kit extract
- 7 pounds high maltose malt extract
- 3 pounds frozen raspberries (steep for 15 minutes after boil)
- 4 ounces raspberry extract
- 1 ounce Saaz hop pellets (60 minutes)
- 3/4 ounce Hallertau hop pellets (10 minutes)
- Red Star champagne yeast
- 2/3 cup dextrose (to prime)

Original gravity:	1.106
Final gravity:	1.036
Boiling time:	60 minutes
Primary fermentation:	6 days at 68 °F (20 °C) in glass
Secondary fermentation:	29 days at 65 °F (18 °C) in glass
Age when judged:	19 months

Brewer's Specifics
Boil for 60 minutes.

Judges' Comments
"Complex aroma—raspberries and plumlike esters, no hops apparent. Some clean alcohol aromas. Good head formation and retention. Clear. Starts with some malt. Has some caramel flavors. Finish is balanced with plenty of alcoholic warmth. Some roasted malts, but the raspberries come through nicely. Beautiful beer. Balanced raspberry character. Lots of malt."

"Good raspberry aroma, but none of the melanoidins that are found in most doppelbocks. There is also a slight roastiness. Beautiful deep ruby color with a creamy pink head. Excellent clarity and head retention."

Wheat 'n' Berry Ale

Bronze Medal, NHC, Fruit Beer, 1995
Ray Taylor, Fargo, North Dakota
(All-Grain)

Ingredients for 6 Gallons
4	pounds German pale malt
4	pounds wheat malt
1	pound flaked wheat
3/4	pound 20 °L Munich malt
1/2	pound CaraPils malt
1/2	pound chocolate malt
1/4	pound German dark caramel malt
1/2	ounce Perle hops, 7.5% alpha acid (40 minutes)
1/4	ounce Perle hops, 7.5% alpha acid (5 minutes)
2 1/2	milliliters Hop Tech raspberry extract added to each bottle
1/2	teaspoon gypsum added to mash
1/4	teaspoon salt added to sparge water
	Rogue ale yeast

Original gravity:	1.054
Final gravity:	1.015
Boiling time:	90 minutes
Primary fermentation:	30 days at 68 °F (20 °C) in glass
Secondary fermentation:	—
Age when judged:	4 months

Brewer's Specifics
Mash grains at 128 °F (53 °C) for 30 minutes and 154 °F (68 °C) for 60 minutes. Mash-out at 168 °F (76 °C) for 10 minutes. Sparge at 185 °F (85 °C) with 3 1/2 gallons.

Judges' Comments
"Strong raspberry bouquet. Good balance between malt and fruit. Slight fruity aftertaste—good."

"Well-balanced fruity flavor. Effervescence of beer brings out fruit! Very nice. Well-balanced fruit beer."

"Good raspberry hint of malt and hops. No off-flavors. Good clean fruit finish. Fine drinkable fruit beer."

Black Kevorkinator

Silver Medal, NHC, Fruit Beer, 1996
Douglas Faynor, Woodburn, Oregon
(All-Grain)

Ingredients for 7 1/2 Gallons

7 1/4	pounds Pilsener malt
6	pounds Munich malt
5	pounds Black Cap raspberries added to secondary fermentation
2	pounds Belgian aromatic malt
1	pound Victory malt
1/2	pound wheat malt
1 3/4	ounces Mt. Hood hops (60 minutes)
1 3/4	ounces Liberty hops (60 minutes)
1/2	ounce Crystal hops (60 minutes)
1/2	ounce Liberty hops (10–15 minutes)
1/2	ounce Liberty hops (2–3 minutes)
3/4	teaspoon salt
	Wyeast No. 2206 Bavarian lager yeast
3/4	corn sugar (to prime)

Original gravity:	1.079–1.080
Final gravity:	1.020
Boiling time:	90 minutes
Primary fermentation:	30 days at 50–52 °F (10–11 °C) in glass
Secondary fermentation:	90 days in glass
Age when judged:	3 months

Brewer's Specifics

Use a double mash. Mash Pilsener and Victory malts at 155 °F (68 °C) for 15 minutes. Raise temperature to 158 °F (70 °C) for 45 minutes. Mash Munich, aromatic, and wheat malts at 149 °F (65 °C) for 60 minutes in a single step infusion. Combine the two mashes in a lauter tun after saccarification and sparge. Add fruit to secondary fermenter.

Cherry Pie

Gold Medal, NHC, Fruit Beer, 1994
Allen Bavry Jr., Sarasota, Florida
(All-Grain)

Ingredients for 5 Gallons

- 10 pounds macerated or crushed fresh sour cherries
- 10 pounds two-row Klages malt
- 2 pounds rolled wheat malt
- 1 ounce Saaz hops, 3.5% alpha acid (60 minutes)
- 1 ounce Saaz hops, 3.5% alpha acid (2 minutes)
- Whitbread ale yeast
- 3/4 cup corn sugar (to prime)

Original gravity:	1.064
Final gravity:	1.015
Boiling time:	60 minutes
Primary fermentation:	5 days at 78 °F (26 °C) in glass
Secondary fermentation:	14 days at 78 °F (26 °C) in glass
Age when judged:	11 months

Brewer's Specifics

Mash grains at 122 °F (50 °C) for 30 minutes. Raise temperature to 154 °F (68 °C) for 30 minutes. Sparge with 170 °F (77 °C) water. Rack beer over cherries in secondary fermenter.

Judges' Comments

"Cherry tart. Well balanced. Very good!"

"Nice, clean, sour-cherry flavor. Dry finish. A little astringent. Great beer! Good balance. Fruit character is strong but blends well."

"Cherry is evident. Nice sour finish. Very nice sour cherry. Good balance. Great job."

Cherry Charlie Barley Wine

Cherry Barley Wine, 1997
Charlie Papazian, Boulder, Colorado
(Extract/Grain)

Ingredients for 5 Gallons

12	pounds macerated or crushed sour cherries
4 3/4	pounds extra light dried malt extract
3	pounds light honey
3	pounds two-row pale malt
2	pounds Munich malt
1	pound 120 °L crystal or caramel malt
1	pound wheat malt
7 1/2	HBU American Nugget hops (90 minutes)
5	HBU American Hersbrucker hops (60 minutes)
4	HBU Kent Goldings hops (45 minutes)
1	ounce American Tettnang hops (1–3 minutes)
1	ounce American Cascade hops (1–3 minutes)
1/4	teaspoon Irish moss
	Wyeast No. 1056 American ale yeast
3/4	cup corn sugar (to prime)

Original gravity:	1.091
Final gravity:	1.024
Boiling time:	90 minutes
Primary fermentation:	7 days at 70 °F (21 °C)
Secondary fermentation:	2 weeks at 65–70 °F (18–21 °C)
Tertiary fermentation:	1–3 months at 50 °F (10 °C)

Brewer's Specifics

Employ a single step infusion mash to mash the grains. Add 7 quarts (6.7 liters) of 165 °F (74 °C) water to the crushed grain, stir, stabilize, and hold the temperature at 150 °F (65.6 °C) for 60 minutes.

After conversion, raise temperature to 167 °F (75 °C), lauter, and sparge with 3 gallons (11.4 liters) of 170 °F (77 °C) water. Collect about 4 gallons (15.1 liters) of runoff. Add first bittering hops, malt extract, honey, 1/2 gallon (2 liters) more of water and bring to a full and vigorous boil.

The total boil time is approximately 90 minutes. When 60 minutes remain, add second bittering hops. When 45 minutes remain, add bittering and flavor hops. When 10 minutes remain, add Irish moss. After a total wort boil of 90 minutes (reducing the wort volume to just over 3.5 gallons [13 liters]) turn off the heat and strain out bittering and flavor hops. Then return wort concentrate to a boil, at which point add 12 pounds of crushed cherries and aroma hops, and turn off heat. Let steep at about 160 °F

(71 °C) for about 15 to 20 minutes to pasteurize fruit. Keep lid securely in place and then place pot in a cold bath of water for 15 minutes to aid cooling. Add the wort, cherries, and aroma hops into 1 large sanitized fermenter or split between 2 6.5-gallon (25-liter) sanitized carboys to which you've added 2 gallons (7.6 liters) of cold water. Total volume is about 7 gallons (26.5 liters) (or 2 times 3.5 gallons [13 L]). If necessary add additional cold water to achieve a 7-gallon (26.5-liter) primary fermentation batch size. Chill the wort to 70 °F (21 °C). Aerate the cooled wort well. Add active yeast and ferment for 7 days in the primary. Then transfer into a secondary fermenter, carefully siphoning to leave the majority of cherries, hops, and sediment behind. The net yield should be about 5 gallons (19 liters) for secondary fermentation. Continue fermenting at 65–70 °F (18.3–21 °C) for 2 more weeks. Rack and transfer a third time into another sanitized carboy, eliminating virtually all cherry and hop remnants from the beer. Chill to 50 °F (10 °C) and age for 1–3 months.

When aging is complete, prime with sugar, and bottle or keg. You may add fresh yeast to help conditioning. Let condition at temperatures above 65 °F (18.3 °C) until clear and carbonated.

Flavor Comments

The flavor intensity of the cherries will dictate much of the final character of this wonderfully complex ale. This is not a highly hopped bitter barley wine. Intentions are to accent the passion of the cherries combined with the complexity of a high-alcohol ale. Specialty malts provide a smooth malt richness, while the honey provides a balancing dryness and helps attenuate this ale. Large doses of aromatically floral, citrusy, fruity hops complement the cherries perfectly. Kent Goldings and Hersbrucker hops provide an earthy, soft, spicy bitterness, while Nugget hops provide a bit of sharpness that begins to pierce through the richness of malt and alcohol. It's a fun fruit barley wine to brew. You can use your favorite fruit if you wish. I used chokecherries in the original recipe. One final note: Let it age . . . hmmmmm. Yes.

Foreplay

Gold Medal, NHC, Chocolate and Raspberry Porter, 1994
Paul Sullivan, Brooklyn, New York
(All-Grain)

Ingredients for 10 Gallons

20	pounds Briess two-row malt
2	pounds 60 °L crystal malt
1	pound Briess chocolate malt
1/2	pound Briess black patent malt
12	ounces Baker's chocolate
1 1/2	ounces Cascade hops, 6% alpha acid (90 minutes)
1	ounce Cascade hops, 6% alpha acid (40 minutes)
1/2	ounce raspberry liqueur added to each bottle
	Wyeast No. 2206 Bavarian lager yeast
	force-carbonate in keg

Original gravity:	1.054
Final gravity:	1.015
Boiling time:	90 minutes
Primary fermentation:	10 days at 68 °F (20 °C) in glass
Secondary fermentation:	2 weeks at 40 °F (4 °C) in keg
Age when judged:	4 months

Brewer's Specifics

Add chocolate malt to boil.

Judges' Comments

"A nice balance of chocolate and raspberry in aroma. A subtle chocolate note is the first flavor, followed quickly by a rich raspberry character. The maltiness hides behind the raspberry. Some astringency in the finish. A very pleasing blend of flavors, lots of complexity."

"Bitter chocolate. Very smooth! Marshmallows. Blackberry. Low hop bitterness for porter. What a great dessert beer. Just delicious. Nice job."

The Tenth Muse
Raspberry Imperial Stout

NHC, Fruit Beer, 1996
Bill Kowalski, Houston, Texas
(All-Grain)

Ingredients for 5 Gallons

18	pounds Klages pale two-row malt
8	pounds raspberries added to secondary fermenter
2	pounds Special "B" malt
1	pound British medium crystal malt
1	pound CaraPils malt
1/2	pound black patent malt
1/2	pound roasted barley
1/4	pound chocolate malt
2	ounces East Kent Goldings hop pellets, 5.2% alpha acid (60 minutes)
	Wyeast No. 1056 American ale yeast
3/4	cup corn sugar (to prime)

Original gravity:	1.085
Final gravity:	1.020
Boiling time:	90 minutes
Primary fermentation:	10 days at 70 °F (21 °C) in glass
Secondary fermentation:	24 days at 70 °F (21 °C) in glass
Age when judged:	7 months

Brewer's Specifics
Mash grains at 154 °F (68 °C) for 90 minutes.

It's a Boy Blueberry Maibock

NHC, Fruit Beer, 1996
Steven Ashton, Indian Hills, Colorado
(All-Grain)

Ingredients for 5 Gallons
11	pounds Durst Pilsener malt
3	pounds crushed blueberries added to secondary
1	ounce Northern Brewer hops, 7.1% alpha acid (60 minutes)
1	ounce Tettnang hops, 2.5% alpha acid (45 minutes)
1/2	ounce Crystal hops, 4.1% alpha acid (15 minutes)
	Wyeast No. 2206 Bavarian Lager yeast

Original gravity:	1.060
Final gravity:	1.030
Boiling time:	90 minutes
Primary fermentation:	8 days at 50 °F (10 °C) in glass
Secondary fermentation:	23 days at 50 °F (10 °C) in stainless steel
Tertiary fermentation:	46 days at 40 °F (4 °C) in stainless steel
Age when judged:	4 months

Brewer's Specifics
Mash grains at 152 °F (67 °C) for 90 minutes. Add 1 1/2 gallons boiling water to mash-out at 170 °F (77 °C) for 15 minutes.

OLD ALE

An English-style beer usually brewed from higher gravities (1.055–1.080 [14–20 °Plato]), old ale has dark, rich, sweet malt characteristics resulting from a fairly low degree of attenuation. Strength varies quite a bit, since an old ale with a high starting gravity may end up with a relatively high finishing gravity as well. But generally, old ale ranges from 5.8–8.5 percent alcohol by volume. Many are enjoyed as winter warmers, but craft the stronger ones early enough in the year to guarantee a proper conditioning period. Traditionally brewed in summer for the following winter, old ale is a provision beer, like Märzen or bière de garde. Color is dark chestnut brown to almost black with heavy malt tones. Medium to heavy body is also appropriate with a full mouthfeel. Old ales have low to medium hop bitterness, aroma, and flavor. Fruitiness or estery flavors are both acceptable with low to medium levels of diacetyl. A warming alcohol character is common for higher-strength versions. These are great beers to age in casks or bottles—just remember when you bottle a beer with a high finishing gravity, you risk a slow secondary fermentation, especially if stored in a warm place for the summer. Beware of overcarbonation!

Old Carcass

Old Ale, 1997
Amahl Turczyn, Boulder, Colorado
(All-Grain)

Ingredients for 10 Gallons

- 25 pounds Harrington two-row malt
- 1 pound 80 °L crystal malt
- 1 pound 55 °L crystal malt
- 8 ounces 120 °L crystal malt
- 8 ounces black malt
- 5 ounces Kent Goldings pelletized hops, 5.4% alpha acid (60 minutes)
- 2 ounces Fuggle pelletized hops, 4.3% alpha acid (15 minutes)
- Wyeast No. 1098 British ale yeast

Original gravity:	1.072
Final gravity:	1.014
Boiling time:	90 minutes
Primary fermentation:	2 weeks at 65 °F (18 °C) in glass
Secondary fermentation:	1 month at 60 °F (16 °C) in oak
Tertiary fermentation:	—

Brewers' Specifics
Mash grains at 152 °F (67 °C) for 60 minutes.

Flavor Comments
If you have the luxury of conditioning your beer in oak casks, this is the beer for it. Old Carcass matures wonderfully with several months of conditioning time, developing caramel, vanilla, and sherryish notes.

Flaming Scrotum

Gold Medal, NHC, English Old Ale, 1994
Bob Gorman, Waltham, Massachusetts
(All-Grain)

Ingredients for 7 3/4 Gallons

16 1/2   pounds Briess two-row malt
2 1/2   pounds DeWolf-Cosyns Munich malt
1 1/2   pounds Munton and Fison crystal malt
1   pound Ireks German wheat malt
2   ounces Kent Goldings hops, 5% alpha acid (60 minutes)
3/5   ounce Galena hops, 13% alpha acid (60 minutes)
1   ounce Kent Goldings hops, 5% alpha acid (30 minutes)
1   ounce Fuggles hops (15 minutes)
1   ounce Cascade hops (5 minutes)
  Boston Brewery ale yeast
  force-carbonate in keg

Original gravity:	1.076
Final gravity:	1.025
Boiling time:	120 minutes
Primary fermentation:	1 month
Secondary fermentation:	—
Age when judged:	17 months

Brewer's Specifics

Mash-in at 154 °F (68 °C). Allow temperature to drop to 150 °F (66 °C) for more than 90 minutes. Raise temperature to 168 °F (76 °C) for 20 minutes. Sparge with 7 gallons of water.

Judges' Comments

"Complex. Some fruitiness. Resinous. Thick, almost syrupy or honeylike. Some residual sweetness. Complex interaction of malt, hops, fruit, honey. Slight huskiness or astringency in the aftertaste. This is good. The best we've had yet. Well done. Good job."

"Rich complex blend with diacetyl—butterscotch elements nicely integrated. Smooth lingering caramel aftertaste. An excellent well-balanced brew that leaves a clean smooth aftertaste. No ragged edges. Jolly good!"

Butchie's Old Ale

NHC, English Old Ale, 1996
Al Korzonas, Palos Hills, Illinois
(Extract/Grain)

Ingredients for 5 Gallons

6	pounds Northwestern Gold malt extract
3	pounds Munton and Fison light dry malt extract
1	pound dextrose (boil)
3/4	pound DeWolf-Cosyns CaraMunich malt
1/4	pound DeWolf-Cosyns CaraVienne malt
4	ounces Mt. Hood hop pellets, 4.1% alpha acid (60 minutes)
1/4	ounce East Kent Goldings hop pellets, 4.65% alpha acid (60 minutes)
3 1/4	ounces East Kent Goldings hop pellets, 4.65% alpha acid (15 minutes)
2	ounces East Kent Goldings hop plugs (dry, 1 1/2 weeks)
5	grams gypsum added to mash water
1 1/4	grams salt added to mash water
	Wyeast No. 1028 London ale yeast
7/16	cup dextrose (to prime)

Original gravity:	1.072
Final gravity:	1.020
Boiling time:	70 minutes
Primary fermentation:	3 weeks at 64 °F (18 °C) in glass
Secondary fermentation:	—
Age when judged:	15 months

Brewer's Specifics
Steep specialty grains at 170 °F (77 °C) for 20 minutes.

Ye Olde Ale

NHC, English and Scottish Strong Ale, 1996
Gene Pribula, Wyndmere, North Dakota
(All-Grain)

Ingredients for 10 Gallons

15	pounds two-row pale malt
1	pound CaraPils malt
1	pound flaked barley
1/2	pound chocolate malt
1/2	pound CaraVienne malt
1/2	pound 95–115 °L crystal malt
1/4	pound Special "B" malt
3	ounces East Kent Goldings hops, 4.8% alpha acid (60 minutes)
1	ounce East Kent Goldings hop pellets, 5% alpha acid (15 minutes)
10	grams chalk
2	grams epsom salts added to mash water
2	grams gypsum added to mash water
	force-carbonate

Original gravity:	1.058
Final gravity:	1.015
Boiling time:	60 minutes
Primary fermentation:	13 days at 68 °F (20 °C) in glass
Secondary fermentation:	10 days at 68 °F (20 °C) in glass
Age when judged:	6 months

Brewer's Specifics
Mash grains at 153 °F (67 °C) for 60 minutes.

Old Slobber Knocker

NHC, English Old Ale, 1996
Charlie Feder, DeSoto, Texas
(All-Grain)

Ingredients for 5 Gallons

12	pounds English two-row malt
1 1/4	pounds 40 °L crystal malt
1/2	pound cane sugar
1	ounce East Kent Goldings hop pellets, 5.8% alpha acid (60 minutes)
1	ounce Fuggles hop pellets, 4.5% alpha acid (30 minutes)
1/2	ounce East Kent Goldings hop pellets, 5.8% alpha acid (30 minutes)
1/2	ounce East Kent Goldings hop pellets, 5.8% alpha acid (10 minutes)
1/2	ounce Fuggles hop pellets, 4.5% alpha acid (finish)
2	teaspoons gypsum added to mash water
1	teaspoon yeast nutrient
	Wyeast No. 1728 Scottish ale yeast
3/4	cup corn sugar (to prime)

Original gravity:	1.075
Final gravity:	1.016
Boiling time:	90 minutes
Primary fermentation:	2 weeks at 60 °F (16 °C) in glass
Secondary fermentation:	2 weeks at 60 °F (16 °C) in glass
Tertiary fermentation:	11 days at 60 °F (16 °C) in glass
Age when judged:	4 months

Brewer's Specifics

Mash grains at 151 °F (60 °C) for 90 minutes.

SUMMER

BELGIAN WHITE

This style is one of the most refreshing and fun-to-brew summer beers. It is traditionally made with roughly equal proportions of unmalted wheat and malted barley, with dried orange peel and/or coriander seed added as flavoring. Whether this was done to add character or to mask undesirable off-flavors is a matter of conjecture, but the increasing popularity of the style attests to its acceptance in today's market. The color of Belgian white, or wit as it's called in Belgium, is bright, almost fluorescent yellow to yellow-orange, with a dense white head. If one uses an authentic yeast strain a slight acidity commonly develops, especially as the beer ages. Clovey phenolic spiciness from the yeast blends well with added spices. A good full mouthfeel comes from using raw wheat, but a relatively dry finish follows from a combination of high carbonation, low finishing gravity, and the very slight bitterness from the orange peel. Hop bitterness is very low, since hops contribute very little to no flavor or aroma. No diacetyl should be detectable.

Hoe Garden—Mow Lawn

Gold Medal, NHC, Belgian-Style Specialty, 1992
Mark Richmond, Springfield, Ohio
(All-Grain)

Ingredients for 5 Gallons

5	pounds Klages two-row malt
4 1/2	pounds wheat malt
1/2	pound oats
1	ounce Hallertau hops, 4.4% alpha acid (60 minutes)
1/2	ounce Tettnang hops, 4.5% alpha acid (20 minutes)
1	ounce Hallertau hops, 4.4% alpha acid (10 minutes)
1	ounce Saaz hops, 3.1% alpha acid (finish)
1	ounce crushed coriander added to boil (60 minutes)
1/2	ounce orange peel added to boil (10 minutes)
1	ounce coriander seed (dry-hop)
1/2	ounce orange peel (dry-hop)
	Wyeast No. 1028 London ale yeast
3/4	cup corn sugar (to prime)

Original gravity:	1.046
Final gravity:	—
Boiling time:	90 minutes
Primary fermentation:	33 days at 65 °F (18 °C) in glass
Secondary fermentation:	—
Age when judged:	5 months

Brewer's Specifics

Use a sour mash technique. Dough-in at 160 °F (71 °C), gradually dropping temperature to 122 °F (50 °C) during a 24-hour period. Sparge with 165 °F (74 °C) water. Dry-hop with 1 ounce coriander seed and 1/2 ounce orange peel.

Judges' Comments

"Clean sharp flavor. Very drinkable."

"Very good white. Spices come through with crispness."

"Great refreshing beer. True to style. With a little less spice and more tartness, it would be unbeatable."

Katarina Wit

Belgian Wheat, 1996
Amahl Turczyn, Boulder, Colorado
(All-Grain)

Ingredients for 15 Gallons

10	pounds Harrington two-row malt
6	pounds malted wheat
5	pounds unmalted wheat flakes
1	pound rice hulls added to mash to help sparge
1	ounce Saaz hop pellets, 3.1% alpha acid (90 minutes)
1/2	ounce Saaz hop pellets, 3.1% alpha acid (60 minutes)
1/2	ounce Saaz hop pellets, 3.1% alpha acid (1 minute)
1/4	ounce crushed coriander seed (1 minute)
1/4	ounce crushed orange peel (1 minute)
	Wyeast No. 3944 Belgian White Beer ale yeast
3/4	cup corn sugar (to prime)

Original gravity:	1.050
Final gravity:	1.010
Boiling time:	90 minutes
Primary fermentation:	1 week at 65 °F (18 °C) in glass
Secondary fermentation:	2 weeks at 60 °F (16 °C) in glass
Tertiary Fermentation:	—

Brewer's Specifics

Use a step infusion mash. The first rest is at 122 °F (50 °C) for 30 minutes. Add boiling water to bring the mash to 150 °F (66 °C) for 60 minutes. Mash-out at 170 °F (77 °C) and sparge. Crush orange peel in a blender and add to boil.

Flavor Comments

This is a light, refreshing, subtly spiced version of the classic Belgian-style wit. To get the tight creamy head, encouraged by the viscosity of malted and unmalted wheat, use slightly more than the recommended 3/4 cup of corn sugar per 5 gallons.

White Beer

Joe Mildenberger, Portland, Oregon
(Extract/Grain)

Ingredients for 5 Gallons

5	pounds domestic two-row pale malt
3	pounds Belgian pale malt
3/4	pound 20 °L crystal malt
1/2	pound light dry malt extract
1/2	pound CaraPils malt
1 1/2	ounces Saaz hop pellets, 3.8% alpha acid (45 minutes)
1 1/2	ounces Hallertau hops, 4.3% alpha acid (30 minutes)
1 1/2	ounces dried orange peel (finish)
3/4	ounce crushed coriander seed (finish)
	Wyeast No. 3944 Belgian White Beer ale yeast
2/3	cup corn sugar (to prime)

Original gravity:	1.043
Final gravity:	1.009
Boiling time:	60 minutes
Primary fermentation:	14 days at 68 °F (20 °C) in glass carboy
Secondary fermentation:	—
Age when judged:	2 1/2 months

Brewer's Specifics
Mash grains at 155 °F (68 °C) for 60 minutes.

Untitled

NHC, White (Wit), 1996
William Krouss, Rancho Palos Verdes, California
(All-Grain)

Ingredients for 5 Gallons

4 1/2	pounds Belgian Pilsener malt
2 1/2	pounds Belgian wheat malt
2	pounds unmalted wheat
1	ounce East Kent Goldings hop pellets, 4.5% alpha acid (90 minutes)
1/2	ounce Saaz hop pellets (5 minutes)
3/4	ounce ground coriander (steep, 5 minutes)
1/4	ounce bitter orange peel (steep, 5 minutes)
	Wyeast No. 3944 Belgian White Beer ale yeast
3/4	cup corn sugar (to prime)

Original gravity:	1.041
Final gravity:	1.009
Boiling time:	90 minutes
Primary fermentation:	8 days at 68 °F (20 °C) in glass
Secondary fermentation:	15 days at 68 °F (20 °C) in glass
Age when judged:	4 months

Brewer's Specifics

Mash grains at 123 °F (51 °C) for 30 minutes and 152 °F (67 °C) for 60 minutes.

Untitled

NHC, White (Wit), 1996
Richard Wenzlik, Carmel, California
(All-Grain)

Ingredients for 5 Gallons

4	pounds two-row lager malt
3	pounds wheat malt
1	pound CaraVienne malt
1/2	ounce Tettnang hop pellets, 3.8% alpha acid (60 minutes)
1	ounce Cluster hop pellets, 6.9% alpha acid (30 minutes)
1/2	ounce Tettnang hop pellets, 3.8% alpha acid (30 minutes)
1	ounce dried orange peel
1/4	ounce ground cumin
1/4	ounce ground coriander
3	teaspoons lactic acid to adjust sparge water's pH to 3.6
1	teaspoon gypsum added to mash water
	Wyeast No. 3944 Belgian White Beer ale yeast
3/4	cup corn sugar (to prime)

Original gravity:	1.050
Final gravity:	1.018
Boiling time:	75 minutes
Primary fermentation:	6 days at 60 °F (16 °C) in glass
Secondary fermentation:	14 days at 60 °F (16 °C) in glass
Age when judged:	9 months

Brewer's Specifics

Use a three-stage step infusion mash. Bring mash to 120 °F (49 °C) for 30 minutes. Raise mash temperature to 145 °F (63 °C) for 60 minutes and 152 °F (67 °C) for 30 minutes. Mash-out at 170 °F (77 °C) for 10 minutes and sparge.

Untitled

Finalist, NHC, White (Wit), 1996
Tom Spaulding, Santa Cruz, California
(All-Grain)

Ingredients for 8 Gallons

8	pounds Belgian Pilsener malt
2 1/4	pounds unmalted wheat
2 1/4	pounds wheat flakes
3/4	pound oat flakes
1 1/2	ounces Willamette hop pellets, 4.3% alpha acid (65 minutes)
1/2	ounce Saaz hops, 3% alpha acid (15 minutes)
1 1/2	ounces crushed coriander (finish)
1	ounce bitter orange peel (finish)
1/4	ounce crushed cumin (finish)
1	teaspoon chalk added to mash water
1	teaspoon calcium chloride added to mash water
3	teaspoons lactic acid added to sparge water
	BreuTek CL-900 Belgian Wheat yeast
18	grams corn sugar (to prime)

Original gravity:	1.049
Final gravity:	1.015
Boiling time:	65 minutes
Primary fermentation:	9 days at 72 °F (22 °C) in glass
Secondary fermentation:	—
Age when judged:	3 1/2 months

Brewer's Specifics

Sour mash at 120 °F (49 °C) for 17 1/2 hours. Mash grains at 152 °F (67 °C) for 125 minutes.

To Wit

NHC, White (Wit), 1996
James Wilts, Richmond, California
(All-Grain)

Ingredients for 5 1/2 Gallons

4	pounds flaked wheat
4	pounds Belgian Pilsener malt
1	pound two-row malt
1	pound flaked oats
1 1/2	ounces Saaz hops, 2.2% alpha acid (60 minutes)
1/2	ounce Hallertau hop pellets, 2.8% alpha acid (30 minutes)
9/10	ounce Hallertau hop pellets, 2.8% alpha acid (5 minutes)
3/5	ounce bitter orange added to boil (20 minutes)
3/5	ounce ground coriander added to boil (5 minutes)
	Wyeast No. 3944 Belgium White Beer ale yeast
1	cup corn sugar (to prime)

Original gravity:	1.050
Final gravity:	1.014
Boiling time:	60 minutes
Primary fermentation:	13 days at 60 °F (16 °C) in glass
Secondary fermentation:	14 days at 60 °F (16 °C) in glass
Age when judged:	6 months

Brewer's Specifics

Step mash at 122 °F (150 °C) for 60 minutes, 131 °F (55 °C) for 45 minutes, and 154 °F (68 °C) for 45 minutes.

BERLINER WEISSE

This light, extremely tart wheat beer is a refreshing style enjoyed in northern Germany and is often served with colored fruit syrups to partially counter the sourness. It is very light with starting gravities of 1.028–1.032 (7–8 °Plato). No hop or malt characteristics are detectable. The *Lactobacillus delbrueckii* bacteria strain produces the intense lactic character. As this character is essential to the uniqueness of this style, you may need to set aside some equipment to use only for sour beer brewing. Otherwise, cross-con-tamination may end up souring all of your beer. Berliner weisse is traditionally made by splitting the wort into two batches. One batch is dosed with a neutral German yeast strain, and the other is inoculated with *Lactobacillus delbrueckii*. The two are then blended after fermentation.

You may choose to do a sour mash. Add ground pale malt to your wort and let it slowly develop the sour bacterial character from the lactic bacteria, which occurs naturally on grain. You may not achieve the intensity of sourness typical of the style, but that may be just as well. Served cold and highly effervescent, Berliner weisse is among the classic summer beers, and though challenging, is well worth the effort.

Shank My Bier

Reprinted from 1996 Winter Issue of *Zymurgy*
Dennis Davison, Greenfield, Wisconsin
(Extract/Grain)

Ingredients for 5 Gallons

3 1/3   pounds Munton and Fison wheat malt extract
2   pounds two-row Pilsener malt
1/2   ounce Hallertau Hersbrucker hops, 3.6% alpha acid (45 minutes)
    Yeast Lab® A04 German ale yeast
1   cup corn sugar (to prime)

Original gravity:	1.030
Final gravity:	1.006
Boiling time:	45 minutes
Primary fermentation:	4 days
Secondary fermentation:	2 weeks
Tertiary fermentation:	6 weeks to 1 year

Brewer's Specifics

Prepare a starter for the liquid yeast 3 days before you plan to brew. The day before brewing, crush the 2 pounds of two-row malt and place in a grain bag. Cover grains with 1 gallon of 95 °F (35 °C) water. Let steep up to 24 hours. To maintain the temperature, place in a gas oven with a pilot light or use a small picnic cooler. Remove the grain bag and run hot water through it to extract some of the trapped sugars. Place all of the liquid on the stove and bring to a boil. Add the wheat malt extract and, once the boil resumes, add the Hersbrucker hops. Boil 45 minutes. Cool and add the wort to a primary fermenter. Bring the volume to 5 1/2 gallons with additional preboiled and cooled water. Pitch yeast when the temperature is approximately 70 °F (21 °C).

Berliner Splits

Reprinted from 1996 Winter Issue of *Zymurgy*
Dennis Davison, Greenfield, Wisconsin
(All-Grain)

Ingredients for 5 Gallons
 3   pounds Durst two-row barley malt
 3   pounds Durst wheat malt
 2   ounces Hallertau Hersbrucker hops, 3.4% alpha acid
     Lactobacillus culture
     Wyeast No. 1007 German ale yeast
 1   cup corn sugar (to prime)

Original gravity:	1.030
Final gravity:	1.004
Boiling time:	see brewer's specifics
Primary fermentation:	4–6 days
Secondary fermentation:	8 weeks
Tertiary fermentation:	—

Brewer's Specifics

Plan your starters ahead. On brew day crush grains, add 1 1/2 gallons of 130 °F (54 °C) water, and hold mash at 122 °F (50 °C) for 20 minutes. Raise the temperature to 150 °F (66 °C) with the addition of boiling water. Boil the hops in the water for 15 minutes before adding it to the mash. Stir the mash gently to incorporate the hops. Hold at 150 °F (66 °C) for 30 minutes or until starch conversion is complete. Again, increase the mash temperature to 165 °F (74 °C) by adding boiling water, then sparge and lauter. Collect 5 1/2 gallons of wort.

Bring the sweet wort to a boil, turn off the heat, and chill to 90 °F (32 °C). Siphon half the volume into 1 fermenter and pitch with the *Lactobacillus* culture. Chill the remainder in the kettle to 65 °F (18 °C), siphon into a second fermenter, and pitch the ale yeast. Keep the *Lactobacillus* fermenter warm at 75–85 °F (24–29 °C), by wrapping it in a blanket. Keep the ale yeast fermenter between 65–70 °F (18–21 °C).

After 4–6 days rack both fermenters into one secondary and allow to age for 8 weeks before bottling. Bottle with corn sugar or fresh kraeusen. Allow 4 weeks in the bottle before sampling. Save a few bottles to try the following year.

Berliner Weisse

Gold Medal, NHC, German-Style Wheat Beer, 1996
Dennis Davison, Greenfield, Wisconsin
(All-Grain)

Ingredients for 5 Gallons
3 1/2 pounds DeWolf-Cosyns wheat malt
3 1/2 pounds DeWolf-Cosyns Pilsener malt
1/4 ounce Tettnang hop pellets, 4.7% alpha acid (60 minutes)
Yeast Lab® 1084 Irish ale yeast
Lactobacillus culture
force-carbonate in keg

Original gravity:	1.034
Final gravity:	—
Boiling time:	120 minutes
Primary fermentation:	2 weeks at 65 °F (18 °C) in glass
Secondary fermentation:	2 years at 65 °F (18 °C) in glass
Age when judged:	5 months

Brewer's Specifics
Mash grains at 150 °F (66 °C) for 90 minutes.

Judges' Comments
"Golden color at dark end of allowed range. Only slight haze. Big head. Aggressively sour, very light body."

"Crisp, clean, lactic sourness. Sourness lasts for most of aftertaste. Fruity esters very subtle—could stand some increase."

"Very intense lactic sourness. Extremely tart and refreshing. This is just a wonderful beer and great example of a most difficult style."

Cranberry Lambic

Bronze Medal, NHC, Classic-Style Berliner Weisse, 1995
Scott Bickham, Ithaca, New York
(All-Grain)

Ingredients for 5 Gallons
6	pounds malted wheat
3 1/2	pounds Pilsener malt
1	ounce Hallertau hops, 2.8% alpha acid (60 minutes)
1/4	ounce Hallertau hops, 2.8% alpha acid (15 minutes)
1/2	ounce orange peel (5 minutes)
5/8	cup glucose (to prime)
1	can cranberry juice concentrate added to secondary
	Wyeast No. 3056 Bavarian Wheat ale yeast

Original gravity:	1.053
Final gravity:	1.018
Boiling time:	75 minutes
Primary fermentation:	10 days at 65 °F (18 °C) in glass
Secondary fermentation:	2 weeks at 65 °F (18 °C) in glass
Age when judged:	3 months

Brewer's Specifics
Employ the following step infusion mash schedule: 30 minutes at 124 °F (50 °C), 60 minutes at 153 °F (67 °C), and 10 minutes at 168 °F (76 °C).

Judges' Comments
"Very nice. A bit sweet for style but a very nice drink!"

"Good head retention, big frothy head. Pretty peach color. A little cloudy. Clean. Strong tartness and sourness. Suggestion of cranberry. Grapefruity. Nice blend of tartness and sourness. Finishes clean and tart."

Weiss Old Owl

NHC, Berliner Weisse, 1996
Mike Hufnagel, Cincinnati, Ohio
(All-Grain)

Ingredients for 5 1/8 Gallons
- 4 pounds Belgian Pilsener malt
- 2 3/4 pounds Belgian wheat malt
- 1/4 ounce Pride of Ringwood hops, 7.5% alpha acid (45 minutes)
- Wyeast No. 3056 Bavarian Wheat ale yeast
- 4 1/2 ounces corn sugar

Original gravity:	1.031
Final gravity:	1.008
Boiling time:	60 minutes
Primary fermentation:	6 days at 63 °F (17 °C) in glass
Secondary fermentation:	7 days at 63 °F (17 °C) in glass
Tertiary fermentation:	13 days at 36 °F (2 °C) in glass
Age when judged:	2 1/2 months

Brewer's Specifics
Mash grains at 153 °F (67 °C) for 60 minutes.

Ich Liebe Berliner

Reprinted from 1996 Winter Issue of *Zymurgy*
Dennis Davison, Greenfield, Wisconsin
(Extract/Grain)

Ingredients for 5 Gallons
   4   pounds Durst wheat malt
2 1/2 pounds Durst two-row barley malt
or
   2   pounds Northwestern dry wheat malt extract
   2   pounds Munton and Fison light dry malt extract

1/2 ounce Hallertau Hersbrucker hops, 3.4% alpha acid (60 minutes)
     Lactobacillus culture
     BreuTek CL-400 Old German ale yeast
  1 cup corn sugar (to prime)

Original gravity:	1.032
Final gravity:	1.004
Boiling time:	60 minutes
Primary fermentation:	5 days
Secondary fermentation:	at least 8 weeks
Tertiary fermentation:	—

Brewer's Specifics

Start *Lactobacillus* culture ahead of time. On brew day crush grains and add 1 1/2 gallons of 130 °F (54 °C) water and allow temperature to stabilize at 122 °F (50 °C) for 20 minutes. Add boiling water to raise temperature to 152 °F (67 °C). Hold for 30 minutes or until starch conversion is complete. Raise temperature to 165 °F (74 °C), then sparge and lauter to collect 6 1/2 gallons.

Boil 60 minutes, chill to 90 °F (32 °C), and pitch the *Lactobacillus* culture. Ferment between 75 and 85 °F (24 and 29 °C). Begin a starter for the ale yeast. After 4 or 5 days allow the fermenter to cool to cellar temperatures and add ale yeast. Ferment for another 5 days in primary and rack to secondary. Leave in secondary at least 8 weeks and bottle with corn sugar or fresh kraeusen.

WEIZEN

One of the most popular summer beers in Bavaria, weizen, notably hefeweizen (with yeast), has begun to catch on in the United States as well. This foamy, spicy wheat beer is very refreshing yet has enough character to be more than just a thirst-quencher. The yeast in the bottle leads enthusiasts to believe, and rightfully so, that hefeweizen is better for you than filtered beer, providing a healthy dose of B-complex and other vitamins. It is pale golden to tawny brown, highly carbonated (necessitating a skillful pour), and made with 50–70 percent wheat malt. The style is of medium strength, usually from an original gravity of 1.045–1.055 (11.5–13.5 °Plato). Clove, banana, pear, vanilla, nutmeg, smoke, and cinnamon flavors are all typical, assuming you have an authentic yeast strain, which is absolutely necessary for this style. At least one major producer of hefeweizen uses a neutral German ale strain, and the resulting product pales in comparison to the real thing. Some strains produce a mild tartness, especially after aging. Cloudiness from proteins in the wheat is acceptable. Very low hop bitterness in flavor and aroma is allowable, but you really want the phenolics and the malt to provide most of the flavor profile. Diacetyl is inappropriate.

Ho Wheat Brew

Gold Medal, NHC, Weizen/Weissbier, 1995
Bert Zelten, Kewaunee, Wisconsin
(All-Grain)

Ingredients for 10 Gallons
- 11 pounds wheat malt
- 7 pounds two-row malt
- 1/2 ounce Saaz hops, 3.6% alpha acid (60 minutes)
- 1/2 ounce Saaz hops, 3.6% alpha acid (15 minutes)
- Brewer's Choice No. 3068 yeast
- 1 1/2 cups corn sugar (to prime)

Original gravity:	1.046
Final gravity:	1.015
Boiling time:	60 minutes
Primary fermentation:	7 days at 66 °F (19 °C) in glass
Secondary fermentation:	10 days at 66 °F (19 °C) in glass
Age when judged:	3 months

Brewer's Specifics
Use a double decoction mashing technique.

Judges' Comments
"Nice sweet flavor. Overcarbonation tingles, taking away some flavor. Good spiciness. Smooth. Sweet. Spicy. A very good beer."

"Wonderful blend of spiciness. Banana. Bubble gum. Fruitiness and malty sweetness. Excellent example."

Untitled

Silver Medal, NHC, Weissbier, 1996
Frank Berry, Hillsboro, Oregon
(All-Grain)

Ingredients for 5 Gallons
 6 pounds German wheat malt
 3 pounds Belgian pale malt
 1 ounce East Kent Goldings hop pellets, 4.5% alpha acid (90 minutes)
 2 teaspoons gypsum added to mash water
    Wyeast No. 3068 Weihenstephan Wheat yeast
 1 cup corn sugar (to prime)

Original gravity:	1.054
Final gravity:	1.014
Boiling time:	90 minutes
Primary fermentation:	7 days at 68 °F (20 °C) in glass
Secondary fermentation:	7 days at 65 °F (18 °C) in glass
Age when judged:	2 1/2 months

Brewer's Specifics
Mash grains at 158–159 °F (70–71 °C) for 60 minutes.

Breakfast Beer

Bronze Medal, NHC, Weissbier, 1995
Todd Kellenbenz, Houston, Texas
(All-Grain)

Ingredients for 10 Gallons

11	pounds German wheat malt
10	pounds U.S. six-row malt
1	pound British CaraPils malt
1	ounce Mt. Hood hops, 5.3% alpha acid (60 minutes)
1 1/2	ounces German Hallertau hops, 4.5% alpha acid (30 minutes)
2	teaspoons gypsum added to mash water
	Wyeast No. 3068 Weihenstephan Wheat yeast
	force-carbonate

Original gravity:	1.047
Final gravity:	1.012
Boiling time:	75 minutes
Primary fermentation:	1 week at 65 °F (18 °C) in plastic
Secondary fermentation:	2 weeks at 65 °F (18 °C) in stainless steel
Age when judged:	3 1/2 months

Brewer's Specifics

Mash grains at 151 °F (66 °C) for 60 minutes.

Colorado Weizen

Gold Medal, NHC, German Weizen, 1991
Michael Croddy, Colorado Springs, Colorado
(Extract)

Ingredients for 5 Gallons

6 2/3 pounds American Brewmaster wheat malt extract
   1 pound American Brewmaster malted rice extract
   4 ounces maltodextrin
   2 ounces Tettnang hops (45 minutes)
   1 ounce Tettnang hops (1 minute)
     Wyeast No. 1028 British ale yeast
 1/2 cup corn sugar (to prime)

Original gravity:	1.050
Final gravity:	1.010
Boiling time:	45 minutes
Primary fermentation:	3 days at 65–70 °F (18–21 °C) in glass
Secondary fermentation:	17 days at 65–70 °F (18–21 °C) in glass
Age when judged:	2 1/2 months

Judges' Comments

"Nice clovelike aroma. Nice color and clarity. Little head, lacks retention. Distinct wheat flavor and lots of clove flavor. Very spicy but well balanced. Medium bodied. Very nice example of German weizen."

"Aroma—fruity, faint hint of cloves. Malt comes through. Hops faint. Appearance—good color, head retention okay, slightly cloudy, but okay for category. Flavor—cloves and green apples. Malt comes through well. Hops are faint. Very good balance. Good conditioning. Very good fruity aftertaste. Body—full, appropriate to style. Overall—excellent weizen. Very drinkable. I love it."

"Nice wheat [and] hop aroma. A bit of sour aroma. Color and clarity good. Not much head. Lovely wheat flavor. A little sour and sweet. Good hopping rate. Quite nice. Very drinkable. Fruity and sour tones in a wonderful combination."

Last Stop Wheezin'

Silver Medal, NHC, Weissbier, 1994
Phil Kaszuba, Essex Junction, Vermont
(Extract/Grain)

Ingredients for 5 Gallons
- 6 pounds wheat malt
- 5 pounds Harrington two-row malt
- 12 ounces Munton and Fison light dry malt extract
- 1/2 ounce Hallertau hops, 2.9% alpha acid (60 minutes)
- 1 ounce Hallertau hops, 2.9% alpha acid (30 minutes)
  - Wyeast No. 3068 Weihenstephan Wheat yeast
- 1 cup corn sugar (to prime)

Original gravity:	1.055
Final gravity:	—
Boiling time:	60 minutes
Primary fermentation:	4 days at 68 °F (20 °C) in glass
Secondary fermentation:	10 days at 68 °F (20 °C) in glass
Age when judged:	6 months

Brewer's Specifics
Mash grains at 152 °F (67 °C) for 120 minutes.

Judges' Comments
"Wheat comes through nicely. Could be more clovey. Finish bit too dry but very nice. Low hop bitterness. Nice hop-malt balance. Beer is very drinkable and clean but a bit too subtle."

"Flavor more harsh than aroma portends. Includes some questionable phenols and harsh bitterness that are not to style."

"Phenolic. Needs more clove [and] more fruit. I get a slightly solvent aroma. Very drinkable, but the clove and banana character need to be bigger."

Old Boots

Gold Medal, NHC, Weissbier, 1993
Walter Dobrowney, Saskatoon, Saskatchewan, Canada
(All-Grain)

Ingredients for 5 Gallons
5 1/2 pounds wheat malt
3 1/4 pounds two-row barley
  1/2 ounce Hallertau hops, 2.9% alpha acid (120 minutes)
  1/4 ounce Hallertau hops, 2.9% alpha acid (50 minutes)
  1/4 ounce Hallertau hops, 2.9% alpha acid (15 minutes)
     Brewers Resource CL62 yeast
1 4/5 quarts wort to prime

Original gravity:	1.050
Final gravity:	1.012
Boiling time:	120 minutes
Primary fermentation:	7 days at 62 °F (17 °C) in glass
Secondary fermentation:	12 days at 62 °F (17 °C) in glass
Age when judged:	4 months

Brewer's Specifics
Use a single decoction mash. Mash-in at 104 °F (40 °C) and heat to 122 °F (50 °C) for 25 minutes. Pull decoction, which is about 40% of the mash volume. While maintaining the rest mash temperature, heat decoction to 160 °F (71 °C) for 15 minutes. Raise decoction temperature to boiling for 20 minutes. Mix the 2 mashes, adjust, and hold temperature at 147 °F (64 °C) for 20 minutes, and then raise temperature to 160 °F (71 °C) until conversion. Heat to 170 °F (77 °C) and sparge.

Judges' Comments
"Gushed when opened. Clove up front then transforms to a sweet finish. Some vanilla and cinnamon flavors too."

"Main problem is gushing. Otherwise nice. Well balanced. Good clean cloves with just a slight sweetness on the finish."

"Foamed over like crazy on opening. Nice aromatics."

"Gusher, but no off-aromas. Slight sweet aftertaste, not overpowering for a wheat beer."

American Wheaten Ale

**Third Place, Club-Only Competition,
American-Style Ale, 1996
Tom Viaene, Kent, Washington
(All-Grain)**

Ingredients for 12 Gallons
- 9 pounds malted wheat
- 9 pounds Klages two-row malt
- 2 pounds Munich 10 °L malt
- 3 ounces Perle hops, 8.4% alpha acid (90 minutes)
- Wyeast No. 1056 American ale yeast

Original gravity:	1.057
Final gravity:	1.020
Boiling time:	90 minutes
Primary fermentation:	3 days in plastic open fermenter
Secondary fermentation:	10 days in glass
Age when judged:	—

Brewer's Specifics
Mash grains at 122 °F (50 °C) for 15 minutes, 150 °F (66 °C) for 30 minutes, 158 °F (70 °C) for 30 minutes, and mash-out at 168 °F (76 °C) for 10 minutes.

WEIZENBOCK

Spicy phenolics are the most noticeable flavor components of this winter wheat beer, which is the strongest of the weizens. This dark brown style may or may not be served with its yeast. Either way it retains its bready clovey character. Brewed to bock strength with an original gravity of 1.064–1.072 (16–18 °Plato), weizenbock is fermented at relatively moderate temperatures (66–68 °F [19–20 °C]) to partially subdue the production of esters and phenolics. Wheat malt gives the beer a heavy viscosity, often making it a trying beer to brew but wonderfully rich and heavy to drink. Though doppelbock is often called liquid bread, this beer better deserves that description. Very low hop bitterness is present with no hop flavor or aroma. Other flavor components mask any diacetyl produced. This is a classic Christmas sipper.

Three-Year Weizenbock

Gold Medal, NHC, German-Style Weizenbock, 1994
Tom O'Connor, Rockport, Maine
(Extract/Grain)

Ingredients for 6 Gallons
6 2/3 pounds Ireks wheat malt extract syrup
3 1/2 pounds Ireks Pilsener malt
  1/2 pound light crystal malt
  1/2 pound maltodextrin
  1/2 ounce Styrian Goldings hops, 5.3% alpha acid (60 minutes)
  1/2 ounce Saaz hops, 3.1% alpha acid (60 minutes)
1 1/5 ounces Saaz hops, 3.1% alpha acid (15 minutes)
       Wyeast No. 3068 Weihenstephan Wheat yeast
    1 cup corn sugar (to prime)

Original gravity:	1.060
Final gravity:	1.020
Boiling time:	60 minutes
Primary fermentation:	21 days at 60 °F (16 °C) in glass
Secondary fermentation:	5 days at 60 °F (16 °C) in glass
Age when judged:	4 1/2 months

Brewer's Specifics
Mash grains at 130 °F (54 °C) for 15 minutes. Raise temperature to 158 °F (70 °C) for 55 minutes.

Judges' Comments
"Malty as appropriate. More of a licorice aspect than clove or banana. Very good. Lacking only the intensity of phenol and esters that can be achieved."

"Maltiness there. Caramelly. Alcoholic. Not much spiciness or cloviness. Some sourness okay. Medicinal phenols detract from an otherwise very good beer."

Husker Championship Brew

NHC, Weizenbock, 1996
Loran Acton, Santa Rosa, California
(Extract/Grain)

Ingredients for 5 Gallons
7	pounds wheat malt
6	pounds The Beverage People™ amber syrup
3	pounds Munich malt
2	pounds Klages malt
1 3/4	pounds 60 °L crystal malt
1 3/4	pounds CaraPils malt
3/4	ounce Northern Brewer hop pellets, 2.4% alpha acid (60 minutes)
1 1/4	ounces Saaz hop pellets, 3.9% alpha acid (30 minutes)
3/4	ounce Saaz hop pellets, 3.9% alpha acid (10 minutes)
	Kent Weizen yeast
	force-carbonate

Original gravity:	1.070
Final gravity:	1.022
Boiling time:	90 minutes
Primary fermentation:	13 days at 70 °F (21 °C) in glass
Secondary fermentation:	45 days at 70 °F (21 °C) in glass
Age when judged:	—

Brewer's Specifics
Mash grains at 112 °F (44 °C) for 10 minutes, 124 °F (51 °C) for 25 minutes, and 154 °F (68 °C) for 30 minutes.

Weizenbock #112

Winner, Club-Only Competition, Weizenbock, 1996
John Griffiths, Fayetteville, Arkansas
(All-Grain)

Ingredients for 5 Gallons

8	pounds malted wheat
4	pounds pale malt
1/2	pound 60 °L crystal malt
1	ounce Perle hops, 6.3% alpha acid (110 minutes)
1	ounce Perle hops, 6.3% alpha acid (60 minutes)
1	ounce Hallertau Mittelfruh hops, 3.6% alpha acid (20 minutes)
	Wyeast No. 3056 Bavarian Wheat ale yeast
2/3	cup corn sugar (to prime)

Original gravity:	1.075
Final gravity:	1.024
Boiling time:	120 minutes
Primary fermentation:	9 days at 65 °F (18 °C) in plastic
Secondary fermentation:	9 days at 60 °F (16 °C) in glass
Age when judged:	7 months

Brewer's Specifics

Use a double decoction mashing schedule for all grains. Mash-in at 104 °F (40 °C) for 5 minutes. Heat to 122 °F (50 °C) for 25 minutes. Pull 1/3 of the thickest part of the mash and heat to 160 °F (71 °C) for 15 minutes. Boil for 20 minutes. Return to rest mash to raise temperature to 145 °F (63 °C) and hold for 10 minutes. Pull 1/3 of the mash's thickest part, heat to 160 °F (71 °C), and hold for 5 minutes. Boil for 20 minutes. Return to rest mash, raise temperature to 147 °F (64 °C), and hold for 15 minutes. Raise temperature to 169 °F (76 °C) and hold for 15 minutes. Sparge with 6 1/2 gallons of 175 °F (79 °C) water.

Judges' Comments

"Outstanding malty, yeasty, Germanic nose. Beautifully balanced malt and other fermentation characteristics. Recipe formulation excellent."

"Wonderful aroma. Great flavor. High maltiness. Low bitterness. Nice yeast character. Phenolics could be increased. A very good beer."

"Wonderful maltiness. Hops appropriate. Excellent balance. Maybe try a more aromatic yeast to produce more esters and phenolics."

Untitled

NHC, Weizenbock, 1996
Tom Spaulding, Santa Cruz, California
(All-Grain)

Ingredients for 5 Gallons
6 1/2 pounds white wheat malt
4 1/2 pounds Munich malt
5 3/4 ounces CaraVienne malt
1 ounce Belgian chocolate malt
1/2 ounce Perle hop pellets, 8.5% alpha acid (90 minutes)
1/2 ounce Mt. Hood hops, 5.3% alpha acid (45 minutes)
1/4 ounce Saaz hop pellets, 3% alpha acid (10 minutes)
1 teaspoon chalk
1/2 teaspoon calcium chloride
1/2 teaspoon lactic acid
Wyeast No. 3068 Weihenstephan Wheat yeast
4 1/4 ounces corn sugar (to prime)

Original gravity:	1.072
Final gravity:	1.020
Boiling time:	150 minutes
Primary fermentation:	4 days at 73 °F (23 °C) in glass
Secondary fermentation:	15 days at 70 °F (21 °C) in glass
Age when judged:	5 1/2 months

Brewer's Specifics
Mash grains at 152 °F (67 °C) for 60 minutes.

Midnight Breeze
Dunkel Weizenbock

Finalist, NHC, Weizenbock, 1996
Steve Nance, Winston-Salem, North Carolina
(Extract/Grain)

Ingredients for 5 Gallons

5	pounds Briess wheat malt
3 3/4	pounds Briess Munich 20 °L malt
3 1/10	pounds Briess weizen dry malt extract
3/5	pound Marie's Munich dry malt extract
1/2	pound Briess 90 °L crystal malt
1/2	pound Briess CaraPils malt
1/4	pound Briess chocolate malt
3	ounces Briess Special "B" roasted malt
1 1/4	ounces Hallertau Hersbrucker hop plugs, 3.5% alpha acid (60 minutes)
	Wyeast No. 3068 Weihenstephan Wheat yeast
	force-carbonate in keg

Original gravity:	1.069
Final gravity:	1.018
Boiling time:	75 minutes
Primary fermentation:	8 days at 68 °F (20 °C) in glass
Secondary fermentation:	10 days at 65 °F (20 °C) in glass
Age when judged:	5 months

Brewer's Specifics

Mash grains at 154 °F (68 °C) for 60 minutes.

Coinzenbok

NHC, Weizenbock, 1996
Joseph Cione, Laurel, Maryland
(All-Grain)

Ingredients for 5 Gallons
4	pounds Munich 10 °L malt
4	pounds malted wheat
3	pounds 10 °L caramel malt
1	pound 120 °L caramel malt
1/3	pound dark brown sugar
2	ounces Styrian Goldings hop plugs, 5.2% alpha acid (32 minutes)
	Wyeast No. 3068 Weihenstephan Wheat yeast
3/4	cup corn sugar (to prime)

Original gravity:	1.070
Final gravity:	1.008
Boiling time:	90 minutes
Primary fermentation:	9 days at 72 °F (22 °C) in plastic
Secondary fermentation:	—
Age when judged:	10 1/2 months

Brewer's Specifics
Mash-in at 160 °F (71 °C). Allow to cool to 150 °F (66 °C) for more than 120 minutes.

Weizmann Weizenbock

NHC, Weizenbock, 1996
Robert Craig, Stevenson, Washington
(All-Grain)

Ingredients for 5 1/2 Gallons

5	pounds German wheat malt
4 1/2	pounds Munich malt
3	pounds Maris Otter pale ale malt
1	pound German 70 °L crystal malt
3/10	pound 40 °L crystal malt
1/4	pound chocolate malt
1/4	pound Belgian Special "B" malt
1/5	pound roasted barley malt
1	ounce Hallertau hop pellets, 3.1% alpha acid (90 minutes)
3/4	ounce Hallertau hop pellets, 3.1% alpha acid (45 minutes)
1/4	ounce Hallertau hop pellets, 3.1% alpha acid (10 minutes)
	Wyeast No. 3068 Weihenstephan Wheat yeast
2/3	cup corn sugar (to prime)

Original gravity:	1.068
Final gravity:	1.024
Boiling time:	120 minutes
Primary fermentation:	10 days at 70–72 °F (21–22 °C)
Secondary fermentation:	3 weeks at 64 °F (18 °C) in glass
Age when judged:	5 months

Brewer's Specifics

Use a double decoction mash.

Son of Weizenbock

NHC, Weizenbock, 1996
Michael Murphy, Bellevue, Nebraska
(All-Grain)

Ingredients for 5 Gallons
- 8 pounds wheat malt
- 2 pounds Munich malt
- 2 pounds pale ale malt
- 1 pound aromatic malt
- 1 pound 120 °L crystal malt
- 3 ounces chocolate malt
- 1 1/2 ounces Tettnang hops, 5.9% alpha acid (60 minutes)
- 1/2 ounce Tettnang hops, 5.9% alpha acid (30 minutes)
- 1/4 ounce Tettnang hops, 5.9% alpha acid (5 minutes)
- 5 grams chalk added to mash water
- 3 grams gypsum added to mash water
- 2 grams salt added to mash water
- 2 grams epsom salt added to mash water
- Wyeast No. 3068 Weihenstephan Wheat yeast
- 3/4 cup corn sugar (to prime)

Original gravity:	1.077
Final gravity:	1.024
Boiling time:	60 minutes
Primary fermentation:	1 week at 60 °F (16 °C) in glass
Secondary fermentation:	1 week at 60 °F (16 °C) in glass
Age when judged:	2 1/2 months

Brewer's Specifics
Mash grains at 154 °F (68 °C) for 60 minutes.

Lots a Wheat

NHC, Weizenbock, 1996
Lindsay Enzminger, Hardin, Montana
(Extract/Grain)

Ingredients for 5 Gallons
6 3/5   pounds Ireks wheat malt extract
3   pounds Hollander light dry malt extract
10   ounces Briess 40 °L crystal malt
4   ounces roasted barley
4   ounces chocolate malt
1   ounce Hallertau Hersbrucker hop pellets,
      5.3% alpha acid (60 minutes)
1/2   ounce Tettnang hop pellets, 4.9% alpha acid (60 minutes)
   Wyeast No. 3056 Bavarian Wheat ale yeast
1   cup corn sugar (to prime)

Original gravity:	1.072
Final gravity:	1.021
Boiling time:	60 minutes
Primary fermentation:	12 days at 62 °F (17 °C) in plastic
Secondary fermentation:	10 days at 62 °F (17 °C) in glass
Age when judged:	7 months

Brewer's Specifics
Add crystal malt, roasted barley, and chocolate malt to 1 1/2 gallons of 160 °F (71 °C) water for 20 minutes. Sparge with 1/2 gallon of 170° F (77 °C) water. Add wheat malt, dry malt, and hop pellets to boil. Boil for 60 minutes. Sparge. Cool in water bath. Pitch yeast. Ferment at 62 °F (17 °C).

BELGIAN STRONG ALE/ TRAPPIST ALE

These styles aren't really the same. Trappist ale is technically a subcategory of Belgian strong ale, but since Trappist ales are becoming so popular to both drink and brew, the name is worth mentioning. Bear in mind that commercially one cannot use the name Trappist for beers not brewed by one of the six authentic monasteries of the Trappist order. The monks are always polite in reminding breweries of this fact, but it is a valid legal consideration. Belgian strong ale, Trappist or not, is one of the most complex and varied categories, as there are so many interpretations available. Indeed, it is the very essence of Belgian brewing to come up with your own personal blend of malts, yeast varieties, hops, and spices to produce a beer with a unique character. By definition, they are strong, ranging from 5.7–12 percent alcohol by volume. They are very complex, as most are fermented fairly warm, with multistrain yeasts that produce a huge variety of estery and phenolic tastes and smells. Hop character varies from minimal to high, and color is very pale to deep brown. Sometimes there is a hint of sourness as well, from lactic or other bacterial activity. One other substyle of Belgian ale, oud bruin, is brewed like a lambic and is very sour. However, in general, strong ales have a restrained tartness, if any. Homebrewers are urged to get an authentic strain of yeast. Several are available as liquid starters, or try culturing out of a bottle. Chimay is perhaps the easiest to culture. Use the lowest-gravity version, the Chimay Rouge, and try to get fresh refrigerated bottles to ensure maximum viability.

Plato Tonic Tripel

Gold Medal, NHC, Tripel, 1995
Eric Munger, Salem, Oregon
(All-Grain)

Ingredients for 5 Gallons
14	pounds Belgian Pilsener malt
2	pounds dextrose
1	ounce Ultra hops, 2.9% alpha acid (50 minutes)
1	ounce Perle hops, 7.3% alpha acid (30 minutes)
	Wyeast No. 3944 Belgian White Beer ale yeast
3/4	cup dextrose (to prime)

Original gravity:	1.081
Final gravity:	1.012
Boiling time:	90 minutes
Primary fermentation:	11 days at 62 °F (17 °C) in glass
Secondary fermentation:	2 weeks at 62 °F (17 °C) in glass
Age when judged:	4 months

Brewer's Specifics
Mash grains at 151 °F (66 °C) for 90 minutes. Boil with 2 pounds dextrose for 40 minutes.

Judges' Comments
"Low to medium malt flavor. Some spicy hop flavor. Good conditioning. Nicely balanced. Good clean tripel. Perhaps a bit astringent."

"Spicy malt flavor. Estery character—more pineapple than banana. Initial sweet spiciness is a little too prominent, but a very nice beer."

"Very nice! Smooth malt foundation leads to big alcoholic and warming finish. A great example. A bit too much of some of the esters and alcohols, but with a big beer like this it's difficult. I prefer a tripel that hides the alcohol better, but this is minor."

"Warming: alcohol presence is noticeable. Slightly sweet, a little clove. Outstanding beer. Perhaps the alcohol is a bit too noticeable, but otherwise a dynamite beer."

Untitled

Gold Medal, NHC, Tripel, 1996
Robert Hall Jr., Salt Point, New York
(All-Grain)

Ingredients for 5 Gallons

13	pounds DeWolf-Cosyns Pilsener malt
1 1/2	pounds turbinado sugar
1 1/5	ounces Northern Brewer hops, 7.5% alpha acid (90 minutes)
1/2	ounce Saaz hops, 3% alpha acid (15 minutes)
	Great Western Kent Trappist Ale No. A08 yeast
3/4	cup corn sugar (to prime)

Original gravity:	1.083
Final gravity:	1.011
Boiling time:	90 minutes
Primary fermentation:	2 weeks at 65 °F (18 °C) in glass
Secondary fermentation:	6 weeks at 65 °F (18 °C) in glass
Age when judged:	4 months

Brewer's Specifics

Mash grains at 67 °F (19°C) for 90 minutes.

Judges' Comments

"Nice beer but only lacks a malty background. Maybe use more malt. Less attenuation."

"Sweet and spicy with an alcohol kick. Good balance. Good overall strong beer, just more maltiness needed."

Tripel Trouble

Second Place, Club-Only Competition, Trappist Ale, 1996
Mike Riddle and Dan Hagewiesche, San Rafael, California
(All-Grain)

Ingredients for 5 Gallons

29	pounds Pilsener malt
2	pounds corn sugar
1	pound candi sugar
1 1/2	ounces Hallertau hops, 2.3% alpha acid (60 minutes)
1 1/2	ounces Hallertau hops, 2.3% alpha acid (45 minutes)
1	ounce Tettnang hops, 4% alpha acid (30 minutes)
1	ounce Tettnang hops, 4% alpha acid (15 minutes)
1	ounce Saaz hops, 3.1% alpha acid (finish)
1	ounce Saaz hops, 3.1% alpha acid (dry)
2	teaspoons gypsum
	Wyeast No. 1214 Belgian Abbey yeast
7	ounces corn sugar (to prime)

Original gravity:	1.096
Final gravity:	1.017
Boiling time:	90 minutes
Primary fermentation:	9 days at 70 °F (21 °C) in glass
Secondary fermentation:	7 days at 70 °F (21 °C) in glass
Age when judged:	2 1/2 months

Brewer's Specifics

Mash grains at 150 °F (66 °C) for 90 minutes. Boil the candi sugar and 2 pounds of corn sugar for 90 minutes. Remove 1/2 gallon of wort, caramelize, and return to main wort.

Judges' Comments

"Good example of the style. Alcohol is warming."

"Good color, clarity, and head retention."

"A fine representation of this style."

Untitled

Bronze Medal, NHC, Belgian Strong Ale, 1995
Paddy Giffen, Rohnert Park, California
(All-Grain)

Ingredients for 5 Gallons

20	pounds Klages malt
8	pounds Belgian Pilsener malt
4	pounds CaraVienne malt
3	pounds Belgian Munich malt
1	pound Special "B" malt
3/4	ounce Northern Brewer hops (60 minutes)
1	ounce Perle hops (30 minutes)
1/2	ounce Perle hops (30 minutes)
1	teaspoon calcium chloride added to mash water
	yeast [*I recommend using the Chimay yeast cultured from the bottle.—Ed.*]
	force-carbonate in keg

Original gravity:	1.087
Final gravity:	1.014
Boiling time:	60 minutes
Primary fermentation:	13 days at 68 °F (20 °C) in glass
Secondary fermentation:	30 days at 66 °F (19 °C) in glass
Age when judged:	—

Icy Hollow Brown Ale

Gold Medal, NHC, Flanders Brown, 1994
Shawn and Joseph Bosch, Wading River, New York
(Extract/Grain)

Ingredients for 5 Gallons

4	pounds Belgian two-row pale malt
2	pounds light dry malt extract
2	pounds Belgian Special "B" malt
1	pound Belgian aromatic malt
1	pound Munich malt
1	pound dark brown sugar
1	ounce Cascade hops, 5.7% alpha acid (75 minutes)
1/2	ounce Liberty hops, 4.6% alpha acid (10 minutes)
1/2	ounce Liberty hops, 4.6% alpha acid (finish)
	cultured bottle-conditioned Belgian brown ale yeast
10	ounces kraeusen (to prime)
3 1/4	ounces dextrose (to prime)

Original gravity:	1.071
Final gravity:	1.024
Boiling time:	90 minutes
Primary fermentation:	1 week at 68 °F (20 °C) in glass
Secondary fermentation:	7 weeks at 68 °F (20 °C) in glass
Tertiary fermentation:	3 weeks at 68 °F (20 °C) in glass
Age when judged:	6 months

Brewer's Specifics

Mash grains for 15 minutes at 123 °F (51 °C). Raise temperature to 152 °F (67 °C) for 60 minutes and 170 °F (77 °C) for 15 minutes.

Judges' Comments

"Beautifully tart and refreshing sourness with good malt roundness. Slightly high conditioning is not unpleasant. A lovely, almost Rodenbachlike beer, with refreshing, slightly sour-cherry palate."

"Slightly too brown. Use less crystal or dark malt. Nice aroma. Good sourness. A little too sweet and malty. Very drinkable."

L' Hommage par Hercule Poirrotté

Third Place, Club-Only Competition, Oud Bruin, 1996
Bruce Hammell, Trenton, New Jersey
(Extract)

Ingredients for 5 Gallons

6 3/5	pounds BrewFerm oud bruin malt extract
1 1/4	pounds Laaglander dark malt extract
2	pounds candi sugar (boil)
1	pound Karo dark syrup added to secondary
1 1/4	ounces Hallertau hops (60 minutes)
1/2	ounce Ultra hops (20 minutes)
180	grams oak chips added to secondary
20	grams gypsum
10	grams epsom salts
	Brewform Diablo Belgian ale yeast
	Radler *Lactobacillus* yeast added to secondary
	M65 *Lactobacillus* yeast added to secondary
	Peynaud *Lactobacillus* yeast added to secondary
	Bitech *Lactobacillus* yeast added to secondary

Original gravity:	1.056
Final gravity:	1.014
Primary fermentation:	45 days at 64 °F (18 °C) in glass
Secondary fermentation:	4 months at 70 °F (21 °C) in steel
Tertiary fermentation:	10 months at 70 °F (21 °C) in steel
Age when judged:	10 months

Judges' Comments

"Strong Spice aroma—very big."

"Very complex. Could spend all day picking different flavors out of this."

"Pleasing spiciness. Strong nose."

"Great beer. You've obviously done this before."

"Intense! Nicely complex—good blend of flavor components."

"Great effort! Please send more. Please, please!"

I Buried Pawl—Abby Road Ale

NHC, Dubbel, 1996
Gunther Jensen, Pacoima, California
(All-Grain)

Ingredients for 5 Gallons

9 1/2	pounds Belgian ale malt
2	pounds Special "B" malt
1	pound Belgian aromatic malt
1	pound Gambrinus Munich 100 °L malt
1	pound dark candi sugar
24	grams Saaz hops, 4.3% alpha acid (60 minutes)
22	grams Tettnang hops, 4.6% alpha acid (60 minutes)
	Chimay Red yeast
	force-carbonate in keg

Original gravity:	1.082
Final gravity:	1.016
Boiling time:	90 minutes
Primary fermentation:	9 days at 65 °F (18 °C) in glass
Secondary fermentation:	15 days at 65 °F (18 °C) in glass
Age when judged:	2 1/2 months

Brewer's Specifics

Mash grains at 132 °F (56 °C) for 30 minutes, 152 °F (67 °C) for 120 minutes, and 168 °F (76 °C) for 10 minutes.

Belgian 2X

NHC, Dubbel, 1996
John Tallarovic, Edwards, California
(All-Grain)

Ingredients for 5 Gallons

9 1/2 pounds Belgian two-row pale malt
1 pound Belgian dark candi sugar
1/2 pound 60 °L crystal malt
1/2 pound English brown malt
1 ounce Liberty hop pellets, 4.2% alpha acid (60 minutes)
3/4 cup dextrose (to prime)
Wyeast No. 1214 Belgian Abbey yeast

Original gravity:	1.072
Final gravity:	—
Boiling time:	60 minutes
Primary fermentation:	9 days at 68 °F (20 °C) in plastic
Secondary fermentation:	7 days at 68 °F (20 °C) in glass
Age when judged:	8 1/2 months

Brewer's Specifics

Mash grains at 152 °F (67 °C) for 90 minutes.

Dundee Bière d'Abbage à la Scourmont

NHC, Belgian Strong Ale, 1996
Scott Parr, Walnut Creek, California
(All-Grain)

Ingredients for 6 1/3 Gallons

11 1/2	pounds DeWolf-Cosyns Pilsener 1.8 °L malt
2 1/6	pounds DeWolf-Cosyns aromatic malt
1	pound DeWolf-Cosyns biscuit malt
1	pound DeWolf-Cosyns CaraMunich malt
3/4	pound Belgian dark candi sugar
7	ounces DeWolf-Cosyns Special "B" malt
2 1/4	ounces Czech Saaz hops, 2% alpha acid (60 minutes)
1	ounce Mt. Hood hops, 5.4% alpha acid (60 minutes)
1/2	ounce Czech Saaz hops (finish, 5 minutes)
2	teaspoons Irish moss (60 minutes)
	Wyeast No. 1214 Belgian Abbey yeast
5	ounces dextrose plus fresh yeast added at bottling (to prime)

Original gravity:	1.074
Final gravity:	1.018
Boiling time:	90 minutes
Primary fermentation:	7 days at 62 °F (17 °C) in glass
Secondary fermentation:	7 days at 62 °F (17 °C) in glass
Tertiary fermentation:	3 days at 62 °F (17 °C) in glass with Polyclar
Age when judged:	3 1/2 months

Brewer's Specifics

Mash grains at 152 °F (67 °C) for 60 minutes and 170 °F (76 °C) for 10 minutes.

Dubbel Play

NHC, Dubbel, 1996
Allen Bavry Jr., Sarasota, Florida
(All-Grain)

Ingredients for 5 Gallons

- 8 1/2 pounds Klages two-row malt
- 1 pound dark candi sugar
- 1/2 pound honey malt
- 1/2 pound aromatic malt
- 1/4 pound 60 °L crystal malt
- 2 ounces Special "B" malt
- 2 ounces chocolate malt
- 1 ounce Hallertau hop pellets, 4.6% alpha acid (60 minutes)
- 1/2 ounce Hallertau hop pellets, 4.6% alpha acid (2 minutes)
- Wyeast No. 1214 Belgian Abbey yeast
- 3/4 cup corn sugar (to prime)

Original gravity:	1.060
Final gravity:	1.008
Boiling time:	60 minutes
Primary fermentation:	7 days at 68 °F (20 °C) in glass
Secondary fermentation:	14 days at 68 °F (20 °C) in glass
Age when judged:	8 1/2 months

Brewer's Specifics

Mash grains at 122 °F (50 °C) for 30 minutes. Raise mash temperature to 154 °F (68 °C) for 45 minutes until conversion is complete.

FALL

BROWN ALE

Some define this style as the bottled equivalent of mild ale, but it may be stronger than the average mild. It generally has an original gravity of 1.035–1.049 (9–12.5 °Plato), resulting in an alcohol content of 3.5–4.5 percent by volume. The color of brown ale is dark amber to chestnut, and it is brewed from a combination of dark caramel malts and a small percentage of black malt. It is lightly hopped for bitterness with little or no hop flavor and no aroma. Very low to low diacetyl is appropriate. American brown ale is similar but often is more heavily hopped and significantly stronger.

Back to Back Double Brown Ale

Gold Medal, NHC, English Brown, 1996
Michael S. Sackett, Wichita, Kansas
(All-Grain)

Ingredients for 5 Gallons
5	pounds Klages malt
3	pounds Munich malt
2	pounds Vienna malt
1	pound 60 °L crystal malt
3/4	pound 20 °L crystal malt
1/4	pound roasted malt
1/4	pound chocolate malt
1	ounce Fuggles hop pellets, 4.4% alpha acid (75 minutes)
1	ounce Willamette hop pellets, 3.7% alpha acid (75 minutes)
1/2	ounce Cascade hop pellets, 4.2% alpha acid (15 minutes)
1	ounce Cascade hop pellets, 4.2% alpha acid (3 minutes)
	Wyeast No. 1056 American ale yeast
1	cup corn sugar (to prime)

Original gravity:	1.068
Final gravity:	1.012
Boiling time:	75 minutes
Primary fermentation:	2 weeks at 70 °F (21 °C) in plastic
Secondary fermentation:	—
Age when judged:	4 months

Brewer's Specifics
Mash grains at 148 °F (64 °C) for 90 minutes.

Judges' Comments
"Nice caramel sweetness in beginning. Astringency from roasted grains is a bit much. Aroma could be better. Oxidized aroma is a problem."

"On the low end of the color scale. Only appears to be about 14 SRM. Very full-flavored beer but overly roasty. Big in the mouth. Try cutting back on the roasted grains."

Get Your Thumb out of Your Butt

Bronze Medal, NHC, English Brown, 1994
Russell Levitt, Bloomington, Indiana
(All-Grain)

Ingredients for 12 Gallons

16	pounds pale ale malt
1	pound wheat malt
1	pound dextrin malt
5 3/4	ounces Belgian biscuit malt
5 1/3	ounces CaraPils malt
5 1/4	ounces Special "B" malt
4 3/4	ounces Munich malt
4 1/2	ounces aromatic malt
4 1/2	ounces CaraMunich malt
3	ounces black patent malt
1 1/2	ounces Goldings hops (60 minutes)
1	ounce Goldings hops (30 minutes)
1/2	ounce Goldings hops (20 minutes)
	Wyeast No. 1028 London ale yeast
	force-carbonate in keg

Original gravity:	1.046
Final gravity:	1.011
Boiling time:	75 minutes
Primary fermentation:	3 weeks at 64 °F (18 °C) in glass
Secondary fermentation:	—
Age when judged:	2 1/2 months

Brewer's Specifics

Mash grains for 60 minutes at 153–154 °F (67–68 °C). Sparge with 170 °F (77 °C) water.

Judges' Comments

"Nice effort! Need more malty sweetness for this style, and a little more hops would make this a great brown."

Buffalo Pass Brown Ale

Bronze Medal, NHC, American Brown, 1995
Dave Shaffer, Lafayette, Colorado
(All-Grain)

Ingredients for 10 Gallons

17	pounds Klages malt
1	pound Ireks dark crystal malt
1	pound 120 °L crystal malt
1	pound Special "B" roasted malt
1	pound CaraPils malt
1	pound Munich malt
1	pound wheat malt
3/8	pound chocolate malt
3/8	pound roasted barley
1 1/2	ounces Cascade hops, 5.5% alpha acid (100 minutes)
1 1/2	ounces Hallertau hops, 5.2% alpha acid (100 minutes)
1 1/2	ounces Hallertau hops, 5.2% alpha acid (15 minutes)
1 1/2	ounces Hallertau Hersbrucker hop pellets, 2.6% alpha acid (15 minutes)
1 1/2	ounces Hallertau hops, 5.2% alpha acid (3 minutes)
1 1/2	ounces Hallertau Hersbrucker hop pellets, 2.6% alpha acid (3 minutes)
3	ounces Hallertau Hersbrucker hop pellets, 2.6% alpha acid (dry)
	Wyeast No. 1056 American ale yeast
3/4	cup corn sugar (to prime)

Original gravity:	1.054
Final gravity:	1.012
Boiling time:	120 minutes
Primary fermentation:	16 days at 62 °F (17 °C) in glass
Secondary fermentation:	5 days at 52 °F (11 °C) in glass
Age when judged:	3 months

Brewer's Specifics

Protein rest is at 130 °F (54 °C) for 25 minutes. Conversion rest is at 151 °F (66 °C) for 25 minutes, 153 °F (67 °C) for 15 minutes, and 157 °F (69 °C) for 20 minutes. Sparge with 170 °F (77 °C) water to collect 13 1/2 gallons wort.

Milestone Mild

NHC, Mild and Brown Ale, 1996
Gene Pribula, Wyndmere, North Dakota
(All-Grain)

Ingredients for 10 Gallons

9	pounds two-row malt
1 1/2	pounds chocolate malt
1	pound 135 °L crystal malt
11	ounces CaraPils malt
6	ounces black patent malt
1 1/2	ounces East Kent Goldings hops, 5.7% alpha acid (60 minutes)
1/2	ounce Fuggles hop pellets, 4.2% alpha acid (5 minutes)
8	grams chalk
2	grams epsom salts
2	grams calcium chloride
	Burton ale yeast
	force-carbonate

Original gravity:	1.040
Final gravity:	1.012
Boiling time:	90 minutes
Primary fermentation:	7 days at 65 °F (18 °C) in glass
Secondary fermentation:	3 days at 65 °F (18 °C) in glass
Age when judged:	4 months

Brewer's Specifics
Mash grains at 153 °F (67 °C) for 60 minutes.

30 CALIFORNIA COMMON

Known as "steam beer" before Prohibition, California common beer is light amber to copper with toasted or caramellike maltiness in its aroma and flavor. Most examples of the style are moderate in strength with original gravities from 1.048–1.058 (12–14 °Plato). Hop bitterness, aroma, and flavor are all medium to high with restrained fruitiness. The special yeast used is technically a lager strain, but it works well at fairly warm temperatures. The beer is fermented at 62–65 °F (17–18 °C), but given a cold conditioning. Its diacetyl character is minimal.

Untitled

Semifinalist, World Homebrew Contest,
California Common, 1997
David Graham, Park Ridge, Illinois
(Extract/Grain)

Ingredients for 5 Gallons

4	pounds Alexander's pale malt extract
3 3/4	pounds Morgan Master rice unhopped malt extract
1	pound domestic 20 °L caramel malt
1	ounce Hallertau hops (50 minutes)
1	ounce Cascade hops (5 minutes)
1	teaspoon Irish moss (15 minutes)
	Wyeast No. 2112 California lager yeast
3/4	cup corn sugar (to prime)

Original gravity:	1.062
Final gravity:	1.022
Boiling time:	90 minutes
Primary fermentation:	3 days at 70–75 °F (21–24 °C), then drop temperature to 60–65 °F (16–18 °C) for 2 days in glass
Secondary fermentation:	6 days at 60–65 °F (16–18 °C) in glass
Age when judged:	—

Brewer's Specifics

Steep caramel malt at 135 °F (57 °C) for 30 minutes and then at 155 °F (68 °C) for 30 minutes.Wring out bag and rinse twice. Add wort to boiling pot with malt extract and water to make 2 1/2 gallons. Boil for 90 minutes. Cool wort and add to primary with water to make 5 gallons.

Judges' Comments

"Decent-sized hop aroma. Toasty aroma is lacking. Color and head retention are good. Clarity is okay. Starts out with some toastiness. Moves into a phenolic middle and finish. Lacks 'toasted- or caramellike maltiness.' Bitterness level is good for this style. Body is fine for this style. Overall you have a nice beer here. It has the basic beginnings of a California common beer. There is an underlying phenolic flavor, however. Check your choice of yeast and try this same recipe again."

Mort's Steamer

Bronze Medal, NHC, California Common Beer, 1996
Steve Rittenhouse, Los Angeles, California
(Extract/Grain)

Ingredients for 5 Gallons

5	pounds Klages malt
3 1/3	pounds gold malt extract
1	pound 40 °L crystal malt
1/2	pound domestic six-row malt
1 1/3	ounces Northern Brewer hops, 8.8% alpha acid (60 minutes)
1/2	ounce Cascade hops, 4.9% alpha acid (10 minutes)
1/2	ounce Chinook hops, 10.7% alpha acid (10 minutes)
1/2	ounce Cascade hop pellets (dry)
	Wyeast No. 1056 American ale yeast
3/4	cup corn sugar (to prime)

Original gravity:	1.050
Final gravity:	1.014
Boiling time:	60 minutes
Primary fermentation:	8 days at 55 °F (13 °C) in glass
Secondary fermentation:	14 days at 55 °F (13 °C) in glass
Age when judged:	6 months

Brewer's Specifics

Mash grains at 155 °F (68 °C) for 60 minutes.

Judges' Comments

"Malt aroma is masked by a light fruitiness. Good amber color. Wonderful head retention. A clean fermentation and a well-made beer. "

"Very bright color—good, maybe just slightly dark. Excellent effort. Great control. Slight recipe tweaks will really make this great!"

"Toasty malt aroma with subtle hops as well. Very drinkable beer. Nice effort. Additional hops in middle end will help."

Off Peak Common II

Bronze Medal, NHC, California Common, 1995
Carl Eidbo, Fargo, North Dakota
(All-Grain)

Ingredients for 11 Gallons

16	pounds two-row American pale malt
3 1/2	pounds 20 °L crystal malt
2 1/2	ounces Northern Brewer hops, 9.5% alpha acid (60 minutes)
1	ounce Northern Brewer hops, 9.5% alpha acid (15 minutes)
1	ounce Northern Brewer hops, 9.5% alpha acid (10 minutes)
1	ounce Northern Brewer hops, 9.5% alpha acid (5 minutes)
	Wyeast No. 2112 California lager yeast
	force-carbonate in kegs

Original gravity:	1.043
Final gravity:	1.011
Boiling time:	60 minutes
Primary fermentation:	3 days at 65 °F (18 °C) in glass
Secondary fermentation:	3 weeks at 65 °F (18 °C) in glass
Tertiary fermentation:	3 months at 42 °F (6 °C) kegged in stainless steel
Age when judged:	2 months

Brewer's Specifics

Mash grains at 152 °F (67 °C) for 60 minutes.

Judges' Comments

"Good hop and malt aroma. Good body. Good hop aftertaste."

"Very clear. Color right on. Good head and retention. Malt and hops well behaved. Some toasted malt—not too sweet. A little dry aftertaste. No fruitiness or diacetyl. Very drinkable beer. Could have more than one. Only fault is a dry aftertaste and finish."

Sonoma Steam

NHC, California Common, 1996
Dave Lewis, Sonoma, California
(All-Grain)

Ingredients for 6 Gallons

8	pounds DeWolf-Cosyns Pilsener malt
4	pounds Great Western Kent lager malt
1 1/2	pounds Belgian Munich malt
1	pound 20 °L caramel malt
1/2	pound 40 °L caramel malt
3/4	ounce Perle hop pellets, 9.5% alpha acid (60 minutes)
1/4	ounce Northern Brewer hop pellets, 6.4% alpha acid (45 minutes)
1/2	ounce Northern Brewer hop pellets, 6.4% alpha acid (30 minutes)
1/4	ounce Perle hop pellets, 9.5% alpha acid (30 minutes)
1/4	ounce Cascade hop pellets, 5.5% alpha acid (30 minutes)
1	ounce Northern Brewer hop pellets, 6.4% alpha acid (2 minutes)
1/2	ounce Cascade hop pellets, 5.5% alpha acid (2 minutes)
	Wyeast No. 2112 California lager yeast
	force-carbonate

Original gravity:	1.054
Final gravity:	1.014
Boiling time:	120 minutes
Primary fermentation:	10 days at 55–60 °F (13–16 °C) in glass
Secondary fermentation:	6 weeks at 34 °F (1 °C) in glass
Age when judged:	3 months

Brewer's Specifics

Mash grains at 152–157 °F (67–69 °C) for 90 minutes and 170 °F (77 °C) for 15 minutes.

Judges' Comments

"Hop aroma medium. Malty aroma somewhat subdued. Slight fruitiness. Excellent clarity. Good amber color. Wonderful head and retention. Maltiness in front gives way to nice hop flavor and strong bitterness. Sulfury flavor lingers on palate."

Strapping Steam Beer

Gold Medal, NHC, California Common, 1996
Philip Gravel, Lisle, Illinois
(All-Grain)

Ingredients for 6 Gallons
9	pounds DeWolf-Cosyns Munich light malt
6	pounds DeWolf-Cosyns Pilsener two-row malt
1/2	pound CaraPils dextrin malt
1/4	pound 40 °L crystal malt
1/4	pound 90 °L crystal malt
1 1/2	ounces Cluster hop pellets, 7.3% alpha acid (60 minutes)
1 1/2	ounces Cluster hop pellets, 7.3% alpha acid (60 minutes)
1/2	ounce Brewers Gold hops, 7.6% alpha acid (60 minutes)
1	ounce Northern Brewer hop plugs, 7.8% alpha acid (20 minutes)
1/2	teaspoon Irish moss (15 minutes) hydrated in 1 cup warm water
	Wyeast No. 2112 California lager yeast
5	ounces corn sugar (to prime)

Original gravity:	1.044
Final gravity:	1.014
Boiling time:	75 minutes
Primary fermentation:	7 days at 60 °F (16 °C) in glass
Secondary fermentation:	7 days at 60 °F (16 °C) in glass
Age when judged:	3 months

Brewer's Specifics
Mash grains at 120 °F (49 °C) for 30 minutes, 138 °F (59 °C) for 25 minutes, and 152 °F (67 °C) for 35 minutes. Heat mash to 175 °F (79 °C) for mash-out. Sparge with 180 °F (82 °C) water to collect 7 gallons.

Judges' Comments
"Very fruity—appropriate for the style but maybe a little too pronounced."

"Wonderfully drinkable beer. Very refreshing. Balance leans a bit far to bitterness. Relatively low hop flavors and caramel does not come through."

"Subtle toffee, sweet plum maltiness with dominant bitter finish. Some astringent citrus rind hints in long finish distract from malt balance. Nicely effervescent."

Steamer

Gold Medal, NHC, California Common, 1994
Walter Dobrowney, Saskatoon, Saskatchewan, Canada
(All-Grain)

Ingredients for 5 Gallons
- 9 pounds Harrington two-row malt
- 4 ounces Munton and Fison crystal malt
- 4 ounces German dark crystal malt
- 4 ounces carastan malt
- 4 ounces biscuit malt
- 1 ounce Northern Brewer hops, 7.5% alpha acid (70 minutes)
- 1/2 ounce Cascade hops, 5.8% alpha acid (25 minutes)
- 1/2 ounce Northern Brewer hops, 7.5% alpha acid (10 minutes)
- 1/2 ounce Northern Brewer hops, 7.5% alpha acid (2 minutes)
- 1/2 ounce Northern Brewer hops, 7.5% alpha acid (dry)
- 1/2 ounce Cascade hops, 5.8% alpha acid (dry)
- Brewers Resource CL-690 yeast
- force-carbonate in keg

Original gravity:	1.051
Final gravity:	1.011
Boiling time:	70 minutes
Primary fermentation:	5 days at 62 °F (17 °C) in glass
Secondary fermentation:	12 days at 62 °F (17 °C) in glass
Age when judged:	6 months

Brewer's Specifics
Mash grains at 152 °F (67 °C) for 60 minutes.

Judges' Comments
"Nice malt up front with hops close behind. Carbonation level good. Maybe a touch more caramel? Aftertaste a bit short. Very nice beer! Could drink this all day. Might benefit from slightly more malt character in nose and flavor."

"Hop bitterness in aftertaste okay. A little sourness. Malt character is not evident. Malt-hop balance needs some adjustment. Good color and carbonation. Body increase would help—needs higher mash temperature."

"Malt and hops evident. Well balanced. Very good. Drinkable. Balance in taste is good. Aftertaste smooth. Aroma is good. Malt is evident."

Steam Roller

Gold Medal, NHC, California Common, 1995
Ed Wolfe and Carol Liquori, Iowa City, Iowa
(All-Grain)

Ingredients for 7 Gallons

10	pounds pale malt
1	pound 60 °L crystal malt
1	pound toasted malt
1 1/2	ounces Centennial hops, 10.9% alpha acid (60 minutes)
1	ounce Cascade hops, 4.9% alpha acid (15 minutes)
1	ounce Fuggles hops, 3.5% alpha acid (15 minutes)
1/2	ounce Cascade hops, 4.9% alpha acid (steep 30 minutes)
1/2	ounce Fuggles hops, 3.5% alpha acid (steep 30 minutes)
1/2	ounce Cascade hops, 4.9% alpha acid (dry, 14 days)
1/2	ounce Fuggles hops, 3.5% alpha acid (dry, 14 days)
	Aeonbrau's California Common yeast
2/3	cup corn sugar (to prime)

Original gravity:	1.050
Final gravity:	1.015
Boiling time:	75 minutes
Primary fermentation:	7 days at 55 °F (13 °C) in glass
Secondary fermentation:	21 days at 55 °F (13 °C) in glass
Age when judged:	4 months

Brewer's Specifics
Mash grains at 147 °F (64 °C) for 90 minutes.

Judges' Comments
"Toasted malt. Sweet. Medium hop bitterness. Good hop flavor. Sweet astringency in aftertaste would keep me from drinking a second. It's much better as it warms."

"Rich and full but with yeast flavors. Good flavor with aftertaste."

EISBOCK

As soon as the weather gets cold, it is time to brew the high-gravity bottom-fermenting eisbock. Deep reddish brown from a combination of light and dark caramel malts, this style has a great deal of alcohol and residual sugar from the brewing process, making it a bit like a liqueur. A classic German example begins with a gravity of 1.006 (24 °Plato), ferments with lager yeast, and is then frozen. When the ice is removed, the alcohol, which has a much lower freezing temperature, is left behind, yielding an alcohol content of 10 percent by volume. Lager this powerful beer for several months. It is traditional to enjoy it on the last Saturday of March.

EKU 27.5

Gold Medal, NHC, Eisbock, 1995
Dennis Davison, Greenfield, Wisconsin
(Extract/Grain)

Ingredients for 10 Gallons

23	pounds Munton and Fison light malt extract
5	pounds DeWolf-Cosyns Pilsener malt
5	pounds DeWolf-Cosyns CaraPils malt
5	pounds DeWolf-Cosyns CaraMunich malt
2	ounces Perle hops, 8.1% alpha acid (60 minutes)
1	ounce Perle hops, 8.1% alpha acid (45 minutes)
1	ounce Hallertau hops, 3.2% alpha acid (10 minutes)
	Wyeast No. 2007 Pilsen lager yeast
	force-carbonate in keg

Original gravity:	1.116
Final gravity:	1.024
Boiling time:	90 minutes
Primary fermentation:	2 weeks at 55 °F (13 °C) in glass
Secondary fermentation:	6 months at 32 °F (0 °C) in glass
Age when judged:	9 months

Brewer's Specifics

Mash grains at 154 °F (68 °C) until conversion. After fermentation is complete, place the keg outdoors at –30 °F (–34 °C) until you can hear the sound of ice crystals hitting the side of the keg. After shaking, siphon under pressure into a clean keg. Repeat procedure until you've collected a total of 1 gallon of ice.

Judges' Comments

"Alcohol apparent. Maltiness rounds it out. Has a high alcohol without the nastiness of fusels—very impressive. A hard style to hit without overdoing the alcohol or getting off-tastes."

"Sweet. Cloying. Strong. Alcohol is soft. Warms all the way down. Hint of hops. Only 50 I've given in 10 years of judging."

"Malt and alcohol. Great balance. The only thing wrong with this beer is that there's only one bottle."

Untitled

Bronze Medal, NHC, Eisbock, 1996
David Lloyd and Richard Dobson, Gainesville, Texas
(All-Grain)

Ingredients for 10 Gallons

  15   pounds two-row Durst malt
   7   pounds Munich 10 °L malt
   2   pounds CaraPils malt
   2   pounds 40 °L crystal malt
  14   AAU Perle hop pellets (60 minutes)
   1   ounce Hallertau hops (20 minutes)
       Wyeast No. 2206 Bavarian lager yeast
       force-carbonate

Original gravity:	1.070
Final gravity:	1.028
Boiling time:	60 minutes
Primary fermentation:	7 days at 48 °F (9 °C) in glass
Secondary fermentation:	7 days at 48 °F (9 °C) in glass
Age when judged:	4 months

Brewer's Specifics

Mash grains at 155 °F (68 °C) for 60 minutes.

Judges' Comments

"Color and clarity good. Excellent head retention for the style. Definite nuttiness in flavor. High alcohol and maltiness. Roughness in flavor may indicate lack of cold aging."

"Nicely brewed beer—very intense flavor—nice and tawny. Beer could have a cleaner flavor. It's more like an ale than a lager but still a nice recipe."

S-K Trubulator

Gold Medal, NHC, Eisbock, 1993
Ron Kribbs and Rick Skillman, Naples, Florida
(Extract/Grain)

Ingredients for 15 Gallons
- 40 pounds Klages two-row malt
- 2 gallons Alexander's amber extract
- 5 ounces Hallertau hops (60 minutes)
- 3 ounces Tettnang hops (15 minutes)
- Wyeast No. 2308 Munich lager yeast

Original gravity:	1.130
Final gravity:	—
Boiling time:	60 minutes
Primary fermentation:	8 months at 38 °F (3 °C)
Secondary fermentation:	4 months at 38 °F (3 °C)
Age when judged:	3 years and 5 months

Brewer's Specifics
Mash grains at 158 °F (70 °C) for 60 minutes. Kraeusen with wort.

Judges' Comments
"Full body. Great for style. Rich and smooth. Would benefit from more alcohol 'warming.' Thanks for entering this beer!"

"Good malt sweetness and alcohol to back it up. Great effort."

"Explosive malt flavor lingers, capped by the expected alcoholic rush at end. Outstanding. Tasty and sweet. This is an outstanding beer."

"Nice malt-alcohol balance. Creamy and full. This is a very well-made beer—be proud."

"Rich malty sweetness with nice warming alcohols behind it. Nice sweet finish. Mild esters in flavor. Very nice. Excellent brew."

Untitled

NHC, Eisbock, 1996
Steven Olson, Duluth, Minnesota
(All-Grain)

Ingredients for 7 Gallons

12 1/2	pounds Harrington two-row malt
5 1/2	pounds Munich 10 °L malt
1 1/2	pounds Belgian pale malt
1 1/2	pounds CaraPils malt
1	pound 60 °L crystal malt
1	ounce Perle hop pellets, 7.3% alpha acid (60 minutes)
1/4	ounce Cluster hop pellets, 7% alpha acid (30 minutes)
1/4	ounce Cluster hop pellets, 7% alpha acid (15 minutes)
1/2	ounce Hallertau hops, 4.5% alpha acid in hop back
	Wyeast No. 2206 Bavarian lager yeast
3/4	cup corn sugar (to prime)

Original gravity:	1.106
Final gravity:	1.026
Boiling time:	70 minutes
Primary fermentation:	18 days at 50 °F (10 °C) in glass
Secondary fermentation:	14 days at 50 °F (10 °C) in glass
Tertiary fermentation:	28 days at 30 °F (–1 °C) in glass
Age when judged:	4 months

Brewer's Specifics

Use single decoction mash schedule. Total time is 185 minutes.

MILD ALE

One of the lowest gravity beers of the season, mild requires little time to brew and condition and is best enjoyed on draught. It is typically dark copper to chestnut brown with an original gravity of 1.030–1.035 (8–9 °Plato), yielding 3–3.5 percent alcohol by volume. Lightly bittered, it possesses low hop flavor and aroma with predominant malt flavors. Fruitiness and esters are typically low with low to moderate diacetyl flavors.

Wild Child Mild

Gold Medal, NHC, English Mild, 1995
John Sullivan, St. Louis, Missouri
(All-Grain)

Ingredients for 10 Gallons
6	pounds Belgian Munich malt
5 1/2	pounds Belgian pale ale malt
2	pounds biscuit malt
1	pound dextrin malt
1/4	pound chocolate malt
1/4	pound black patent malt
1/4	pound Belgian aromatic malt
1/4	pound CaraVienne malt
1/4	pound CaraMunich malt
1/4	pound Special "B" malt
3	ounces Willamette hops, 4.2% alpha acid (60 minutes)
1	teaspoon gypsum added to sparge
1/2	teaspoon gypsum added to mash
	Wyeast No. 1728 Scottish ale yeast
3/4	cup corn sugar (to prime)

Original gravity:	1.041
Final gravity:	1.010
Boiling time:	60 minutes
Primary fermentation:	6 days at 62 °F (17 °C) in glass
Secondary fermentation:	8 days at 62 °F (17 °C) in glass
Age when judged:	5 months

Brewer's Specifics
Mash grains at 152 °F (67 °C) for 120 minutes.

Judges' Comments
"Roasty flavor as in the aroma. Some hop flavor. A little bitterness. No residual sweetness. Nice drinkable beer."

"Too much roastiness in flavor. Cut back on black patent malt. This beer is fine with very few flaws."

Thirty Beer

Silver Medal, NHC, English Dark Mild, 1996
James Weiner, La Jolla, California
(Extract/Grain)

Ingredients for 5 Gallons

8	pounds Great Western two-row pale malt
1/2	pound 60 °L crystal malt
1/4	pound chocolate malt
1/4	pound black patent malt
1 1/4	cups dry malt extract
32	grams Fuggles hops, 4.4% alpha acid (60 minutes)
20	grams Northern Brewer hops, 7% alpha acid (60 minutes)
14	grams Fuggles hops, 4.4% alpha acid (1 minute)
1/4	teaspoon Irish moss (20 minutes)
	Wyeast No. 1084 Irish ale yeast

Original gravity:	1.045
Final gravity:	1.010
Boiling time:	60 minutes
Primary fermentation:	7 days at 68 °F (20 °C) in glass
Secondary fermentation:	7 days at 65 °F (18 °C) in glass
Age when judged:	5 months

Brewer's Specifics

Mash grains at 155 °F (68 °C) for 60 minutes.

Judges' Comments

"Some roast in the nose, no hop, pretty delicate aroma. Malty, roasty flavor. Some residual sweetness. Some bitterness possibly from the grain. Reasonably well-balanced flavors. Very high carbonation for a mild."

Kick in the Rear Mild Ale

Mild Ale, 1997
Charlie Papazian, Boulder, Colorado
(All-Grain)

Ingredients for 5 Gallons

2 1/2 pounds English two-row pale malt
  2 pounds English mild malt
  1 pound English 40 °L crystal malt
 1/2 pound wheat malt
 1/2 pound English carastan malt
 1/2 pound English chocolate malt
4 1/2 HBU English Fuggles hops (75 minutes)
2 1/2 HBU English Kent Goldings hops (30 minutes)
 1/4 teaspoon Irish moss
     Wyeast No. 1968 Special London yeast
 3/4 cup corn sugar (to prime)

Original gravity:	1.036
Final gravity:	1.006
Boiling time:	75 minutes
Primary fermentation:	4–6 days
Secondary fermentation:	2 weeks at 60 °F (15.6 °C)
Tertiary fermentation:	—

Brewer's Specifics

Employ a single step infusion mash to mash the grains. Add 7 quarts (6.6 liters) of 168 °F (75.6 °C) water to the crushed grain, stir, stabilize, and hold the temperature at 153 °F (67 °C) for 60 minutes.

After conversion, raise temperature to 167 °F (75 °C), lauter, and sparge with 3 gallons (11.4 liters) of 170 °F (77 °C) water. Collect about 3.5 gallons (11.4 liters) of runoff, add bittering hops, and bring to a full and vigorous boil.

The total boil time will be 75 minutes. When 30 minutes remain, add flavor hops. When 10 minutes remain, add Irish moss. After a total wort boil of 75 minutes (reducing the wort volume to just over 2.5 gallons [9.5 liters]) turn off the heat, keep lid securely in place, and place pot in cold bath water for 15 minutes to aid in cooling. Then separate or strain out and sparge hops. Direct the hot wort into a sanitized fermenter containing 2 gallons (7.6 liters) of very cold water. If necessary add additional cold water to achieve a 5-gallon (19-liter) batch size. Chill the wort to 70 °F (21 °C). Aerate the cooled wort well. Add active yeast and ferment.

Flavor Comments

Deep reddish brown. Strong, malty-sweet, toasted, and aromatic crystal malt characters predominate in the aroma. The aromatic maltiness does not overpower the flavor. This beer is wonderfully balanced with suggestions of roasted malt dryness and cocoa character. This light-bodied dry ale with high drinkability is well attenuated and very quenching with lightness in the mouthfeel. Hop bitterness is evident but is not a central theme. It provides a counterpoint to the malt character. Aftertaste is clean. Diacetyl is absent in the flavor. Shakespeare would have liked it.

English Mild

Gold Medal, NHC, Brown Ale, 1993
Douglas Brown, Redondo Beach, California
(Extract/Grain)

Ingredients for 5 Gallons
4	pounds Williams Australian dry malt extract
1	pound Klages malt
1/2	pound domestic two-row malt
5	ounces CaraPils malt
3 1/2	ounces black patent malt
3 1/2	ounces 80 °L crystal malt
2	ounces chocolate malt
7/10	ounce Fuggles hops, 3.1% alpha acid (60 minutes)
	Kent English ale yeast (dry)
1/2	cup dextrose (to prime)

Original gravity:	1.034
Final gravity:	1.011
Boiling time:	60 minutes
Primary fermentation:	14 days at 68 °F (20 °C) in plastic
Secondary fermentation:	—
Age when judged:	7 months

Brewer's Specifics
Mash grains with 2 1/2 gallons of water at 140 °F (60 °C) for 40 minutes. Raise temperature to 155 °F (68 °C) for 20 minutes. Sparge with 1 gallon water at 170 °F (77 °C). Boil 3 1/2 gallons water and extract for 60 minutes.

Judges' Comments
"Malt sweetness low, very thin. Needs more maltodextrin for body."

"Nice clean brown. No apparent defects. Body a bit thin."

"More hop bitterness than appropriate for style. Aftertaste is astringent and too lasting."

"Slight astringency. Maltiness slightly low even for style. Aftertaste lingers, detracts from enjoying beer."

"Malt character predominates. Slightly sweet, but also a slight astringent aftertaste. Light body but not inappropriate."

Dangerfield Mild
(It don't get no respect!)

Winner, Club-Only Competition, English Mild, 1993
Vince Shumski, York, Pennsylvania
(All-Grain)

Ingredients for 5 1/2 Gallons
7 1/2 pounds Hugh Baird pale ale malt
    1 pound Gambrinus honey malt
    1 pound CaraVienne malt
 1/4 pound black malt
 1/4 pound Hugh Baird chocolate malt
 1/4 pound Munton and Fison torrefied wheat
    1 ounce East Kent Goldings hops, 4.9% alpha acid (70 minutes)
    1 ounce Liberty hops, 3.4% alpha acid (70 minutes)
      Yeast Culture Kit Co. Whitbread ale yeast
      force-carbonate in keg

Original gravity:	1.036
Final gravity:	1.011
Boiling time:	90 minutes
Primary fermentation:	10 days at 68 °F (20 °C) in glass
Secondary fermentation:	14 days at 55–58 °F (13–14.4 °C) in glass
Age when judged:	1 month

Brewer's Specifics
Mash grains at 154 °F (68 °C) for 60 minutes. Raise temperature to 162 °F (72 °C) for 10 minutes. Sparge with 4 1/2 gallons of 165 °F (74 °C) water.

Judges' Comments
"Very drinkable—I could drink several of these. My preference would be to back off on hops to let your wonderful malt come through."

"Chocolate malt and hop flavors are evident. No off-flavors are present. Good drinkable beer."

"A touch of roastiness is nice. Good hop balance with a fairly smooth malt flavor. Maybe just a little too much hop bittering in the aftertaste."

"Roasted malt flavor. Possibly a little too much hop in flavor. Some sweetness at end is appropriate."

"Nice malt and hop balance. A roasted grain bitterness. Very good beer."

Mild

NHC, English Dark Mild, 1996
Davy Davis, Denver, Colorado
(All-Grain)

Ingredients for 5 Gallons

4 1/8	pounds mild ale malt
10	ounces 50 °L crystal malt
6	ounces barley flakes
2	ounces black patent malt
1 1/2	ounces East Kent Goldings hop pellets, 6% alpha acid (60 minutes)
1/4	ounce East Kent Goldings hop pellets, 6% alpha acid (15 minutes)
1/2	teaspoon gypsum
1/3	teaspoon noniodized table salt
	Wyeast No. 1318 London III ale yeast
3/4	cup corn sugar (to prime)

Original gravity:	1.032
Final gravity:	1.007
Boiling time:	90 minutes
Primary fermentation:	8 days at 64 °F (18 °C) in glass
Secondary fermentation:	8 days at 64 °F (18 °C) in glass
Age when judged:	2 1/2 months

Brewer's Specifics

Mash grains at 145 °F (63 °C) for 90 minutes.

Mightily Mild

NHC, English Dark Mild, 1996
John Huie, Lakewood, Colorado
(All-Grain)

Ingredients for 3 Gallons

4	pounds mild ale malt
1/2	pound pale ale malt
1/2	pound brown malt
1/4	pound 80 °L crystal malt
1/4	pound Belgian CaraVienne malt
2 1/2	ounces Fuggles hops, 4.7% alpha acid (60 minutes)
2	ounces chocolate malt
1	ounce Fuggles hops, 4.7% alpha acid (30 minutes)
1	ounce East Kent Goldings hops, 5% alpha acid (15 minutes)
4	teaspoons Burton salts to 6 gallons brewing water
	Wyeast No. 1098 British ale yeast
2 1/2	ounces corn sugar (to prime)

Original gravity:	1.040
Final gravity:	1.016
Boiling time:	90 minutes
Primary fermentation:	7 days at 67 °F (19 °C) in glass
Secondary fermentation:	14 days at 67 °F (19 °C) in glass
Tertiary fermentation:	7 days at 60 °F (16 °C) in glass
Age when judged:	2 months

Brewer's Specifics

Mash-in at 122 °F (50 °C) and hold for 30 minutes. Add water, raise temperature to 150 °F (66 °C), and hold for 20 minutes. Add heat, raise temperature to 158 °F (70 °C), and hold for 20 minutes or until conversion. Raise temperature to 168–170 °F (76–77 °C) and hold for 10 minutes. Sparge with 170 °F (77 °C) water for 45 minutes.

CFA

English Dark Mild, 1997
John Evans, Portland, Oregon
(All-Grain)

Ingredients for 5 Gallons

8 1/2 pounds British two-row malt
1/2 pound British 55 °L crystal malt
6 ounces roasted barley
1 ounce East Kent Goldings hops, 5.2% alpha acid (60 minutes)
1/2 ounce Hallertau hops, 3.5% alpha acid (30 minutes)
1/4 ounce East Kent Goldings hops, 5.2% alpha acid (10 minutes)
1 ounce Hallertau hops, 3.5% alpha acid (5 minutes)
2 teaspoons gypsum added to mash water
Wyeast No. 1968 Special London ale yeast
force-carbonate in keg

Original gravity:	1.055
Final gravity:	1.008
Boiling time:	60 minutes
Primary fermentation:	7 days at 68 °F (20 °C) in glass
Secondary fermentation:	7 days at 65 °F (18 °C) in glass

Brewer's Specifics
Mash grains at 150 °F (66 °C) for 90 minutes.

Flavor Comments
On the strong side for a mild ale, CFA, nonetheless, captures the essence of the style's smoothness and drinkability. Enjoy this wonderfully British formulation at cellar temperatures, on draught, with steak and kidney pie, or perhaps a Cornish pastie. Cheers!

SCOTTISH ALE

This style is also called Scottish export and doesn't have quite the same strength as its counterpart, Scotch ale. Gold amber to dark brown in color, Scottish ale has low carbonation and bitterness with no hop flavor or aroma. It possesses medium maltiness, often with some smoky character from the use of peated malt. Low to medium diacetyl without any fruitiness or estery character is acceptable. It is best enjoyed on draught at cellar temperatures (55 °F [13 °C]).

Scottish Export Ale

Gold Medal, NHC, Scottish Export, 1995
Dan Gates, Franklin, Vermont
(Extract/Grain)

Ingredients for 4 3/4 Gallons

8	pounds DeWolf-Cosyns two-row malt
1	pound DeWolf-Cosyns biscuit malt
1	pound Laaglander amber dried malt extract
1/2	pound CaraMunich malt
1/4	pound medium crystal malt
1/4	pound dark crystal malt
1	ounce roasted barley
1/4	ounce Goldings hops, 5.4% alpha acid (70 minutes)
1/2	ounce Pride of Ringwood hops, 6.7% alpha acid (60 minutes)
3/4	ounce Goldings hops, 5.4% alpha acid (45 minutes)
	Wyeast No. 1728 Scottish ale yeast
	force-carbonate in keg

Original gravity:	1.069
Final gravity:	—
Boiling time:	70 minutes
Primary fermentation:	2 weeks at 52–54 °F (11–12 °C) in glass
Secondary fermentation:	2 weeks at 48–52 °F (9–11 °C) in glass
Tertiary fermentation:	1 month at 46–48 °F (8–9 °C) in keg
Age when judged:	6 months

Brewer's Specifics

Mash grains at 155 °F (68 °C) for 60 minutes.

Judges' Comments

"Malt and caramel up front with a bit of hop bitterness in middle and finish. Lingering bitterness a bit off-style. A nice beer with a hair too much hops in finish. Cut back a bit on bittering and keep everything else as is."

"Some grain taste with big hops in flavor. Very drinkable beer with a bit too much hops and a mild phenolic taste."

"Malty roastiness in flavor, otherwise clean. Excellent beer. I would try to cut down on roastiness, otherwise don't change a thing."

Untitled

Bronze Medal, NHC, Scottish Export, 1996
Darwin Harting, Pekin, Indiana
(All-Grain)

Ingredients for 5 Gallons
10 1/4   pounds DeWolf-Cosyns pale malt
1 1/2   pounds bulgar wheat
  3/4   pound DeWolf-Cosyns caramel Pils malt
  1/4   pound DeWolf-Cosyns biscuit malt
2 2/5   ounces chocolate malt
1 3/4   ounces Liberty hops, 3.8% alpha acid (65 minutes)
1 3/5   ounces roasted barley
    1   ounce Tettnang hop pellets, 4.1% alpha acid (35 minutes)
      Wyeast No. 1728 Scottish ale yeast
      force-carbonate

Original gravity:	1.064
Final gravity:	1.018
Boiling time:	80 minutes
Primary fermentation:	14 days at 58–60 °F (14–16 °C) in glass
Secondary fermentation:	13 days at 56–60 °F (13–16 °C) in glass
Tertiary fermentation:	7 days at 38 °F (3 °C) in keg
Age when judged:	2 months

Brewer's Specifics
Mash grains at 152 °F (67 °C) for 60 minutes. Bring mash to 162 °F (72 °C) for 30 minutes. Mash-out at 170 °F (77 °C) for 10 minutes.

Judges' Comments
"Smooth caramel hops flavor. Hops are good for style—low but balanced. Maybe a tad cloying. A bit rich for an export. A good export but it could be more drinkable. Try lowering gravity or CaraPils just a hair."

What's under the Kilt?

Gold Medal, NHC, Scottish Heavy, 1994
Michael Byers, Santa Cruz, California
(All-Grain)

Ingredients for 5 Gallons
     12 pounds Belgian Pilsener malt
      5 pounds British pale malt
 19 1/2 ounces CaraVienne malt
 19 1/2 ounces 40 °L crystal malt
     10 ounces Belgian Special "B" malt
    4/5 ounce Kent Goldings hops, 5.6% alpha acid (60 minutes)
   3/10 ounce Kent Goldings hops, 4.9% alpha acid (30 minutes)
         Scottish ale yeast
         force-carbonate in keg

Original gravity:	1.086
Final gravity:	1.030
Boiling time:	60 minutes
Primary fermentation:	1 week at 60 °F (16 °C) in glass
Secondary fermentation:	2 weeks at 32 °F (0 °C) in stainless steel
Age when judged:	2 1/2 months

Brewer's Specifics
Mash grains at 155 °F (68 °C) for 60 minutes.

Judges' Comments
"Scottish ale! All style descriptors present in a well-balanced and well-rounded flavor. Outstanding effort. Recipe formulation, alcohol, sweetness, balance all fine.

"Pears, delicious. Peaty, hint of smoke. Rich malt. The Scottish ale multiflavors are all good. Rounded and delicious."

"Beautiful malty sweetness. Hops present but perfect for style. Slight estery flavors blend very well with the malt and hops. Excellent balance! Outstanding beer! Can't give you any tips on how to improve this beer because I don't think it can be improved."

Pay the Piper II

Gold Medal, NHC, Scottish Light, 1996
Wendy Parker-Wood and Bev Nulman,
Albuquerque, New Mexico
(All-Grain)

Ingredients for 7 3/4 Gallons
5 5/8 pounds Hugh Baird two-row malt
    5 pounds German Munich 6 °L malt
  10 ounces peated malt
  10 ounces carastan 32 °L malt
    4 ounces 2 °L wheat malt
    2 ounces 50 °L roasted malt
    1 ounce East Kent Goldings hop plugs, 5.2% alpha acid (60 minutes)
 1/10 ounce East Kent Goldings hop pellets, 5.2% alpha acid (60 minutes)
    1 ounce East Kent Goldings hop plugs, 5.2% alpha acid (5 minutes)
      Wyeast No. 1728 Scottish ale yeast
  7/8 cup corn sugar (to prime)

Original gravity:	1.048
Final gravity:	1.013
Boiling time:	60 minutes
Primary fermentation:	6 days at 65 °F (18 °C) in glass
Secondary fermentation:	5 days at 58 °F (14 °C) in glass
Age when judged:	15 months

Brewer's Specifics
Mash grains at 132 °F (56 °C) for 30 minutes. Boil for 60 minutes at 154–156 °F (68–69 °C) and 168 °F (76 °C) for 10 minutes.

Judges' Comments
"A little astringent. Good caramel flavor. Hop bitterness a bit too high for the style. A very drinkable beer."

"Smokiness more evident in the flavor than aroma, perhaps a bit too strong. Good level of dark malt flavor. Very nice. This is exceptionally malty for a 1.035 beer. Very drinkable."

T. Duck's Scottish Ale

NHC, Scottish Export, 1996
Tom O'Connor, Rockport, Maine
(All-Grain)

Ingredients for 5 Gallons
- 7 pounds pale malt
- 1/2 pound English crystal malt
- 7/16 pound black treacle
- 1/8 pound roasted barley
- 1 ounce Fuggle hops, 4% alpha acid (60 minutes)
- 1 teaspoon Irish moss (20 minutes)
- Wyeast No. 1728 Scottish ale yeast
- 1 teaspoon Fermax yeast nutrient
- force-carbonate in keg

Original gravity:	1.055
Final gravity:	1.016
Boiling time:	60 minutes
Primary fermentation:	24 days at 55 °F (13 °C) in glass
Secondary fermentation:	—
Age when judged:	5 months

Brewer's Specifics
Mash grains at 128 °F (53 °C) for 35 minutes and 158 °F (70 °C) for 160 minutes.

Judges' Comments
"Smoked malt evident but subtle and pleasing. Nice, smooth, clean maltiness with hints of roast and smoke weaving in and out. A hair overcarbonated. Hair too much smoke."

McDouglas Export

Silver Medal, NHC, Scottish Export, 1995
Robert Douglas, St. Helens, Oregon
(All-Grain)

Ingredients for 5 Gallons

- 10 pounds Belgian Pilsener malt
- 6 pounds British pale malt
- 1 pound 40 °L crystal malt
- 12 ounces CaraVienne malt
- 8 ounces Belgian Special "B" malt
- 1 ounce Kent Goldings hops, 5% alpha acid (60 minutes)
- 1/2 ounce Kent Goldings hops, 5% alpha acid (30 minutes)
  - Wyeast No. 1728 Scottish ale yeast
- 3/4 cup corn sugar (to prime)

Original gravity:	1.070
Final gravity:	1.026
Boiling time:	60 minutes
Primary fermentation:	3 days at 60 °F (16 °C) in glass
Secondary fermentation:	19 days at 60 °F (16 °C) in glass
Age when judged:	6 months

Brewer's Specifics

Mash grains at 158 °F (70 °C) for 60 minutes.

Judges' Comments

"Smooth. Malty. I find the smokiness to be a bit too much. It should be faint. Hop level is okay as is the maltiness."

"Some malt and roast in nose with slight spiciness and smoke. Malt sweetness up front with slight vegetal character. Hop balance okay with spicy character. Finish on malty side. Some papery oxidation."

SMOKED BEER

The German version of this style, rauchbier, originated in Bamberg. Malt is smoked over hardwood fires, usually beech or alder. For Scottish-style ales, malt that's been smoked over peat is also used. Color varies from deep amber to reddish copper, and strength varies from 1.055–1.065 (13.5–16.2 °Plato). Hop character is very subdued in favor of the malt. Smoke usually dominates the flavor and aroma of rauchbier and its variations, so it is not a beer for everyone but is a wonderful complement to heavier holiday cuisine.

Geschmack Rauchbier

Gold Medal, NHC, Bamberg-Style Rauchbier, 1996
Chris Kaufman, Derby, Kansas
(All-Grain)

Ingredients for 5 1/2 Gallons
5 1/2 pounds DeWolf-Cosyns Pilsener malt
   3 pounds Hugh Baird home-smoked two-row malt over hickory chips
1 1/2 pounds DeWolf-Cosyns Munich malt
  1/2 pound dextrin malt
1 1/4 ounces Spalt hops, 4.8% alpha acid (60 minutes)
  3/4 ounce Spalt hops, 4.8% alpha acid (25 minutes)
      Wyeast No. 2206 Bavarian lager yeast
1 1/4 cup light dry malt extract (to prime)

Original gravity:	1.056
Final gravity:	1.019
Boiling time:	75 minutes
Primary fermentation:	4 days at 55 °F (13 °C) in glass
Secondary fermentation:	20 days at 40 °F (4 °C) in glass
Tertiary fermentation:	40 days at 40 °F (4 °C) in stainless steel
Age when judged:	2 1/2 months

Brewer's Specifics
Mash grains at 122 °F (50 °C) for 30 minutes. Mash at 145 °F (63 °C) for 30 minutes, 150 °F (66 °C) for 30 minutes, and 165 °F (74 °C) for 15 minutes.

Judges' Comments
"Low smoke flavor. Low malt sweetness. Smoke flavor does not match aroma. Needs more smoke flavor and body."

"Very smooth. Nice balance. Good smoke flavor. Good malt flavor. Just a little too sweet for style."

Old Smoky

Silver Medal, NHC, Peat-Smoked Scottish Wee Heavy, 1994
Morris Schademan, Portland, Oregon
(All-Grain)

Ingredients for 10 Gallons
25	pounds pale malt
5	pounds Vienna malt
1	pound peat-smoked malt
1/2	pound black patent malt
1	ounce Chinook hops (90 minutes)
2	ounces Chinook hops (30 minutes)
	Wyeast No. 1728 Scottish ale yeast

Original gravity:	1.090
Final gravity:	1.028
Boiling time:	90 minutes
Primary fermentation:	7 days at 60 °F (16 °C) in glass
Secondary fermentation:	3 weeks at 60 °F (16 °C) in glass
Age when judged:	4 months

Brewer's Specifics
Mash grains at 155 °F (68 °C) for 60 minutes. Double mash—also makes 5 gallons of 1.052 original gravity beer.

Judges' Comments
"Sweet. Smoky. Alcoholic. Smooth. Good balance. A slight ashy coating of the tongue in the aftertaste. Great beer, but the aftertaste goes out of balance."

"Good smoke flavor. Very slight astringency in background. Very good. Tastes like a smoked Belhaven."

"Sweet, burnt malt, and licorice flavors. Alcohol is there. Has a bitter aftertaste. Slight sulfur, but beer is good. Slight sour taste."

Smoke This!

Gold Medal, NHC, Bamberg-Style Rauchbier, 1995
Carlos Kelley, Fort Worth, Texas
(All-Grain)

Ingredients for 10 Gallons
- 12 pounds two-row pale malt
- 5 pounds Belgian Munich malt
- 5 pounds smoked two-row malt
- 4 ounces Hallertau Hersbrucker hops, 4.2% alpha acid (60 minutes)
- 1 ounce Hallertau Hersbrucker hops, 4.2% alpha acid (10 minutes)
  - Wyeast No. 2206 Munich lager yeast
- 1 1/2 cup corn sugar (to prime)

Original gravity:	1.056
Final gravity:	1.014
Boiling time:	60 minutes
Primary fermentation:	30 days at 45 °F (7 °C) in glass
Secondary fermentation:	60 days at 40 °F (4 °C) in glass
Age when judged:	5 months

Brewer's Specifics
Smoke grain over cool sugar maple smoke at 110–120 °F (43–49 °C) for 90 minutes. Mash grains at 152 °F (67 °C) for 90 minutes.

Judges' Comments
"Very nice balance of smoke and malt sweetness. Astringency noticeable. Good conditioning. Long aftertaste. A better than average example."

"Malt is a little low for style. Good low hop flavor. Slight astringent aftertaste."

"Good smoke flavor. Astringent aftertaste. Nice drinking beer. Could use a little work."

Smoky Scotch

Finalist, NHC, Classic-Style Smoked Beer, 1996
Ross Frederiksen, Loomis, Colorado
(All-Grain)

Ingredients for 5 Gallons

- 10 pounds English pale malt
- 2 pounds Scottish peat malt
- 1 pound Munich malt
- 1 pound 37 °L crystal malt
- 1/2 pound chocolate malt
- 3/4 ounce Kent Goldings hop pellets, 4.2% alpha acid (60 minutes)
- 3/4 ounce Kent Goldings hop pellets, 4.2% alpha acid (45 minutes)
- 3/4 ounce Fuggles hop pellets, 3.4% alpha acid (30 minutes)
- 1/2 ounce Fuggles hop pellets, 3.4% alpha acid (15 minutes)
- 1/2 ounce Kent Goldings hop pellets, 4.2% alpha acid (steep)
- Wyeast No. 1728 Scottish ale yeast
- 4 ounces corn sugar (to prime)

Original gravity:	1.064
Final gravity:	1.018
Boiling time:	90 minutes
Primary fermentation:	5 days at 75 °F (24 °C) in glass
Secondary fermentation:	10 days at 75 °F (24 °C) in glass
Age when judged:	4 months

Brewer's Specifics

Mash grains at 154 °F (68 °C) for 60 minutes.

Judges' Comments

"Needs more smoke character throughout. The toastiness is really good."

"Smoke bouquet is excellent. Malt evident."

"Rich dark color—beautiful. Good head retention. Nice carbonation. Excellent. Rich, chocolate, smoky flavor."

Untitled

Silver Medal, NHC, Smoked/Irish Red, 1995
Paddy Giffen, Rohnert Park, California
(All-Grain)

Ingredients for 10 Gallons
- 24 pounds Klages malt
- 4 pounds CaraVienne malt
- 4 pounds smoked two-row malt
- 3 pounds Belgian Munich malt
- 3/4 ounce Perle hops (60 minutes)
- 1 ounce Perle hops (30 minutes)
- 2 teaspoons chalk added to mash water
- 2 teaspoons salt added to mash water
- Wyeast No. 1968 Special London ale yeast
- force-carbonate in keg

Original gravity:	1.076
Final gravity:	1.028
Boiling time:	60 minutes
Primary fermentation:	5 days at 67 °F (19 °C) in glass
Secondary fermentation:	1 month at 67 °F (19 °C) in glass
Age when judged:	—

Brewer's Specifics
Mash grains at 152 °F (67 °C) for 75 minutes.

Judges' Comments
"Sweet caramel with smokey undertones. Pleasant enough. More hops might help balance. Caramel and smoke come through. Long aftertaste with obvious alcoholic strength. Mild astringency."

On Top with Ol' Smoky

Finalist, World Homebrew Contest, Smoked Beer, 1997
Carlos Kelley, Fort Worth, Texas
(All-Grain)

Ingredients for 11 Gallons

- 12 pounds DeWolf-Cosyns pale malt
- 5 pounds DeWolf-Cosyns CaraMunich malt
- 5 pounds smoked DeWolf-Cosyns pale malt
  (home-smoked over pecan shells)
- 3 ounces Hallertau Hersbrucker plugs, 4.5% alpha acid (60 minutes)
- 1 ounce Hallertau Hersbrucker plugs, 4.5% alpha acid (10 minutes)
  Wyeast No. 2112 California Common yeast
- 1 1/2 cups dextrose (to prime)

Original gravity:	1.056
Final gravity:	1.012
Boiling time:	75 minutes
Primary fermentation:	4 days at 58–62 °F (17 °C) in glass
Secondary fermentation:	10 days at 58–62 °F (17 °C) in glass
Age when judged:	6 months

Brewer's Specifics

Mash grains at 152 °F (67 °C) for 60 minutes. Smoke grains the day before brew day. Use 1 of the 2-foot-tall round patio smokers with 2 grills. Place some aluminum screen over the upper grill, making a basket to keep the grain from falling off the sides. Do not moisten the grains first because it reduces the husk's ability to absorb the smoke. Spread the grain evenly in a layer 1–2 inches thick. Start the fire with some charcoal and add water-soaked pecan shells (or wood) to keep it burning. It should be a slow, cool, smoking fire so as to not overheat the grain. Keep a thermometer in the bed of grains to monitor the temperature. Keep the temperature between 100–130 °F (38–54 °C). Total smoking time is 120 minutes. Stir and relevel the grain bed about every 15–20 minutes and add freshly soaked pecan shells to the fire as needed to keep a good smoke going. Keep the water pan full of the same pecan shells and water. Leave grains on the grill to cool overnight and then mix with the other grains the next morning for milling.

Smoky Logger

Bronze Medal, NHC, Bamberg-Style Rauchbier, 1995
Robert Drousth, Madison, Wisconsin
(All-Grain)

Ingredients for 12 Gallons
- 17 pounds Weyermann smoked malt
- 5 pounds Schrier two-row malt
- 2 pounds DeWolf-Cosyns CaraPils malt
- 2 ounces Hallertau hops, 6.3% alpha acid (60 minutes)
- 2 ounces Spalt Select hops, 4.7% alpha acid (30 minutes)
  Advanced Brewers Scientific-005 Czech lager yeast
  force-carbonate in keg

Original gravity:	1.050
Final gravity:	1.018
Boiling time:	60 minutes
Primary fermentation:	7 days at 60 °F (16 °C) in stainless steel
Secondary fermentation:	6 weeks at 40–33 °F (4–1 °C) in stainless steel
Age when judged:	2 months

Brewer's Specifics
Add 20 quarts of 133 °F (56 °C) water to grain and hold temperature at 121 °F (49 °C) for 30 minutes. Raise temperature to 128 °F (53 °C). Add 6 quarts of 194 °F (90 °C) water and hold temperature at 155 °F (68 °C) for 60 minutes. Mash-out at 170 °F (80 °C). Sparge with 64 quarts of 170 °F (80 °C) water.

Judges' Comments
"Good smoke flavor. Could use some hop-malt balance."

"A little low on malt. Very nice smoky flavor."

"A little too bitter. Nice smoke and malt balance. Nice effort."

Verdigris Valley Foreign-Style Stout

**Winner, Club-Only Competition,
Smoked Foreign-Style Stout, 1995
Mark Taylor, Independence, Kansas
(All-Grain)**

Ingredients for 10 Gallons
- 16 pounds two-row malt
- 3 pounds roasted barley
- 1 pound 90 °L crystal malt
- 1/2 pound chocolate malt
- 1/2 pound black malt
- 1/2 pound wheat malt
- 1 1/2 ounces Galena hops, 12.4% alpha acid (60 minutes)
- 1 ounce Perle hops, 7.5% alpha acid (60 minutes)
- 3/4 ounce Centennial hops, 9.9% alpha acid (60 minutes)
- Wyeast No. 1084 Irish ale yeast
- force-carbonate in keg, counterpressure fill bottles
- 3 drops Wright's Natural Hickory Seasoning per 12-ounce bottle added at bottling

Original gravity:	1.076
Final gravity:	1.030
Boiling time:	90 minutes
Primary fermentation:	14 days at 68 °F (20 °C) in glass
Secondary fermentation:	1 month at 65 °F (18 °C) in stainless steel
Age when judged:	1 month

Brewer's Specifics
Mash two-row malt and roasted barley at 156 °F (69 °C) for 60 minutes. Steep remaining grain until boil.

Judges' Comments
"Nice smokiness. Creamy, sweet, and malty. Could use more smoke because it fades quickly."

"Malty with slight sourness. Roasted barley character is evident. Smoky flavor is subtle and complementary."

"Smoke more noticeable in taste than aroma. Malts also very noticeable. Clean well-made beer but very light on the smoke for a smoked beer."

ALTBIER

This German ale style comes from the word for old, referring to the method of top-fermenting, which predated the relatively new lagering methods widely adapted in the South. Altbier is deep amber to copper and brewed from dark high-kilned malts. It has a medium to high hop bitterness with low hop flavor and no hop aroma. It often displays a restrained fruity or estery character and is light to medium in body, at 4.4–5 percent alcohol by volume. Very low to no diacetyl should be present. Like California common, altbier is fermented fairly warm but is cold conditioned.

Kowabungtie Düsseldorf-Style Altbier

Gold Medal, NHC, German-Style Ale, 1996
Gil Hantzsch, John Bowman, Scott Spevacek,
and Dave Anderson, Baraboo, Wisconsin
(Extract/Grain)

Ingredients for 10 Gallons
6	pounds Northwestern light malt extract syrup
4	pounds Munich malt
3	pounds Vienna malt
2	pounds dextrin malt
2	pounds light dry extract
1	pound toasted Victory malt
6	ounces chocolate malt
2	ounces Tettnang hop pellets, 4.3% alpha acid (60 minutes)
1 1/2	ounces Saaz hop pellets, 5.4% alpha acid (60 minutes)
2	ounces Tettnang hop pellets, 4.3% alpha acid (30 minutes)
1 1/2	ounces Saaz hop pellets, 5.4% alpha acid (30 minutes)
2	ounces Hallertau hop pellets, 3.8% alpha acid (finish)
	Wyeast No. 1007 German ale yeast
3/4	cup corn sugar (to prime)

Original gravity:	1.050
Final gravity:	1.012
Boiling time:	60 minutes
Primary fermentation:	4 days at 68 °F (20 °C) in glass
Secondary fermentation:	14 days at 68 °F (20 °C) in glass
Age when judged:	4 months

Brewer's Specifics
Mash grains at 120 °F (49 °C) for 30 minutes and at 158 °F (70 °C) for 30 minutes.

Judges' Comments
"Well balanced. Malt expression is balanced with clean hops. Bitterness lingers a bit. Smooth and well crafted."

"Roasty malt flavor is too predominant. Too sweet for the style. Closer to an American brown ale. An okay beer but lacks the crispness and cleanness that are hallmarks of this style."

"Nice balance. Bitterness on the high side, which is okay. Fine brew!"

Salisbury Strong Alt

Silver Medal, NHC, Düsseldorf-Style Altbier, 1995
LaMar Hill, Delmar, New York
(All-Grain)

Ingredients for 5 Gallons

8	pounds Belgian pale ale malt
3/4	pound Ireks Vienna malt
3/4	pound Ireks Munich malt
3/4	pound English 50 °L crystal malt
1/8	pound black patent malt
2 1/2	ounces Spalt hops, 5.5% alpha acid (60 minutes)
1 1/2	ounces Hallertau Hersbrucker hops, 3.5% alpha acid (15 minutes)
4/5	ounces Hallertau Hersbrucker hops, 3.5% alpha acid (5 minutes)
1	teaspoon gypsum added to mash water
	BreuTek Altbier yeast
30	ounces 1.050 gyle (unfermented wort) (to prime)

Original gravity:	1.048
Final gravity:	1.010
Boiling time:	75 minutes
Primary fermentation:	1 week at 65 °F (18 °C) in plastic
Secondary fermentation:	1 week at 65 °F (18 °C) in glass
Tertiary fermentation:	2 weeks at 38 °F (3 °C) in glass
Age when judged:	5 months

Brewer's Specifics
Mash grains at 154 °F (68 °C) for 90 minutes.

Judges' Comments
"Good balance but a little buttery. Good hoppiness but a slight sourness. Nicely balanced beer that emphasizes hops—as it should. Formulation on target—keep making this until you get it right and you'll have a great beer."

"Hop-malt balance okay. Needs a higher attenuation. Diacetyl taste is inappropriate for style. A little sourness. Watch sterility."

Alt 2 B-A-Law

Gold Medal, NHC, Düsseldorf-Style Altbier, 1993
Bill Yearous, Galt, California
(All-Grain)

Ingredients for 5 Gallons
8	pounds two-row malt
2	pounds Munich malt
1	pound crystal malt
1	pound wheat malt
1/2	pound CaraPils malt
2	ounces chocolate malt
1/2	ounce Northern Brewer hops, 7.1% alpha acid (65 minutes)
1/2	ounce Cascade hops, 5.7% alpha acid (45 minutes)
1/4	ounce Cluster hops, 6.8% alpha acid (30 minutes)
1/2	ounce Cluster hops, 6.8% alpha acid (25 minutes)
1/4	ounce Cluster hops, 6.8% alpha acid (20 minutes)
1/2	ounce Saaz hops, 3.7% alpha acid (7 minutes)
1	ounce Saaz hops, 3.7% alpha acid (5 minutes)
1/2	ounce Saaz hops, 3.7% alpha acid (3 minutes)
	Edme dry yeast
3/4	cup corn sugar (to prime)

Original gravity:	1.051
Final gravity:	1.017
Boiling time:	75 minutes
Primary fermentation:	5 days in plastic at 60 °F (16 °C)
Secondary fermentation:	60 days in glass at 60 °F (16 °C)
Age when judged:	3 months

Brewer's Specifics
Mash grains at 158 °F (70 °C) for 60 minutes.

Judges' Comments
"Medium malt. Low to medium bitterness. Needs more bitterness."

"Malt predominates. I taste a little hint of chocolate! Nice dry finish and hops. Great beer. No major flaws. The chocolate detracts. Might try a lower Lovibond malt."

"Dryness appropriate. Clean hop bitter finish. This beer could use a little more complexity."

"Slight clovelike flavor, not unpleasant. Malt good. Well-rounded altbier."

Uller's Alt

Second Place, Club-Only Competition, Altbier, 1996
Kirk Olsen, Erie, Pennsylvania
(Extract/Grain)

Ingredients for 5 Gallons
6 3/5   pounds Ireks amber malt extract
1/2   pound 40 °L crystal malt
1   ounce black patent malt
2   ounces Perle hops, 7.8% alpha acid (60 minutes)
1   ounce Perle hops, 7.8% alpha acid (15 minutes)
  Wyeast No. 1338 European ale yeast
  force-carbonate

Original gravity:	1.052
Final gravity:	1.015
Boiling time:	60 minutes
Primary fermentation:	1 week at 73 °F (23 °C) in glass
Secondary fermentation:	3 weeks at 60 °F (16 °C) in glass
Age when judged:	—

Brewer's Specifics
Steep specialty malts in water at 150 °F (66 °C) for 30 minutes.

T. Duck's Alt No. 115

Reprinted from 1996 Special Issue of *Zymurgy*
Tom O'Connor, Rockport, Maine
(All-Grain)

Ingredients for 5 Gallons
- 2 pounds Durst Pilsener malt
- 2 pounds light Munich malt
- 2 pounds dark Munich malt
- 1 pound German wheat malt
- 4 ounces German dark crystal malt
- 1 ounce black malt
- 1 ounce Hallertau Northern Brewer hops, 7.8% alpha acid (60 minutes)
- 1 teaspoon Irish moss (15 minutes)
- 5 yeast energizer tablets
  - Wyeast No. 1007 German ale yeast

Original gravity:	1.049
Final gravity:	1.012
Boiling time:	60 minutes
Primary fermentation:	1 week at 65 °F (18 °C) in glass
Secondary fermentation:	2 weeks at 65 °F (18 °C) in glass
Age when judged:	—

Brewer's Specifics
Mash grains at 129 °F (54 °C) for 45 minutes and 152 °F (67 °C) for 120 minutes. Adjust the mash pH to 5.4 if necessary. Sparge with water to make 6 gallons of wort then boil wort for 60 minutes.

Allmans Alt

Third Place, Club-Only Competition, Altbier, 1996
Ronald E. Alleman, Bolton, Connecticut
(All-Grain)

Ingredients for 5 Gallons

6	pounds Belgian two-row malt
1	pound Munich malt
1/2	pound dextrin
1/2	pound flaked barley
1/2	pound wheat
2	ounces chocolate malt
2	ounces Cluster hops, 6.4% alpha acid (60 minutes)
1	ounce Willamette hops, 5% alpha acid (60 minutes)
1	ounce Cascade hops, 4.7% alpha acid (5 minutes)
	Wyeast No. 1028 London ale yeast
3/4	cup corn sugar (to prime)

Original gravity:	1.046
Final gravity:	1.008
Boiling time:	60 minutes
Primary fermentation:	6 days at 65 °F (18 °C) in plastic
Secondary fermentation:	9 days at 65 °F (18 °C) in glass
Age when judged:	2 1/2 months

Brewer's Specifics

Mash grains at 147 °F (64 °C) for 60 minutes.

BITTER

This is a moderate-strength autumn style with some ester character allowed. British bitter can be made in late summer for enjoyment in fall. Bitter is best on draught, so now's the time to invest in that keg system you've always wanted. It's golden to copper to dark brown and highly hopped in bitterness, flavor, and aroma. Most commercial bitters are brewed with 5–15 percent sugar adjunct to give it a dry rummy character, and it is served relatively warm, by American standards, at 122–131 °F (50–55 °C). Bitter comes in three different strengths: ordinary, at an original gravity of 1.035–1.039 (9–10 °Plato); best, at 1.040–1.047 (10–12 °Plato); and special, at 1.048–1.056 (12–14 °Plato). Moderate levels of diacetyl and fruitiness are allowable. A still stronger style of bitter is called extra special bitter.

Rose Blossom Bitter

Bronze Medal, NHC, English Ordinary Bitter, 1995
Chuck Allen, Westminster, Colorado
(Extract/Grain)

Ingredients for 5 Gallons

5	pounds Hugh Baird English pale malt
2	pounds Geordie English light dry malt extract
1/2	pound Hugh Baird 50–60 °L English crystal malt
1/8	pound Hugh Baird roasted barley
1	ounce Nugget hops, 12.6% alpha acid (40 minutes)
1	ounce Cascade hops, 5.7% alpha acid (15 minutes)
1	ounce Fuggles hops, 4.3% alpha acid (5 minutes)
2	teaspoons Irish moss (40 minutes)
1	teaspoon gypsum added to boil
1 1/4	cups dry malt extract (to prime)
1	package gelatin (for fining)
	Wyeast No. 1968 Special London ale yeast

Original gravity:	1.040
Final gravity:	1.014
Boiling time:	60 minutes
Primary fermentation:	7 days at 68 °F (20 °C) in glass
Secondary fermentation:	7 days at 68 °F (20 °C) in plastic
Age when judged:	3 months

Brewer's Specifics

Add 5 quarts warm water (130 °F [54 °C]) to malt. Let stand at 122 °F (50 °C) for 30 minutes (protein rest). Add 5 pints boiling water, bringing temperature to 145 °F (63 °C). Heat to 156 °F (69 °C) and let stand for 20 minutes. Sparge with 6 quarts water at 170 °F (77 °C). Add malt extract, Irish moss, and gypsum. Boil for 40 minutes. Add gelatin after primary fermentation.

Judges' Comments

"Alcohol comes through in first sip. Too malty for ordinary—perhaps a special. Complexity is very interesting."

"Nice ripe fruit expression, with grassy hop—some malt. Attractive copper. Excellent clarity. Soft fluffy head."

Muddy Mo Amber Ale

Gold Medal, NHC, English Best Bitter, 1996
John Fahrer, Omaha, Nebraska
(All-Grain)

Ingredients for 5 Gallons

8 1/2   pounds Schrier two-row malt
10   ounces 120 °L crystal malt
1   ounce chocolate malt
1/2   ounce Nugget hops, 12% alpha acid (60 minutes)
1/2   ounce Fuggles hop plugs, 4.2% alpha acid (30 minutes)
1/2   ounce Fuggles hop plugs, 4.2% alpha acid (10 minutes)
1   ounce Tettnang hop pellets, 4.7% alpha acid (finish)
   Wyeast No. 1028 London ale yeast
66   ounces 1.050 gravity wort (to prime)

Original gravity:	1.050
Final gravity:	1.012
Boiling time:	75 minutes
Primary fermentation:	7 days at 68 °F (20 °C) in stainless steel
Secondary fermentation:	16 days at 66 °F (19 °C) in stainless steel
Age when judged:	7 months

Brewer's Specifics

Mash grains at 122 °F (50 °C) for 25 minutes, 152 °F (67 °C) for 60 minutes, 157 °F (69 °C) for 20 minutes, and 169 °F (76 °C) for 10 minutes.

Judges' Comments

"Very nice flavor. Slight astringency and phenolics detract a little from this beer's flavor. This is a very good special bitter. Possibly the sparge water pH could be adjusted to avoid the slight astringency."

"Some slight astringency on finish. Balance great."

"Phenol up front disappears very quickly. Malt sweetness is present. Very pleasant to drink."

Real Bitter

Gold Medal, NHC, English Special, 1995
Rhett Rebold, Burke, Virginia
(All-Grain)

Ingredients for 11 1/2 Gallons
15 1/2 pounds British pale malt
1 1/3 pounds 60 °L crystal malt
1/4 pound unrefined sugar (boil)
6 2/5 ounces demerara sugar (boil)
6 ounces Belgian biscuit malt
6 ounces flaked wheat
2 1/5 ounces Belgian aromatic malt
2 ounces East Kent Goldings hops, 5.1% alpha acid (55 minutes)
1 1/3 ounces Fuggles hops, 4% alpha acid (55 minutes)
1 4/5 ounces East Kent Goldings hops, 5.1% alpha acid (15 minutes)
Wyeast No. 1728 Scottish ale yeast
force-carbonate in keg

Original gravity:	1.045
Final gravity:	1.012
Boiling time:	90 minutes
Primary fermentation:	8 days at 64 °F (18 °C) in glass
Secondary fermentation:	23 days at 64 °F (18 °C) in glass
Age when judged:	3 months

Brewer's Specifics
Mash grains at 152 °F (67 °C) for 120 minutes.

Judges' Comments
"Malt dominates balance with plenty of expression up front. Middle reveals a solid kettle hop addition, which lasts through a dry firm finish. It may be a bit 'big' for a special—indeed, it could do well as an ESB."

"Chocolate. Crystal. Some smoke. Good bitterness. A very complex beer. May be a little too much body for style. A very good example of style."

"Malt expressed clearly. A little heavy flavor characteristic that reminds me of pipe tobacco. Nice balance. Body very full for style."

Baby's Best Bitter

Gold Medal, NHC, English Special, 1993
Donna Lynn and Brian Johnson, Palo Alto, California
(All-Grain)

Ingredients for 10 Gallons
13	pounds Munton and Fison pale ale malt
1	pound CaraPils malt
1	pound 20 °L crystal malt
1	pound Victory malt
1/2	pound flaked barley
1/3	pound Hugh Baird pale malt
1/4	pound flaked red wheat
2	ounces Perle hops, 7.6% alpha acid (45 minutes)
1	ounce Cascade hops, 6.5% alpha acid (1 minute)
	Wyeast No. 1028 London ale yeast
	force-carbonate in keg

Original gravity:	1.047
Final gravity:	1.012
Boiling time:	60 minutes
Primary fermentation:	21 days at 68 °F (20 °C) in glass
Secondary fermentation:	—
Age when judged:	2 months

Brewer's Specifics
Mash grains at 157 °F (69 °C) for 90 minutes.

Judges' Comments
"Clean. Sweet with some bitterness in the finish. Nice bitter."

"Fairly good malt-hop balance. Some bitterness in aftertaste. Rather buttery flavor. Could use a bit more malt. Perhaps a bit too much diacetyl."

"Good malt and hop balance. Nice drinking beer. Good beer."

"The malt profile could come up just a bit, perhaps with less attenuative yeast. Some fruitiness would also be nice."

Bag-End Bitter

NHC, English Best Bitter, 1996
Hal Buttermore, Ann Arbor, Michigan
(All-Grain)

Ingredients for 5 Gallons
6 1/2   pounds Schrier pale malt
1/2   pound English crystal malt
1/2   pound wheat malt
1 1/2   ounces Northern Brewer whole hops or plugs,
           7.8% alpha acid (60 minutes)
1   ounce black malt
1   ounce Kent Goldings whole hops or plugs,
           5.2% alpha acid (60 minutes)
1   ounce Styrian Goldings whole hops or plugs (15 minutes)
2   teaspoons gypsum added to mash
1/2   teaspoon epsom salts added to mash
1/4   teaspoon salt added to mash
     Yeast Lab® No. 1187 yeast
1/2   cup corn sugar (to prime)

Original gravity:	1.040
Final gravity:	1.011
Boiling time:	90 minutes
Primary fermentation:	5 days at 66 °F (19 °C) in glass
Secondary fermentation:	—
Age when judged:	8 months

Brewer's Specifics
Use a single infusion mash at 152–154 °F (67–68°C) for 60 minutes.

Spiny Norman's Special Bitter

Finalist, NHC, English Best Bitter, 1996
Al Korzonas, Palos Hills, Illinois
(All-Grain)

Ingredients for 3 4/5 Gallons
5 2/5   pounds Munton and Fison pale ale malt
1/2   pound Munton and Fison mild ale malt
1/4   pound DeWolf-Cosyns CaraVienne 22 °L malt
1/4   pound DeWolf-Cosyns CaraMunich 77 °L malt
1/4   pound DeWolf-Cosyns wheat malt
2 1/2   ounces Fuggles hop pellets, 3% alpha acid (60 minutes)
2/5   ounce East Kent Goldings hop pellets, 4.6% alpha acid (15 minutes)
2   ounces East Kent Goldings hops (dry, 2 weeks)
9   teaspoons gypsum added to mash water
Wyeast No. 1275 Thames Valley ale yeast
force-carbonate

Original gravity:	1.045
Final gravity:	1.011
Boiling time:	75 minutes
Primary fermentation:	3 weeks at 64 °F (18 °C) in glass
Secondary fermentation:	—
Age when judged:	2 months

Brewer's Specifics
Mash grains at 150 °F (66 °C) for 17 minutes and 158 °F (70 °C) for 60 minutes.

MacCaney High Country Bitter

Special Bitter, 1997
Amahl Turczyn, Boulder, Colorado
(All-Grain)

Ingredients for 10 Gallons

14	pounds two-row Scottish malt
2	ounces Northern Brewer hop pellets, 7% alpha acid (90 minutes)
1	ounce roasted barley
1	ounce Kent Goldings hop pellets, 6% alpha acid (10 minutes)
1 1/2	pounds sucanat (dried cane sugar juice) added to boil
	Wyeast No. 1098 British ale yeast
	force-carbonate in keg

Original gravity:	1.051
Final gravity:	1.007
Boiling time:	2 hours
Primary fermentation:	1 week at 68 °F (20 °C)
Secondary fermentation:	3 weeks at 60–65 °F (16–18 °C)
Tertiary fermentation:	—

Brewer's Specifics

Mash grains at 156 °F (69 °C) for 60 minutes. Use direct fire heat under kettle to maximize caramelization of malt sugars. After primary fermentation is complete, rack into secondary with 2 teaspoons gelatin finings. When yeast has fallen out, carbonate in kegs with forced carbonation.

Flavor Comments

This tawny amber bitter relies on a scant amount of roasted barley and kettle caramelization for color. The sucanat also contributes quite a bit of color, as well as caramel, treacle, toffee flavors reminiscent of many authentic British examples. A slight fruitiness complements these sugary notes in the nose, yet a liberal dose of Northern Brewer hops provides a dry refreshing finish.

EXTRA SPECIAL BITTER (ESB)

This style is little more than a strong bitter, ranging from 1.056–1.064 (14–16 °Plato) in strength. It has a more pronounced estery fruity character than its lighter-strength counterparts. ESB is usually copper to dark brown with a pronounced hop profile from kettle and dry-hopping. Low levels of diacetyl are expected. This is a great beer to help prepare for the approaching cold season.

Amberly Ale

Extra Special Bitter, 1997
Amahl Turczyn, Boulder, Colorado
(All-Grain)

Ingredients for 9 Gallons
16	pounds two-row malt
2	pounds British 80 °L crystal malt
1 1/2	pounds Briith 30 °L crystal malt
3	ounces British black malt
3	ounces British brown malt
2	ounces Willamette hop pellets, 5% alpha acid (60 minutes)
2	ounces Willamette hop pellets, 5% alpha acid (30 minutes)
2	ounces Willamette hop pellets, 5% alpha acid (10 minutes)
	Wyeast No. 1056 American ale yeast

Original gravity:	1.065
Final gravity:	1.012
Boiling time:	60 minutes
Primary fermentation:	10 days at 65 °F (18 °C)
Secondary fermentation:	1 week at 65 °F (18 °C)
Tertiary fermentation:	—

Brewer's Specifics
Mash grains at 150 °F (66 °C) for 60 minutes.

Flavor Comments
This ale has a deep tawny red color with fragrant hops and a big malty palate. There's a sharp tangy finish from the Willamette hops.

Be Bop Bitter

Silver Medal, NHC, English Extra Special Bitter, 1994
Michael Byers, Santa Cruz, California
(All-Grain)

Ingredients for 5 Gallons

12 1/4	pounds two-row malt
1 1/2	pounds Belgian CaraVienne malt
1	pound British 30–37 °L malt
1/3	pound Belgian CaraMunich malt
1/8	pound Belgian Special "B" malt
1	ounce Kent Goldings hops, 5.4% alpha acid (60 minutes)
1 1/3	ounces Kent Goldings hops, 5.4% alpha acid (30 minutes)
	Wyeast No. 1968 Special London yeast
	force-carbonate in keg

Original gravity:	1.070
Final gravity:	1.020
Boiling time:	60 minutes
Primary fermentation:	1 week at 68 °F (20 °C) in stainless steel
Secondary fermentation:	2 weeks at 32 °F (0 °C) in stainless steel
Age when judged:	2 1/2 months

Brewer's Specifics

Mash grains at 156 °F (69 °C) for 60 minutes.

Judges' Comments

"Malty sweet. Low hop bitterness. Great beer! Needs a bit more hop bitterness to balance the malt."

"Appropriate ESB taste. This is a good job of balance. Very nice job. True to style in almost every way—try to get a touch more bitterness next time."

"Good beer. Maltiness correct. Hops lacking for ESB category. Hop it up next time."

Bob's Flywater Ale

Winner, World Homebrew Contest, Extra Special Bitter, 1997
Robert Gordash, Fort Lauderdale, Florida
(All-Grain)

Ingredients for 11 Gallons
- 13 pounds Briess pale ale malt
- 3 pounds DeWolf-Cosyns Munich malt
- 2 pounds DeWolf-Cosyns aromatic malt
- 2 pounds DeWolf-Cosyns biscuit malt
- 2 pounds DeWolf-Cosyns CaraVienne malt
- 1 pound DeWolf-Cosyns CaraPils malt
- 1 pound DeWolf-Cosyns wheat malt
- 1 1/2 ounces East Kent Goldings hops, 4.5% alpha acid (90 minutes)
- 2 1/2 ounces Fuggles hops, 4.5% alpha acid (45 minutes)
- 1 1/2 ounces Fuggles hops, 4.5% alpha acid (25 minutes)
- 2 1/2 ounces Cascade hops, 4.5% alpha acid (15 minutes)
- 4 ounces Willamette hops, 4.2% alpha acid (1 minute)
- 4 ounces East Kent Goldings hops, 4.5% alpha acid (1 minute)
- 1/2 ounce Cascade hops, 4.5% alpha acid (finish)
- 1 teaspoon gypsum added to mash water
- Wyeast No. 1968 Special London yeast
- force-carbonate

Original gravity:	1.057
Final gravity:	1.018
Boiling time:	90 minutes
Primary fermentation:	7 days at 68 °F (20 °C)
Secondary fermentation:	21 days at 40 °F (4 °C)
Tertiary fermentation:	7 months

Brewer's Specifics
Mash grains at 156 °F (69 °C) for 90 minutes.

Wet Nose in the Ear ESB

Bronze Medal, NHC, English Strong Bitter, 1996
Mark E. Hall, Athens, Georgia
(All-Grain)

Ingredients for 5 Gallons

  8 pounds Munton and Fison British pale two-row malt
  1 pound Munton and Fison flaked barley
  1 pound Munton and Fison 50 °L crystal malt
  3 ounces Cascade hops, 5% alpha acid (60 minutes)
1/2 ounce Fuggles hops, 3.6% alpha acid (20 minutes)
1/2 ounce Fuggles hops, 3.6% alpha acid (15 minutes)
1/2 ounce Fuggles hops, 3.6% alpha acid (10 minutes)
1/2 ounce Fuggles hops, 3.6% alpha acid (5 minutes)
1/3 ounce Burton water salts added to mash water
     Wyeast No. 1968 Special London yeast
     force-carbonate in keg

Original gravity:	1.051
Final gravity:	1.006
Boiling time:	60 minutes
Primary fermentation:	10 days at 68 °F (20 °C) in plastic
Secondary fermentation:	11 days at 68–70 °F (20–21 °C) in glass
Age when judged:	3 months

Brewer's Specifics

Mash grains at 152 °F (67 °C) for 90 minutes.

SPECIALTY STOUT

Enjoyed around the holidays, this is an open style category, usually reserved for "kitchen sink" beers (in which everything but is used as an ingredient). As variety and amount of ingredients are entirely up to the imagination of the brewer, strengths vary quite a bit but are usually stronger than examples of the classic dry stout. Fruit, especially cherries, is often used with great success in specialty stout, making this category overlap somewhat with fruit beers.

Molasses Coffee Stout II

Winner, World Homebrew Contest, Stout, 1997
Paul Karasiewicz, Dayton, New Jersey
(Extract/Grain)

Ingredients for 5 Gallons

6	pounds Dutch dry malt extract
3/4	pound Belgian roasted barley
1/2	pound CaraPils malt
1/2	pound Belgian chocolate malt
1/2	pound Belgian aromatic malt
1/4	pound special roasted malt
1/4	pound Belgian biscuit malt
1/4	pound Special "B" malt
1 1/2	ounces Northern Brewer hop plugs, 8.4% alpha acid
1	ounce Liberty hop pellets, 3.3% alpha acid (30 minutes)
1/2	inch shaved brewers licorice added to boil
3/4	cup black strap molasses added to boil
1/3	cup French roasted coffee and chicory added at the end of the 65-minute boil—remove from heat and steep 10 minutes
	Wyeast No. 1318 London ale yeast
2	tablespoons black strap molasses (to prime)
4 1/2	ounces corn sugar (to prime)

Original gravity:	1.070
Final gravity:	1.030
Boiling time:	65 minutes
Primary fermentation:	2 weeks at 68–70 °F (20–21 °C)
Secondary fermentation:	3 1/2 weeks at 68–70 °F (20–21 °C)
Age when judged:	—

Brewer's Specifics

Mash grains at 155 °F (68 °C) for 30 minutes.

Chocolate Chambord Stout

Gold Medal, NHC, Classic-Style Specialty Beer, 1993
Ron Page, Middletown, Connecticut
(All-Grain)

Ingredients for 4 1/2 Gallons

7 1/2 pounds pale malt
1 1/2 pounds wheat malt
1/2 pound crystal malt
1/2 pound chocolate malt
1/2 pound flaked barley
1/4 pound Hershey's cocoa powder (30 minutes)
4 AAU Cascade hops (60 minutes)
4 AAU Perle hops (60 minutes)
1 tablespoon Chambord liqueur added to each bottle at capping force-carbonate

Original gravity:	1.051
Final gravity:	—
Boiling time:	60 minutes
Primary fermentation:	3 weeks at 65 °F (18 °C) in stainless steel
Secondary fermentation:	6 weeks at 35 °F (2 °C) in stainless steel
Age when judged:	—

Brewer's Specifics

Mash grains at 152 °F (67 °C) for 60 minutes. Use chocolate in boil for 30 minutes.

Judges' Comments

"Nice balance. Long-lasting aftertaste."

"Nice chocolate-raspberry flavor with bitter aftertaste of hops and raspberry."

"Delicious raspberry-vanilla flavor. Slight charcoal flavor. Should have more hop bitterness for a dry stout."

XXXmas Stout

Gold Medal, NHC, Foreign-Style Stout, 1996
Dan Morley, Calgary, Alberta, Canada
(All-Grain)

Ingredients for 6 Gallons
10	pounds two-row malt
1 1/2	pounds roasted barley
1 1/2	pounds flaked barley
1	pound wheat malt
1	pound instant oatmeal
1/2	pound Munich malt
1/2	pound chocolate malt
1/2	pound 120 °L crystal malt
2	ounces Northern Brewer hop pellets, 7.9% alpha acid (75 minutes)
1	ounce Styrian Goldings hop pellets, 4.2% alpha acid (35 minutes)
1	ounce Styrian Goldings hop pellets, 4.2% alpha acid (15 minutes)
1	teaspoon Irish moss (20 minutes)
	Wyeast No. 1084 Irish ale yeast
1	cup corn sugar (to prime)

Original gravity:	1.069
Final gravity:	1.020
Boiling time:	75 minutes
Primary fermentation:	5 days at 68 °F (20 °C) in glass
Secondary fermentation:	18 days at 62 °F (17 °C) in glass
Age when judged:	5 months

Brewer's Specifics
Mash grains at 122 °F (50 °C) for 30 minutes. Raise temperature to 140 °F (60 °C) with boiling water and then to 152 °F (67 °C) for 120 minutes. Sparge with 170 °F (77 °C) water.

Judges' Comments
"Roasty malt flavor. Balance of malt and bitterness good. A good, clean, well-balanced beer."

Oatmeal Stout

Silver Medal, NHC, Oatmeal Stout, 1996
Randy Johnson, Alton, Illinois
(All-Grain)

Ingredients for 6 1/2 Gallons
- 5 pounds American two-row malt
- 1 pound English crystal malt
- 1 pound oatmeal
- 1/2 pound English two-row chocolate malt
- 1/2 pound American six-row malt
- 1/4 pound Belgian biscuit malt
- 1/4 pound DeWolf-Cosyns Belgian Special "B" malt
- 1/4 pound roasted barley
- 1 ounce Styrian Goldings hop pellets, 4.5% alpha acid (60 minutes)
- 1 ounce East Kent Goldings hop plugs, 5% alpha acid (45 minutes)
- 1 ounce East Kent Goldings hop plugs, 5% alpha acid (30 minutes)
- 1 ounce East Kent Goldings hop plugs, 5% alpha acid (15 minutes)
- 2 ounces Fuggles hop plugs, 4% alpha acid (steep)
- Irish moss
- Wyeast No. 1098 British ale yeast
- 1 1/2 cups light dry malt extract (to prime)

Original gravity:	1.060
Final gravity:	1.022
Boiling time:	60 minutes
Primary fermentation:	1 week at 68 °F (20 °C) in glass
Secondary fermentation:	3 weeks at 38 °F (3 °C) in glass
Tertiary fermentation:	2 weeks at 68 °F (20 °C) in glass
Age when judged:	3 months

Brewer's Specifics
Soak grains at 90 °F (32 °C) for 240 minutes. Bring mash temperature to 120 °F (49 °C) for 30 minutes. Bring mash to 145 °F (63 °C) for 60 minutes. Mash-out at 160 °F (71 °C) for 10 minutes.

Judges' Comments
"Good head and head retention. Black color good. Clarity fine."

"Good black color. Good clarity. Roasted barley and malt flavor on low side. Oatmeal flavor should be more pronounced."

Steve's Stout

Reprinted from 1996 Special Issue of *Zymurgy*
Steve Gomes, Denver, Colorado
(All-Grain)

Ingredients for 5 Gallons

10	pounds Briess two-row malt
3/4	pound roasted barley
1/2	pound chocolate malt
1/2	pound 60 °L crystal malt
1/8	pound black patent malt
1 1/3	ounces Centennial hops (60 minutes)
2	packets Lallemand Nottingham dry ale yeast
	force-carbonate

Original gravity:	—
Final gravity:	—
Boiling time:	60 minutes
Primary fermentation:	14 days
Secondary fermentation:	—
Tertiary fermentation:	—

Brewer's Specifics

Mash grains at 155 °F (68 °C) for 120 minutes. The long mash circumvents the need to check for conversion. Sparge with 6 gallons of 170 °F (77 °C) water. Boil for 60 minutes. Chill and pitch yeast. Ferment for 14 days then keg.

New Stout II

Gold Medal, NHC, Foreign-Style, 1993
David and Melinda Brockington, Seattle, Washington
(All-Grain)

Ingredients for 5 Gallons
- 9 pounds English pale two-row malt
- 3 pounds roasted barley
- 1/2 pound 40 °L crystal malt
- 1/2 pound black patent malt
- 2 ounces Goldings hops (60 minutes)
- Wyeast No. 1084 Irish ale yeast
- 3/4 cup corn sugar (to prime)

Original gravity:	1.060
Final gravity:	1.016
Boiling time:	60 minutes
Primary fermentation:	15 days at 65 °F (18 °C) in glass
Secondary fermentation:	—
Age when judged:	4 months

Brewer's Specifics
Mash grains at 155 °F (68 °C) for 60 minutes.

Judges' Comments
"Roasted flavor not quite there. No strong off-flavors."

"Very good! Work on conditioning to fix the head."

"Malt evident, but needs more hops. Slightly out of balance to sweet side."

Untitled

NHC, Foreign-Style Stout, 1996
James Womack, Las Cruces, New Mexico
(All-Grain)

Ingredients for 5 1/2 Gallons
- 8 pounds English 4 °L pale malt
- 1 pound DeWolf-Cosyns Belgian CaraPils 8 °L malt
- 1 pound Hugh Baird 575 °L roasted barley
- 1/2 pound DeWolf-Cosyns Special "B" 220 °L malt
- 2 ounces Centennial hop pellets, 6.6% alpha acid (130 minutes)
- Wyeast No. 1084 Irish ale yeast
- 2/3 cup dextrose (to prime)

Original gravity:	1.074
Final gravity:	1.022
Boiling time:	130 minutes
Primary fermentation:	14 days at 55–65 °F (13–18 °C) in glass
Secondary fermentation:	6 days at 55–65 °F (13–18 °C) in glass
Age when judged:	6 months

Brewer's Specifics
Mash grains at 153 °F (67 °C) for 80 minutes.

DOPPELBOCK

During the forty days of Lent prior to Easter and during the four weeks of Advent following Christmas, the followers of Saint Paula in Munich fasted. No solid food was allowed, but liquids were. Doppelbock was produced as a nutritious and sustaining beverage to substitute for food. In the 1800s, this double bock had a much higher finishing gravity, making it richer and less alcoholic (around 6 percent by volume) than it is now. Today, its original gravity is still 1.072–1.084 (18–21 °Plato), but it finishes with 7.7 percent alcohol by volume. Because of this strength, brew it early enough in the year to allow a lengthy lagering time. Doppelbock ranges from light to very dark and has a very full body. Malty sweetness predominates in both aroma and flavor with obvious levels of alcohol. Very low bitterness is usually present, though a slight "noble-type" hop flavor is tolerated for the style. No hop aroma, fruitiness, or diacetyl should be detectable. Doppelbock is usually served with low carbonation.

Hallucinator

Gold Medal, NHC, Doppelbock, 1994
David Cooke and James Prince, Yorktown, Virginia
(Extract/Grain)

Ingredients for 5 Gallons

3 1/3	pounds Munton and Fison amber malt extract syrup
3 1/3	pounds Munton and Fison light malt extract syrup
3	pounds Laaglander extra light dry malt extract
2	pounds 50 °L crystal malt
1	pound Laaglander amber dry malt extract
1/2	pound 338 °L chocolate malt
2	ounces Saaz hops, 3.5% alpha acid (60 minutes)
1	ounce Saaz hops, 3.5% alpha acid (5 minutes)
	Wyeast No. 2206 Bavarian lager yeast
1 1/4	cups Laaglander extra light dry malt extract (to prime)

Original gravity:	1.081
Final gravity:	1.022
Boiling time:	60 minutes
Primary fermentation:	8 days at 50 °F (10 °C) in glass
Secondary fermentation:	39 days at 50 °F (10 °C) in glass
Age when judged:	3 1/2 months

Brewer's Specifics
Steep grains for 60 minutes at 160 °F (71 °C).

Judges' Comments
"An obvious metallic character—maybe from hops? Sweet. Malty. A bit of roastiness comes through. Nice carbonation feel. Perhaps a bit bitter on finish. Metallic character moderates after first sip. Good maltiness, you got that perfect."

"Malty. Roasty. Sweet. Low hop bitterness. Conditioning okay. Sherrylike. Balance toward malt finish. Warming, alcoholic. Watch for falling goats! This beer might be a little old but it's the best so far. Try to get less yeast in the bottle and you'll have a great one."

Untitled

Silver Medal, NHC, Doppelbock, 1995
Thomas Altenbach, Tracy, California
(All-Grain)

Ingredients for 10 Gallons
18	pounds pale malt
6	pounds Munich malt
2	pounds toasted pale malt
2	pounds German crystal malt
1 1/2	pounds chocolate malt
1	pound wheat malt
1	pound American crystal malt
1/2	pound brown malt
1/2	ounce Centennial hops, 11.8% alpha acid (60 minutes)
1/4	ounce Hallertau hops, 5.2% alpha acid (60 minutes)
1	ounce Hallertau hops, 5.2% alpha acid (30 minutes)
1/2	ounce Hallertau hops, 5.2% alpha acid (10 minutes)
2	ounces Hallertau hops, 5.2% alpha acid (finish)
1	ounce Mt. Hood hops, 6.3% alpha acid (finish)
	filtered tap water
	Wyeast No. 2007 Pilsen lager yeast
3/4	cup corn sugar (to prime)

Original gravity:	1.096
Final gravity:	1.032
Boiling time:	120 minutes
Primary fermentation:	22 days at 50 °F (10 °C) in glass
Secondary fermentation:	11 days at 50 °F (10 °C) in glass
Age when judged:	6 months

Brewer's Specifics
Mash grains at 158 °F (70 °C) for 90 minutes.

Judges' Comments
"Great look with just a hint of ruby in color."

"Nice blend of malt, molasses, and roast. Good strength. Licorice in tail. Chocolatey. Rich."

The Debilitator

<hr>

Winner, Club-Only Competition, Doppelbock, 1995
Timothy Dalton, North Reading, Massachusetts
(All-Grain)

Ingredients for 5 Gallons

10 1/2 pounds Munich malt
    2 pounds CaraVienne malt
    1 pound CaraMunich malt
    1 pound aromatic malt
  1/2 pound CaraPils malt
  1/4 pound wheat malt
    2 ounces Hallertau Hersbrucker hops, 2.3% alpha acid (60 minutes)
    1 ounce Saaz hops, 2.4% alpha acid (60 minutes)
      Wyeast No. 2206 Bavarian lager yeast
  3/4 cup corn sugar (to prime)

Original gravity:	1.077
Final gravity:	1.026
Boiling time:	120 minutes
Primary fermentation:	4 weeks at 43 °F (6 °C) in glass
Secondary fermentation:	1 week at 50 °F (10 °C) in glass
Age when judged:	1 1/2 months

Brewer's Specifics

Mash grains with 15 quarts of 146 °F (63 °C) water. Hold mash at 133 °F (56 °C) for 30 minutes. Remove 7 quarts of thick mash and heat to boiling for more than 15 minutes. Boil for 30 minutes and then return to main mash to raise the temperature to 150 °F (66 °C). Hold temperature for 30 minutes. Add boiling water to raise the temperature to 168 °F (76 °C). Hold the temperature for 10 minutes. Sparge with 5 gallons of 167 °F (75 °C) water and collect 7 1/2 gallons wort.

Judges' Comments

"Roasted malt flavor. Good malt flavor, well-balanced with hops. Alcoholic warmth evident. Very good beer. Could use fuller body."

"Full round malty sweetness. Subdued hops. Slight bitter finish. Controlled alcohol. Could use some more malt and less hop bitterness."

"Lots of alcohol. Nice balance. Could use a bit more malt."

"Clean doppel. Overall very nice though roasty flavor is not totally to style."

Educator

Third Place, Club-Only Competition, Doppelbock, 1996
Bill Campbell, North East, Pennsylvania
(Extract/Grain)

Ingredients for 5 Gallons

6	pounds six-row malt
6	pounds dark malt extract
3 1/3	pounds Hansberg Dortmunder malt extract
2 1/2	pounds honey
1/2	pound 40 °L crystal malt
1/2	pound CaraPils malt
3/8	pound roasted malt
1/4	pound chocolate malt
1/8	pound black patent malt
3/4	ounce Cluster hops (60 minutes)
2	teaspoons gypsum added to mash water
1/2	teaspoon Irish moss (last 5 minutes)
	CL680 lager yeast
	Pasteur champagne yeast
1/2	cup corn sugar (to prime)

Original gravity:	1.115
Final gravity:	1.040
Boiling time:	60 minutes
Primary fermentation:	7 days at 65 °F (18 °C) in plastic
Secondary fermentation:	30 days at 55 °F (13 °C) in glass
Age when judged:	7 months

Brewer's Specifics

Mash grains at 150 °F (66 °C) for 120 minutes.

DORTMUNDER

Named after the German city of its origin, this lager is golden in color and mashed at high enough temperatures to achieve a fuller body than a Pilsener. It also has less hop character than a Pilsener. With medium bitterness and very low levels of "noble-type" hop aroma and flavor, its maltiness is less pronounced than that of a Munich helles. Strength is also relatively high (up to 1.054 [13.5 °Plato]) with an alcohol content around 5.5 percent. The style is produced worldwide, but usually there is some reference to Dortmunder, Dort, or export. No fruitiness, esters, or perceptible levels of diacetyl are allowable for the style. Some alcoholic warmth is permissible. Carbonation is usually moderate for a beer of this color and strength.

Dortmund 357

**Third Place, Club-Only Competition, Dortmund/Export, 1995
Keith Weerts, Windsor, California
(All-Grain)**

Ingredients for 6 1/5 Gallons
11 1/2 pounds German Pilsener malt
  45 grams Saaz hops, 2.5% alpha acid (60 minutes)
  15 grams Northern Brewer hops, 7.4% alpha acid (60 minutes)
  20 grams Saaz hops, 2.5% alpha acid (30 minutes)
  15 grams Saaz hops, 2.5% alpha acid (10 minutes)
  10 grams Saaz hops, 2.5% alpha acid (finish)
     tap water
     Wyeast No. 2278 Czech Pils lager yeast
     force-carbonate

Original gravity:	1.050
Final gravity:	1.012
Boiling time:	90 minutes
Primary fermentation:	11 days at 50 °F (10 °C) in stainless steel
Secondary fermentation:	3 weeks at 44–32 °F (7–10 °C) in glass
Age when judged:	2 months

Brewer's Specifics
Mash-in at 120 °F (49 °C) for 30 minutes. Raise temperature to 144 °F (62 °C) for 20 minutes. Mash grains at 152 °F (67 °C) for 60 minutes.

Judges' Comments
"Malty with complex German malt aroma characteristic of this style. A touch of spicy hops comes through nicely. Assertive maltiness up front with sense of 'husky' astringency coming through, then ends slightly bitter for this style. Alcohol warming is evident."

Dork-Munder

Finalist, NHC, Dortmunder/Export, 1996
Mike Hufnagel, Cincinnati, Ohio
(All-Grain)

Ingredients for 5 Gallons

8 3/4	pounds Belgian Pilsener malt
1	pound Belgian Munich malt
8	ounces Belgian CaraPils malt
2	ounces 10 °L crystal malt
5/8	ounce Pride of Ringwood hops, 7.5% alpha acid (60 minutes)
1/8	ounce Pride of Ringwood hops, 7.5% alpha acid (45 minutes)
1	ounce Ultra hops, 2.9% alpha acid (15 minutes)
1	ounce Ultra hops, 2.9% alpha acid (10 minutes)
	Wyeast No. 2308 Munich lager yeast

Original gravity:	1.057
Final gravity:	1.008
Boiling time:	90 minutes
Primary fermentation:	18 days at 50 °F (10 °C) in glass
Secondary fermentation:	17 days at 50 °F (10 °C) in glass
Tertiary fermentation:	5 days at 33 °F (1 °C) in glass
Age when judged:	3 months

Brewer's Specifics

Mash grains at 152 °F (67 °C) for 60 minutes.

Judges' Comments

"Hint of sourness leaves a clean dry finish. Nice well-made beer. Grassy hop finish detracts. Could use more malt and body to round out the flavors. Try higher mash temperature."

Fill'er Up with High Test

Silver Medal, NHC, Dortmund/Export, 1995
George Fix, Arlington, Texas
(All-Grain)

Ingredients for 13 1/2 Gallons
18 pounds Durst Pilsener malt
5   pounds Durst Munich malt
2   ounces Tettnang hops, 4.5% alpha acid (45 minutes)
2   ounces Hallertau hops, 4.2% alpha acid (30 minutes)
1   ounce Liberty hops, 3.5% alpha acid (finish)
    Wyeast No. 2206 Bavarian lager yeast

Original gravity:	1.056
Final gravity:	1.014
Boiling time:	90 minutes
Primary fermentation:	10 days at 50 °F (10 °C) in stainless steel
Secondary fermentation:	6 weeks at 35 °F (2 °C) in stainless steel
Age when judged:	3 months

Brewer's Specifics
Mash grains at 122 °F (50 °C) for 30 minutes. Raise temperature to 140 °F (60 °C) for 30 minutes and 158 °F (70 °C) for 30 minutes.

Judges' Comments
"Well balanced with malt up front and hops sticking. Well-made beer that lacks some complexity. Could use about 5–10% more bitterness."

"Malty and very rounded up front with DMS coming through in taste. Continues with malty sweetness and ends balanced but bland."

Von Schnookulas Export

Gold Medal, NHC, Dortmund/Export, 1993
Robert Henke, Whitefish Bay, Wisconsin
(All-Grain)

Ingredients for 5 Gallons

6	pounds two-row malt
1 1/2	pounds rice
1 1/4	ounces Cascade hops, 5% alpha acid (60 minutes)
1/2	ounce Saaz hops, 4.4% alpha acid (5 minutes)
	Wyeast No. 2042 Danish lager yeast
3/4	cup corn sugar (to prime)

Original gravity:	1.040
Final gravity:	1.012
Boiling time:	90 minutes
Primary fermentation:	10 days at 55 °F (13 °C) in glass
Secondary fermentation:	14 days at 50 °F (10 °C) in glass
Tertiary fermentation:	7 days at 35 °F (2 °C) in glass
Age when judged:	5 months

Brewer's Specifics

Boil rice for 45 minutes prior to mashing. Mash grains at 120 °F (49 °C) for 45 minutes. Raise temperature to 140 °F (60 °C) for 45 minutes, 155 °F (68 °C) for 90 minutes, and 170 °F (77 °C) for 20 minutes. Sparge with 4 gallons of 180 °F (82 °C) water.

Judges' Comments

"Very clean with good hop flavor and balance. Very good aftertaste. Nice conditioning."

"Light and soft. Quite clean with nice conditioning. Needs to have just a bit more hop assertiveness and a bit more body."

"Slightly light in color. Clean flavor. Very pleasant. Malt-to-hop balance is slightly light for style. Excellent—I love it."

Fallen Oak Dortmund

Gold Medal, NHC, Dortmund/Export, 1994
Keith Weerts, Windsor, California
(All-Grain)

Ingredients for 11 1/2 Gallons
16	pounds German Pilsener malt
7	pounds Klages malt
3	ounces Saaz hops, 2.4% alpha acid (60 minutes)
2 4/5	ounces Saaz hops, 5% alpha acid (60 minutes)
1 1/5	ounces Saaz hops, 2.4% alpha acid (30 minutes)
3/5	ounce Saaz hops, 5% alpha acid (15 minutes)
1 1/5	ounces Saaz hops, 2.4% alpha acid (finish)
	Wyeast No. 2278 Czech Pils lager yeast
	force-carbonate in keg

Original gravity:	1.051
Final gravity:	1.018
Boiling time:	90 minutes
Primary fermentation:	10 days at 45 °F (7 °C) in glass
Secondary fermentation:	35 days at 33 °F (1 °C) in glass
Age when judged:	2 1/2 months

Brewer's Specifics
Mash grains at 122 °F (50 °C) for 20 minutes. Raise temperature to 144 °F (62 °C) for 25 minutes and 154 °F (68 °C) for 30 minutes. Sparge with 8 gallons of 175 °F (79 °C) water.

Judges' Comments
"Alcohol warmth evident. Malt aftertaste really nice. No big defects. Too much hop bitterness. Real nice beer. Just on the high side of bitterness for style."

"Just a bit too bitter for style. Very tasty beer. Just a bit too highly hopped."

Emily's Export

Gold Medal, NHC, Dortmunder/European-Style Export, 1996
Ted Johnston, Phoenixville, Pennsylvania
(All-Grain)

Ingredients for 5 Gallons

6	pounds Durst Pilsener malt
1	pound HDM CaraPils malt
1	pound Briess six-row pale malt
1/2	pound Durst Munich malt
1 1/2	ounces Hallertau Hersbrucker hops, 3.5% alpha acid (60 minutes)
1/2	ounce Hallertau Hersbrucker hops, 3.5% alpha acid (30 minutes)
1/2	ounce Hallertau Hersbrucker hops, 3.5% alpha acid (10 minutes)
	Wyeast No. 2206 Bavarian lager yeast
3/4	cup corn sugar (to prime)

Original gravity:	1.051
Final gravity:	1.020
Boiling time:	90 minutes
Primary fermentation:	4 days at 65 °F (18 °C) and 11 days at 48 °F (9 °C) in glass
Secondary fermentation:	30 days at 48 °F (9 °C) in glass
Tertiary fermentation:	16 days at 35–40 °F (2–4 °C) in glass
Age when judged:	6 months

Brewer's Specifics

Mash grains at 132 °F (56 °C) for 30 minutes, 154 °F (68 °C) for 90 minutes, and 168 °F (76 °C) for 5 minutes. Raise temperature by decocting 1/3 of the mash to boiling and returning it to the main mash.

Judges' Comments

"Slight malt flavor with pleasant hop finish. Some sour-metallic finish detracts from flavor. Could use a little more malt."

"Nice malty sweetness—tastes like a decoction mash. Body a bit thin."

Boogie's Export

Gold Medal, NHC, Dortmund/Export, 1991
Dave Woodruff, Sebatopol, California
(All-Grain)

Ingredients for 5 Gallons
- 10 pounds Klages malt
- 3/4 pound Munich malt
- 1/2 pound Vienna malt
- 1/2 pound dextrin malt
- 1/2 ounce Northern Brewer hops, 8% alpha acid (60 minutes)
- 1/4 ounce Northern Brewer hops, 8% alpha acid (40 minutes)
- 1/2 ounce Hallertau hops, 5.3% alpha acid (30 minutes)
- 1 ounce Tettnang hops, 3.3% alpha acid (7 minutes)
- 1/2 teaspoon gypsum added to mash water
- 1/2 teaspoon chalk added to mash water
- Wyeast No. 2206 Bavarian lager yeast

Original gravity:	1.058
Final gravity:	—
Boiling time:	60 minutes
Primary fermentation:	11 days at 48 °F (9 °C) in glass
Secondary fermentation:	3 weeks at 35 °F (2 °C) in glass
Age when judged:	1 1/2 months

Brewer's Specifics
Mash all grains at 152 °F (67 °C) for 90 minutes.

Judges' Comments
"Good. Clean nose. Excessive hop aroma. Good taste. Good balance of malt and bittering hops."

"Too much flavor hops. Aftertaste is a little bitter. A little astringent. Great beer. Tastes right! Reduce flavor and finish to get true-to-style Dortmunder."

SPICED ALE

Brewing for the holidays usually means the use of unorthodox ingredients for many homebrewers. Historically herbs and spices lent bitterness to beer before hops were favored for this purpose. Gale, juniper, heather, ginger, and anise were once used. Now, more commercial brewers take advantage of spices like cardamom, nutmeg, and cinnamon to produce holiday ales. This is a very wide category of styles, so use your imagination. Some words of advice: Don't overdo it. For example, chili beer is a great novelty, but you need to ask yourself if you really want to drink 5 gallons of it. Also, some spices like cloves come through much stronger than others. You might want to make a fairly neutral ale and blend a little of it with a few spices to see what it tastes like. From there, depending on what you like, you can devise a recipe.

Untitled

Bronze Medal, NHC, Herb and Spice Beer, 1996
David Archambeau, Jamestown, North Dakota
(All-Grain)

Ingredients for 5 Gallons
9	pounds Belgian pale malt
1 1/2	pounds Harrington two-row malt
1	pound 60 °L crystal malt
1	pound brown sugar
1/2	pound dark brown sugar
2	ounces Tettnang hop pellets, 2.6% alpha acid (45 minutes)
1	ounce cowslip (primrose flowers) (20 minutes)
1	ounce dried mug wort (15 minutes)
1/2	ounce crushed coriander seeds added to secondary fermentation
1/2	ounce crushed coriander seeds (10 minutes)
1/2	ounce crushed cardamom seeds (10 minutes)
1/4	ounce grated ginger root (10 minutes)
	Wyeast No. 1214 Belgian ale yeast
3/4	cup corn sugar

Original gravity:	1.057
Final gravity:	1.006
Boiling time:	80 minutes
Primary fermentation:	17 days at 61 °F (16 °C) in plastic
Secondary fermentation:	44 days at 60 °F (16 °C) in glass
Age when judged:	4 months

Brewer's Specifics
Mash-in at 157 °F (69 °C). Stabilize at 152 °F (67 °C) for 90 minutes. Mash-out at 165 °F (74 °C) for 10 minutes. Sparge with 4 1/4 gallons of 170 °F (77 °C) water.

Judges' Comments
"Clarity okay but not crystal clear. Medium golden to amber in color. Sweet balance. Interesting complexity in spice blend. Are there any hops in here or is all bitterness from herbs? Very floral."

Chautauqua Holiday Ale

Gold Medal, NHC, Herb Beer, 1994
Dan Rabin and Gabriella Hess, Boulder, Colorado
(Extract)

Ingredients for 6 Gallons

8	pounds Alexander's pale malt extract syrup
2	pounds dark dry malt extract
1	pound honey
3 1/2	ounces finely chopped ginger
2	ounces Northern Brewer hops, 7.4% alpha acid (60 minutes)
1	ounce Willamette hops (15 minutes)
1	tablespoon whole cloves
1/2	tablespoon ground coriander
8	medium grated orange peels
7	3-inch cinnamon sticks
1	pinch Irish moss (15 minutes)
	Wyeast No. 1056 American ale yeast
1	cup corn sugar (to prime)

Original gravity:	1.052
Final gravity:	1.020
Boiling time:	60 minutes
Primary fermentation:	1 week at 65 °F (18 °C) in glass
Secondary fermentation:	4 weeks at 65 °F (18 °C) in glass
Age when judged:	6 1/2 months

Brewer's Specifics

To make a spice tea, boil 1 gallon of water and turn off heat. Add honey, orange peel, and all spices. Cover and steep for 60 minutes at 180 °F (82 °C). Add to boiled wort.

Judges' Comments

"Effervescence on tongue. Nice marriage of spices. They all blend together with one spice dominating. Sweet finish. A great beer to sip by the fireplace."

"This is a smooth brew that goes down easy and is followed by some very nice spice flavor. The aftertaste is packed with clove and some ginger. Very clean. I enjoyed this brew. It was smooth, tasty, and left my mouth with a wonderful spicy aftertaste. Good job!"

Xmas Ale 1994

Gold Medal, NHC, Specialty Beer, 1995
Strom Thacker, Gainesville, Georgia
(All-Grain)

Ingredients for 6 Gallons

8	pounds Briess two-row pale malt
1	pound Briess Special "B" roasted malt
1	pound Briess 20 °L crystal malt
1	pound Briess CaraPils malt
1	pound wildflower honey added to boil
1/2	ounce Northern Brewer hops, 7.1% alpha acid (60 minutes)
1/2	ounce Northern Brewer hops, 6.5% alpha acid (60 minutes)
1/2	ounce British Columbia Goldings hops, 4.6% alpha acid (30 minutes)
1/2	ounce British Columbia Goldings hops, 4.6% alpha acid (2 minutes)
1 1/2	teaspoons cinnamon added to secondary
3/4	teaspoon nutmeg added to secondary
3/4	teaspoon allspice added to secondary
3/4	teaspoon mace added to secondary
1/4	teaspoon cloves added to secondary
	Wyeast No. 1056 American ale yeast
3/4	cup corn sugar (to prime)

Original gravity:	1.061
Final gravity:	1.017
Boiling time:	90 minutes
Primary fermentation:	10 days at 65 °F (18 °C) in glass
Secondary fermentation:	16 days at 65 °F (18 °C) in glass
Age when judged:	7 months

Brewer's Specifics
Mash grains at 158 °F (70 °C) for 60 minutes.

Judges' Comments
"Not at all disappointed. Great balance of specialties with malt and hops displaying a complex taste profile with wonderful finish."

"Very tasty. A nicely balanced blend of ingredients. Honey character manages to come through all the rest. With all those ingredients it is still possible to detect almost all."

Gingerella

NHC, Herb and Spice Beer, 1996
Christopher DePerno, Rapid City, South Dakota
(Extract)

Ingredients for 5 Gallons

3 3/4	pounds Morgan's malt
3 1/3	pounds Blue Mountain lager hopped malt extract
2	pounds raw unfiltered clover honey (15 minutes)
2 1/2	ounces fresh grated ginger root (15 minutes)
	Morgan's dried lager yeast
1 1/4	cups Laaglander unhopped extra-light dried malt extract (to prime)

Original gravity:	1.051
Final gravity:	1.014
Boiling time:	30 minutes
Primary fermentation:	8 days at 65–75 °F (18–24°C) in glass
Secondary fermentation:	12 days at 65–75 °F (18–24°C) in glass
Age when judged:	10 months

Brewer's Specifics

Bring 1 1/4 gallons of cold water to a boil in the brewpot. Add the malt extract syrup to the brewpot and boil for 30 minutes. Add ginger root and honey 15 minutes into the boil. Sparge the hot wort into 3 gallons of cold water within the glass carboy. Pitch the yeast starter. Add cold water to the carboy to fill the remaining space. Shake the carboy to aerate the wort and the overflow tube attached. Place into a vent bucket half filled with chlorine water to catch the overflow. Ferment the brew at approximately 65–75 °F (18–24 °C). Attach the fermentation lock 2 days after the initial brewing date. Rack to the secondary fermenter 8 days after the initial brewing date. Bottle with 1 1/4 cups malt extract (dissolved in 2 cups boiling water) 20 days after the initial brewing date.

Clean Christmas Ale

NHC, Herb and Spice Beer, 1996
Brent Stromness, Salt Lake City, Utah
(All-Grain)

Ingredients for 5 Gallons
    7   pounds two-row malt
    2   pounds Hugh Baird brown malt
    1   pound 70–80 °L crystal malt
  1/2   pound American dextrin malt
  1/2   pound wheat malt
    7   ounces honey malt
    1   ounce black patent malt
  1/2   ounce chocolate malt
    1   ounce Cascade hop pellets, 5.6% alpha acid (95 minutes)
  1/4   ounce Columbus hop pellets, 13.6% alpha acid (95 minutes)
  1/3   ounce East Kent Goldings hop pellets, 5.4% alpha acid (10 minutes)
  1/3   ounce East Kent Goldings hop pellets, 5.4% alpha acid (3 minutes)
  1/4   teaspoon gypsum added to sparge water
  1/8   teaspoon citric acid added to sparge water
        Wyeast No. 1968 Special London yeast
  1/2   cup brewers sugar (to prime)

Original gravity:	1.074
Final gravity:	1.028
Boiling time:	120 minutes
Primary fermentation:	8 days at 65 °F (18 °C) in glass
Secondary fermentation:	25 days at 65 °F (18 °C) in glass
Age when judged:	6 months

Brewer's Specifics
Mash grains at 152 °F (67 °C) for 75 minutes.

India Chai Beer

NHC, Herb and Spice Beer, 1996
Brian Rezac, Boulder, Colorado
(Extract/Grain)

Ingredients for 5 Gallons

8	pounds Munton and Fison light malt extract
1	pound English 55 °L crystal malt
8	ounces Belgian Munich malt
4	ounces Belgian CaraPils malt
4	ounces Briess chocolate malt
4	ounces Briess roasted barley
2	ounces Cascade, 4.9% alpha acid (70 minutes)
3/4	ounce Saaz, 3.0% alpha acid (15 minutes)
1/2	ounce Saaz, 3.0% alpha acid (2 minutes, finish)
120	cracked cardamom pods
11	teaspoons cinnamon chips
11	teaspoons whole coriander
5 1/2	teaspoons whole cloves
5 1/2	teaspoons whole peppercorns
1	teaspoon Irish moss (15 minutes)
1	teaspoon Burton salts (15 minutes)
11	inches fresh, sliced, peeled ginger
	Wyeast No. 1007 German ale yeast
	force-carbonate

Original gravity:	1.060
Final gravity:	1.016
Boiling time:	60 minutes
Primary fermentation:	8 days in 6 1/2-gallon glass carboy
Secondary fermentation:	25 days in 5-gallon glass carboy
Age when judged:	6 months

Brewer's Specifics

Boil spices for 20 minutes, then let sit for 20 minutes. Add tea to wort at 20 minutes.

Appendix A BEER LOG

Name of Brew _____

Brewing Location _____

Special Ingredients _____

Batch Size _____

Water Source _____

Water Treatment _____

Boiling Time _____

Chilling Method _____

Yeast Culture _____

Yeast Starter _____

Yeast Nutrients _____

Carbonation _____

Brewing Date _____ Racking Date_____ Bottling/Kegging Date _____

Specific Gravities: Original _____ Terminal _____

Flavor Comments _____

Hops

Type	Pellets or Whole?	Amount (oz.)	% Alpha Acid	Use (Boil, Dry, Etc.)	Time

Malt (Grain, Extracts, and/or Other Fermentables)

Type/Brand	Amount (lbs.)	Use (Steep/Mash)	Time	Temperature

Fermentation

	Duration (Days)	Temperature	Type of Fermenter (Glass, Plastic, Etc.)
Primary			
Secondary			
Tertiary			

Appendix B FORMULAS AND CONVERSIONS

Here are some basic formulas to help calculate conversions.

Bittering Units

For a one-hour boil, percent utilization is usually 25 to 30. The constant that converts these formulas from metric to U.S. units is 1.34.

$$IBU = \frac{\text{Ounces of Hops x \%Alpha Acid of Hops x \%Utilization}}{\text{Gallons x 1.34}}$$

$$HBU = \frac{\text{IBU x gallons x 1.34}}{\text{\%Utilization}}$$

Homebrew Bittering Units are a measure of the total amount of bitterness in a given volume of beer. Calculate bittering units by multiplying the percent of alpha acid in the hops by the number of ounces. For example, if 2 ounces of Northern Brewer hops (9 percent alpha acid) and 3 ounces of Cascade hops (5 percent alpha acid) were used in a 10-gallon batch, the total amount of bittering units would be 33: (2 x 9) + (3 x 5) = 18 + 15. Bittering units per gallon would be 3.3 in a 10-gallon batch or 6.6 in a 5-gallon batch, so it is important to note volumes whenever expressing bittering units.

Alcohol Content

Alcohol by Weight = (Original Gravity − Final Gravity) x 105

Alcohol by Volume = Alcohol by Weight x 1.25

Alcohol by Weight = Alcohol by Volume x 0.80

For example, the original gravity of your beer was 1.060, and the final gravity is 1.015. So, the equation reads (1.060 − 1.015) x 105 = 4.7% alcohol by weight. Alcohol by volume = 4.7 x 1.25 = 5.9% alcohol by volume.

Using Dry Malt Extract and Malt Extract Syrup

Malt extract syrup is 15–18 percent water. Therefore, the amount of dry extract to use in a recipe calling for extract syrup is about 85 percent of the quantity of syrup given in the recipe. Use the following two formulas to convert extract recipes from one type of extract to another.

Amount of Liquid Extract Given x 0.85 = Amount of Dry Extract to Use

Amount of Dry Extract Given x 0.85 = Amount of Liquid Extract to Use

Converting an All-Grain Recipe to Extract

The amount of extract to substitute in a recipe using all-grain is about 75 percent of the amount of grain given in the recipe. Use the following two formulas to convert between extract recipes and all-grain recipes.

Amount of Grain Given x 0.75 = Amount of Extract to Use

Amount of Extract Given ÷ 0.75 = Amount of Grain to Use

Note that "grain" in these formulas refers to the grain that will provide the fermentable constituents in your wort. They won't work for converting specialty grains to extract.

Estimating Original Gravity

$$\text{Pounds of Malt Needed} = \frac{(OG - 1) \times \text{Number of Gallons}}{(\text{Extraction Rating} - 1)}$$

For example, you brew 5 gallons of an Oktoberfest beer with an original gravity of about 1.054. You know your extraction rating is about 1.025, so the equation reads: $(1.054 - 1) \times 5 \div (1.025 - 1) = 10.8$ pounds of malt for your batch. The extraction rating of a malt is the specific gravity of 1 gallon of wort made from 1 pound of the malt. Therefore, extraction ratings can vary according to the kind of malt you use. A malt extract syrup will have a rating of about 1.033, dried malt about 1.038 to 1.042, Vienna malt about 1.025, etc. You can often find these ratings at your homebrew supply shop. Also note: your extraction rating varies according to your brewing system.

Estimating Color

(Pounds of Malt A x Color Rating of Malt A) + (Pounds of Malt B x Color Rating of Malt B) + . . . = (Gallons of Beer) x (Color of Beer)

For example, you brew 5 gallons of beer with a desired color rating of 12. This means the right side of the equation equals 60. By substituting the color ratings and weights for the malts you use, you can figure how much of each malt is needed for the desired color. For instance, Munich malt has a color rating of 10, and Vienna malt has a color rating of 4. So, it will take 7 1/2 pounds of Vienna malt and 3 pounds of Munich malt to give you a color rating of 12 in your finished beer. Your homebrew supply shop should be able to give you color values for the malts you purchase. Different malts have different color ratings. For more details, check *Zymurgy*, 1992 Spring Issue.

Unit Conversion Chart

Index	lb. to kg	oz. to g	fl. oz. to mL	gal. to L US	gal. to L UK	qt. to L US	qt. to L UK	pt. to L US	pt. to L UK	tsp. to mL	tbsp. to mL	cup to mL
0.25	0.11	7	7	0.95	1.14	0.24	0.28	0.12	0.14	1.2	3.7	59
0.50	0.23	14	15	1.89	2.27	0.47	0.57	0.24	0.28	2.5	7.4	118
0.75	0.34	21	22	2.84	3.41	0.71	0.85	0.35	0.43	3.7	11.1	177
1.00	0.45	28	30	3.79	4.55	0.95	1.14	0.47	0.57	4.9	14.8	237
1.25	0.57	35	37	4.73	5.68	1.18	1.42	0.59	0.71	6.2	18.5	296
1.50	0.68	43	44	5.68	6.82	1.42	1.70	0.71	0.85	7.4	22.2	355
1.75	0.79	50	52	6.62	7.96	1.66	1.99	0.83	0.99	8.6	25.9	414
2.00	0.91	57	59	7.57	9.09	1.89	2.27	0.95	1.14	9.9	29.6	473
2.25	1.02	64	67	8.52	10.23	2.13	2.56	1.06	1.28	11.1	33.3	532
2.50	1.13	71	74	9.46	11.36	2.37	2.84	1.18	1.42	12.3	37.0	591
2.75	1.25	78	81	10.41	12.50	2.60	3.13	1.30	1.56	13.6	40.2	651
3.00	1.36	85	89	11.36	13.64	2.84	3.41	1.42	1.70	14.8	44.4	710
3.25	1.47	92	96	12.30	14.77	3.08	3.69	1.54	1.85	16.0	48.1	769
3.50	1.59	99	103	13.25	15.91	3.31	3.98	1.66	1.99	17.3	51.8	828
3.75	1.70	106	111	14.19	17.05	3.55	4.26	1.77	2.13	18.5	55.4	887
4.00	1.81	113	118	15.14	18.18	3.79	4.55	1.89	2.27	19.7	59.1	946
4.25	1.93	120	126	16.09	19.32	4.02	4.83	2.01	2.42	20.9	62.8	1,005
4.50	2.04	128	133	17.03	20.46	4.26	5.11	2.13	2.56	22.2	66.5	1,065
4.75	2.15	135	140	17.98	21.59	4.50	5.40	2.25	2.70	23.4	70.2	1,124
5.00	2.27	142	148	18.93	22.73	4.73	5.68	2.37	2.84	24.6	73.9	1,183
5.25	2.38	149	155	19.87	23.87	4.97	5.97	2.48	2.98	25.9	77.6	1,242
5.50	2.49	156	163	20.82	25.00	5.20	6.25	2.60	3.13	27.1	81.3	1,301
5.75	2.61	163	170	21.77	26.14	5.44	6.53	2.72	3.27	28.3	85.0	1,360
6.00	2.72	170	177	22.71	27.28	5.68	6.82	2.84	3.41	29.6	88.7	1,419
6.25	2.84	177	185	23.66	28.41	5.91	7.10	2.96	3.55	30.8	92.4	1,479
6.50	2.95	184	192	24.60	29.55	6.15	7.39	3.08	3.69	32.0	96.1	1,538
6.75	3.06	191	200	25.55	30.69	6.39	7.67	3.19	3.84	33.3	99.8	1,597
7.00	3.18	198	207	26.50	31.82	6.62	7.96	3.31	3.98	34.5	103.5	1,656
7.25	3.29	206	214	27.44	32.96	6.86	8.24	3.43	4.12	35.7	107.2	1,715
7.50	3.40	213	222	28.39	34.09	7.10	8.52	3.55	4.26	37.0	110.9	1,774
7.75	3.52	220	229	29.34	35.23	7.33	8.81	3.67	4.40	38.2	114.6	1,834
8.00	3.63	227	237	30.28	36.37	7.57	9.09	3.79	4.55	39.4	118.3	1,893
8.25	3.74	234	244	31.23	37.50	7.81	9.38	3.90	4.69	40.7	122.0	1,952
8.50	3.86	241	251	32.18	38.64	8.04	9.66	4.02	4.83	41.9	125.7	2,011
8.75	3.97	248	259	33.12	39.78	8.28	9.94	4.14	4.97	43.1	129.4	2,070
9.00	4.08	255	266	34.07	40.91	8.52	10.23	4.26	5.11	44.4	133.1	2,129
9.25	4.20	262	274	35.01	42.05	8.75	10.51	4.38	5.26	45.6	136.8	2,188
9.50	4.31	269	281	36.96	43.19	9.99	10.80	4.50	5.40	46.8	140.5	2,248
9.75	4.42	276	288	37.91	44.32	9.23	11.08	4.61	5.54	48.1	144.2	2,307
10.00	4.54	283	296	37.85	45.46	9.46	11.36	4.73	5.68	49.3	147.9	2,366
10.25	4.65	291	303	38.80	46.60	9.70	11.65	4.85	5.82	50.5	151.6	2,425
10.50	4.76	298	310	39.75	47.73	9.94	11.93	4.97	5.97	51.8	155.3	2,484
10.75	4.88	305	318	40.69	48.87	10.17	12.22	5.09	6.11	53.0	159.0	2,543
11.00	4.99	312	325	41.64	50.01	10.41	12.50	5.20	6.25	54.2	162.6	2,602
11.25	5.10	319	333	42.58	51.14	10.65	12.79	5.32	6.39	55.4	166.3	2,662
11.50	5.22	326	340	43.53	52.28	10.88	13.07	5.44	6.53	56.7	170.0	2,721
11.75	5.33	333	347	44.48	53.41	11.12	13.35	5.56	6.68	57.9	173.7	2,780
12.00	5.44	340	355	45.42	54.55	11.36	13.64	5.68	6.82	59.1	177.4	2,839

By Philip W. Fleming and Joachim Schüring.
Reprinted with permission from *Zymurgy*®.

GLOSSARY

adjunct. Any unmalted grain or other fermentable ingredient that is added to the mash.

aeration. The action of introducing air to the wort at various stages of the brewing process. Proper aeration before primary fermentation is vital to a vigorous ferment.

airlock. *See* **fermentation lock.**

airspace. *See* **ullage**.

alcohol by volume (v/v). The percentage of volume of alcohol per volume of beer. To calculate the approximate volumetric alcohol content, subtract the final gravity from the original gravity and divide the result by 0.0075. For example: $1.050 - 1.012 = 0.029 \div 0.0075 = 3\%$ v/v.

alcohol by weight (w/v). The percentage weight of alcohol per volume of beer. To calculate the approximate alcohol content by weight, subtract the final gravity from the original gravity and multiply by 105. For example: $1.050 - 1.021 = 0.029 \times 105 = 3\%$ w/v.

ale. 1. Historically, an unhopped malt beverage. 2. Now, a generic term for hopped beers produced by top fermentation, as opposed to lagers, which are produced by bottom fermentation.

all-extract beer. A beer made with only malt extract as opposed to one made from barley or a combination of malt extract and barley.

all-grain beer. A beer made with only malted barley as opposed to one made from malt extract or from malt extract and malted barley.

all-malt beer. A beer made with only barley malt with neither adjuncts nor refined sugars.

alpha acid. A soft resin in hop cones. When boiled, alpha acids are converted to iso-alpha-acids, accounting for 60 percent of a beer's bitterness.

alpha-acid unit. A measurement of the potential bitterness of hops, expressed by their percentage of alpha acid. Low is 2–4 percent; medium is 5–7 percent; high is 8–12 percent. Abbreviation is AAU.

attenuation. The reduction in the wort's specific gravity caused by the transformation of sugars into alcohol and carbon dioxide.

autolysis. A process in which yeast feed on each other, producing a rubbery odor. To avoid this, rack beer to remove excess yeast as soon as possible after fermentation.

Bitterness Units (BU). A measurement of the American Society for Brewing Chemists for bittering substances in beer, primarily iso-alpha-acids, but also including oxidized beta acids. *See also* **International Bitterness Units**.

blow-by (blow-off). A single-stage homebrewing fermentation method in which a plastic tube is fitted into the mouth of a carboy, and the other end is submerged in a pail of sterile water. Unwanted residues and carbon dioxide are expelled through the tube, while air is prevented from coming into contact with the fermenting beer, thus avoiding contamination.

carbonation. The process of introducing carbon dioxide into a liquid by: (1) injecting the finished beer with carbon dioxide; (2) adding young fermenting beer to finished beer for a renewed fermentation (kraeusening); (3) priming (adding sugar) to fermented wort prior to bottling, creating a secondary fermentation in the bottle.

carboy. A large glass, plastic, or earthenware bottle.

chalk (calcium carbonate). Often added to sparge water to achieve a more efficient extraction of sugars.

chill haze. Haziness caused by protein and tannin during the secondary fermentation.

cold break. The flocculation of proteins and tannins during wort cooling.

decoction. A method of mashing that raises the temperature of the wash by removing a portion, boiling it, and returning it to the mash tun.

diacetyl. A strong aromatic compound in beer that adds a butterlike flavor.

dimethyl sulfide (DMS). A major sulfur compound of lagers. DMS is released during boiling as a gas that dissipates into the atmosphere.

dry-hopping. The addition of hops to the primary fermenter, the secondary fermenter, or to casked beer to add aroma and hop character to the finished beer without adding significant bitterness.

dry malt. Malt extract in powdered form.

European Brewery Convention (EBC). *See* **Standard Reference Method**.

esters. A group of compounds in beer, which impart fruity flavors.

extract. The amount of dissolved materials in the wort after mashing and lautering malted barley and/or malt adjuncts such as corn and rice.

fermentation lock. A one-way valve, which allows carbon dioxide to escape from the fermenter while excluding contaminants.

final gravity. The specific gravity of a beer when fermentation is complete.

fining. The process of adding clarifying agents to beer during secondary fermentation to precipitate suspended matter.

flocculant yeast. Yeast cells that form large colonies and tend to come out of suspension before the end of fermentation.

flocculation. The behavior of yeast cells joining into masses and settling out toward the end of fermentation.

fusel alcohol. High molecular weight alcohol, which results from excessively high fermentation temperatures. Fusel alcohol can impart harsh bitter flavors to beer as well as contribute to hangovers.

gelatin. A fining agent added to secondary fermentation to clarify the beer.

Homebrew Bittering Units. A formula invented by the American Homebrewers Association to measure bitterness of beer. Calculate bittering units by multiplying the percent alpha acid in the hops by the number of ounces. Example: if 1.5 ounces of 10 percent alpha acid hops were used in a 5-gallon batch, the total homebrew bittering units would be 1.5 x 10 = 15 HBU per 5 gallons.

hop back. A large sieving vessel fitted with a perforated false bottom to separate the spent hops from the bitter wort after boiling.

hop pellets. Finely powdered hop cones compressed into tablets. Hop pellets are 20–30 percent more bitter by weight than the same variety in loose form.

hydrometer. A glass instrument used to measure the specific gravity of liquids as compared to water, consisting of a graduated stem resting on a weighted float.

infusion mash. *See* **step infusion.**

IBU (International Bitterness Units). The measurement of the European Brewing Convention for the concentration of iso-alpha-acids in 34 milligrams per liter (parts per million) in wort and beer. *See also* **Bitterness Units**.

Irish moss. Copper "finings" that help precipitate proteins in the kettle. *See also* **cold break**.

isinglass. A gelatinous substance made from the swim bladder of certain fish and added to beer as a fining agent.

kraeusen. *n.* The rocky-looking head of foam which appears on the surface of the wort during fermentation. *v.* To add fermenting wort to fermented beer to induce carbonation through a secondary fermentation.

lager. *n.* A generic term for any bottom-fermented beer. Lager brewing is now the predominant brewing method worldwide except in Britain where top-fermented ales dominate. *v.* To store beer at near-zero temperatures in order to precipitate yeast cells and proteins and improve taste.

lauter tun. A vessel in which the mash settles and the grains are removed from the sweet wort through a straining process. It has a false slotted bottom and spigot.

liquefaction. The process by which alpha-amylase enzymes degrade soluble starch into dextrin.

Lovibond (°L). The scale used to measure beer color. *See also* **Standard Reference Method**.

malt. Barley that has been steeped in water, germinated, then dried in kilns. This process converts insoluble starches to soluble substances and sugars.

malt extract. A thick syrup or dry powder prepared from malt.

mashing. Mixing crushed malt with water to extract the fermentables, degrade haze-forming proteins, and convert grain starches to fermentable sugars and nonfermentable carbohydrates.

modification. 1. The physical and chemical changes in barley as a result of malting. 2. The degree to which these changes have occurred, as determined by the growth of the acrospire.

original gravity. The specific gravity of wort previous to fermentation. A measure of the total amount of dissolved solids in wort.

pH. A measure of acidity or alkalinity of a solution, usually on a scale of 1 to 14, where 7 is neutral.

phenolic. Compounds that give a spicy character to beer, as in the hefeweizen style.

pitching. The process of adding yeast to the cooled wort.

Plato. A saccharometer that expresses specific gravity as extract weight in a 100-gram solution at 68 °F (20 °C). A revised, more accurate version of Balling, developed by Dr. Plato.

primary fermentation. The first stage of fermentation, during which most fermentable sugars are converted to ethyl alcohol and carbon dioxide.

priming sugar. A small amount of corn, malt, or cane sugar that is added to bulk beer prior to racking or at bottling to induce a new fermentation and create carbonation.

racking. The process of transferring beer from one container to another, especially into the final package (bottles, kegs).

recirculation. Clarifying the wort before it moves from the lauter tun into the kettle by recirculating it through the wash bed.

saccharification. The naturally occurring process in which malt starch is converted into fermentable sugars, primarily maltose.

saccharometer. An instrument that determines the sugar concentration of a solution by measuring the specific gravity.

secondary fermentation. 1. The second slower stage of fermentation, lasting from a few weeks to many months depending on the type of beer. 2. A fermentation occurring in bottles or casks and initiated by priming or by adding yeast.

sparging. Spraying the spent grains in the mash with hot water to retrieve the remaining malt sugar.

specific gravity. A measure of a substance's density as compared to that of water, which is given the value of 1.000 at 39.2 °F (4 °C). Specific gravity has no accompanying units because it is expressed as a ratio.

Standard Reference Method (SRM) and European Brewery Convention (EBC). Two different analytical methods of describing color developed by comparing color samples. Degrees SRM, approximately equivalent to degrees Lovibond, are used by the American Society of Brewing Chemists (ASBC), while degrees EBC are European units. The following equations show approximate conversions: $°EBC = 2.65 \times °Lovibond - 1.2$ and $°Lovibond = 0.377 \times °EBC + 0.45$.

starter. A batch of fermenting yeast that is added to the wort to help initiate fermentation.

step infusion. A method of mashing whereby the temperature of the mash is raised by adding very hot water, and then stirring and stabilizing the mash at the target step temperature.

strike temperature. The initial temperature of the water when the malted barley is added to it to create the mash.

torrefied wheat. Wheat which has been heated quickly at a high temperature, causing it to puff up, which renders it easily mashed.

trub. Suspended particles resulting from the precipitation of proteins, hop oils, and tannins during boiling and cooling stages of brewing.

tun. Any open tank or vessel.

ullage. The empty space between a liquid and the top of its container. Also called airspace or headspace.

v/v. *See* **alcohol by volume.**

vorlauf. To recirculate the wort from the mash tun back through the grain bed to clarify.

w/v. *See* **alcohol by weight.**

water hardness. The degree of dissolved minerals in water.

whirlpool. A method of bringing cold break material to the center of the kettle by stirring the wort until a vortex is formed.

wort. The mixture that results from mashing the malt and boiling the hops, before it is fermented into beer.

INDEX